P9-DZY-952

WITHOUT AUTHORITY

KIERKEGAARD'S WRITINGS, XVIII

WITHOUT AUTHORITY

THE LILY IN THE FIELD AND THE BIRD OF THE AIR

TWO ETHICAL-RELIGIOUS ESSAYS

THREE DISCOURSES AT THE COMMUNION ON FRIDAYS

AN UPBUILDING DISCOURSE

TWO DISCOURSES AT THE COMMUNION ON FRIDAYS

by Søren Kierkegaard

Edited and Translated
with Introduction and Notes by

Howard V. Hong and
Edna H. Hong

PRINCETON UNIVERSITY PRESS
PRINCETON, NEW JERSEY

Published by Princeton University Press,
41 William Street, Princeton, New Jersey 08540
In the United Kingdom: Princeton University Press,
Chichester, West Sussex

Library of Congress Cataloging-in-Publication Data

Kierkegaard, Søren, 1813–1855
[Uden Myndighed. English]
Without Authority / by Søren Kierkegaard ;
edited and translated with introduction and notes by
Howard V. Hong and Edna H. Hong.
p. cm. — (Kierkegaard's writings ; 18)
Translation of: Uden Myndighed
Includes bibliographical references and index.
ISBN 0-691-01239-3 (cloth)
1. Devotional literature. 2. Christian ethics.
3. Authority—Religious aspects—Christianity.
I. Hong, Howard Vincent, 1912–.
II. Hong, Edna Hatlestad, 1913–.
III. Title. IV. Series: Kierkegaard, Søren,
1813–1855. Works. English. 1978 ; 18.
BV4836.K53 1997
242—dc20

Preparation of the volume has been made possible in part by a grant from
the Division of Research Programs of the National Endowment
for the Humanities, an independent federal agency

Princeton University Press books are printed
on acid-free paper and meet the guidelines for permanence and durability
of the Committee on Production Guidelines for Book Longevity
of the Council on Library Resources

Designed by Frank Mahood

Printed in the United States of America
by Princeton Academic Press

1 3 5 7 9 10 8 6 4 2

CONTENTS

HISTORICAL INTRODUCTION

The common title of the present volume of five short works is Kierkegaard's own disclaimer for himself and his writings: "without authority." He saw himself as one who "has something of a poet in his nature, in other respects is a thinker, but—yes, how often I have repeated this, to me so important and crucial, my first statement about myself—*without authority*."[1] The disavowal of authority first appeared in the preface to *Two Upbuilding Discourses* (1843), the initial volume in the signed series offered with his right hand and the companion volume to *Either/Or*, the initial volume in the pseudonymous series offered with his left hand.[2] In the preface he states that the book "is called 'discourses,' not 'sermons,' because its author does not have authority to *preach*; 'upbuilding discourses,' not 'discourses for upbuilding,' because the speaker by no means claims to be a *teacher*."[3]

Kierkegaard had intended to cease being an author (except for perhaps some reviews of the writing of others, such as Thomasine Gyllembourg's *Two Ages*) with *Concluding Unscientific Postscript to* Philosophical Fragments (February 27, 1846) and to seek

[1] *Pap.* IX B 10, p. 311. See pp. 99, 165; Supplement, pp. 216, 226–27, 235 (*Pap.* IX B 22, p. 321; VIII^2 B 9:17; X^1 A 328, p. 218). See also, for example, *For Self-Examination*, p. 3, *KW* XXI (*SV* XII 295); *On My Work as an Author*, in *The Point of View*, *KW* XXII (*SV* XIII 494, 501, 505); *The Point of View for My Work as an Author*, in *The Point of View*, *KW* XXII (*SV* XIII 494, 501, 505, 563, 571, 604); *JP* II 1258; VI 6220, 6577 (*Pap.* X^2 A 159; IX A 189; X^2 A 375). On the concept of authority in Kierkegaard's works, see *The Book on Adler*, Historical Introduction, *KW* XXIV.

[2] See Supplement, pp. 237–38 (*Pap.* X^1 A 351). See also *Two Upbuilding Discourses* (1844), in *Eighteen Upbuilding Discourses*, p. 179, *KW* V (*SV* IV 73); *Point of View*, *KW* XXII (*SV* XIII 527); *JP* V 5639, 5648 (*Pap.* IV A 75, 89). On the two parallel lines of publication, see *Eighteen Discourses*, Historical Introduction, pp. ix-xi.

[3] *Two Discourses* (1843), in *Eighteen Discourses*, p. 5, *KW* V (*SV* III 11). The phrase "its author does not have authority" is repeated in the prefaces to the other five volumes included in *Eighteen Discourses*, pp. 53, 107, 179, 231, 295, *KW* V (*SV* III 271; IV 7, 73, 121; V 79).

an appointment as a country pastor or a teacher.[4] The *Corsair* affair convinced him to stay in place and to continue writing,[5] which he did for five years on a prodigious scale, a second authorship after retirement as a writer at the age of thirty-two!

During this second period, the two parallel series were continued, but with a quantitative and a qualitative shift of emphasis to the works of the right hand. After the signed *Upbuilding Discourses in Various Spirits* (March 13, 1847) and *Works of Love* (September 29, 1847) came *Christian Discourses* (April 26, 1848), which was accompanied by *The Crisis and a Crisis in the Life of an Actress* (July 24–27, 1848), by Inter et Inter. At this point Kierkegaard was again inclined to terminate his work as an author,[6] and therefore it was important to him that the esthetic piece on the actress Luise Heiberg appear in the series of the left hand.

But Kierkegaard's mind was too active to permit a cessation. In the years 1849 to 1851 there appeared not only the five works in the present volume but also *The Sickness unto Death* (July 30, 1849) and *Practice in Christianity* (September 25, 1850), both under a new pseudonym, Anti-Climacus, and the signed works *On My Work as an Author* (August 7, 1851) and *For Self-Examination* (September 12, 1851). In addition "The Book on Adler" was written and revised, as were "The Point of View for My Work as an Author," "Armed Neutrality," "Judge for Yourself!" and "A Cycle of Ethical-Religious Essays,"[7] all of which he did not publish at the time, with the exception of two parts of "A Cycle," the *Two Ethical-Religious Essays* by H. H. (May 19,1849).

During this second period, the original parallelism of left-hand and right-hand series was continued symbolically by the simultaneous publication (May 14, 1849) of the signed *The Lily in the Field and the Bird of the Air* and the second edition of *Either/Or*, the first title in the pseudonymous series. Two parallel series, signed and pseudonymous, were continued thereafter, but with

[4] See, for example, *JP* V 5873, 5877, 5887, 5888, 6016, 6062; VI 6157 (*Pap.* VII¹ A 4, 9, 98, 99; VIII¹ A 171, 352; IX A 54); *Point of View*, *KW* XXII (*SV* XIII 570).

[5] See *The* Corsair *Affair*, Historical Introduction, pp. xxxi-xxxiii, *KW* XIII.

[6] See Supplement, pp. 216–17 (*Pap.* X¹ A 79); see also *Pap.* X⁶ B 249, p. 412.

[7] See Supplement, p. 213 (*Pap.* IX B 1–6).

a difference. The new pseudonym, Anti-Climacus, belongs to a higher plane than Johannes Climacus of *Philosophical Fragments, or A Fragment of Philosophy*; *Johannes Climacus, or De omnibus dubitandum est*; and *Postscript*.[8] In the four published volumes by Climacus and Anti-Climacus, Kierkegaard is listed as the editor. The signed companion volume to *Sickness unto Death* (July 30, 1849) was *Three Discourses at the Communion on Fridays* (November 14, 1849),[9] and *Practice in Christianity* (September 25, 1850) and *An Upbuilding Discourse* (December 20, 1850) constituted a similar pairing.

Pseudonymous	Signed
1848	1848
The Crisis and a Crisis in the Life of an Actress, by Inter et Inter, *Fædrelandet*, July 24, 25, 26, 27, 1848	*Christian Discourses*, by S. Kierkegaard, April 26, 1848
1849	1849
**Two Ethical-Religious Essays*, by H. H., May 19, 1849	**The Lily in the Field and the Bird of the Air*, by S. Kierkegaard, May 14, 1849
The Sickness unto Death, by Anti-Climacus, July 30, 1849	**Three Discourses at the Communion on Fridays: The High Priest, The Tax Collector,*

[8] "Johannes Climacus and Anti-Climacus have several things in common; but the difference is that whereas Johannes Climacus places himself so low that he even says that he himself is not a Christian, one seems to be able to detect in Anti-Climacus that he considers himself to be a Christian on an extraordinarily high level, at times also seems to believe that Christianity really is only for daimons, but with this word taken in a nonintellectual sense.

"His personal guilt, then, is to confuse himself with ideality (this is the daemonic in him), but his portrayal of ideality can be absolutely sound, and I bow to it.

"I would place myself higher than Johannes Climacus, lower than Anti-Climacus." —*JP* VI 6433 (*Pap.* X^1 A 517) *n.d.*, 1849

[9] See *On My Work*, in *Point of View*, *KW* XXII (*SV* XIII 494).

Pseudonymous	Signed
	The Woman Who Was a Sinner, by S. Kierkegaard, November 14, 1849
1850	1850
Practice in Christianity, by Anti-Climacus, September 25, 1850	**An Upbuilding Discourse*, by S. Kierkegaard, December 20, 1850

1851

**Two Discourses at the Communion on Fridays*, by S. Kierkegaard, August 7, 1851

For Self-Examination, by S. Kierkegaard, September 12, 1851

* works included in *Without Authority, Kierkegaard's Writings*, XVIII

In a retrospective entry in 1849, Kierkegaard stated that the movement of the entire complex authorship was "from 'the poet,' from the esthetic—from the philosopher, from the speculative—to the intimation of the most inward interpretation of the essentially Christian; **from** the **pseudonymous** *Either/Or*, which was immediately accompanied by *Two Upbuilding Discourses* with *my name* as author, **through** *Concluding Postscript* with my name as editor, to *Discourses at the Communion on Fridays*,[10] the latest work I have written, and of which two were delivered in Frue Church."[11] Later in 1849, after considerable additional writing and after the completion of the pseudonymous *Practice*, he wrote with regard to *Three Discourses at the Communion on Fridays*: "I must have a place of rest, but I cannot use a pseudonym as a place of rest; they are parallel to Anti-Climacus, and the position of 'Discourses at the Communion on Fridays'[12] is once and for all designated as the place of rest of the author-

[10] Part IV of *Christian Discourses*, *KW* XVII (*SV* X 245–317).

[11] *Pap*. X^5 B 201, p. 382. See also, for example, *On My Work*, in *Point of View*, *KW* XXII (*SV* XIII 493–99); *Point of View*, *KW* XXII (*SV* XIII 521–28).

[12] The three discourses: "The High Priest," "The Tax Collector," and "The Woman Who Was a Sinner," pp. 109–60.

ship."[13] *Two Discourses at the Communion on Fridays*[14]—also written in 1849, although published August 7, 1851, a few weeks prior to the last work, *For Self-Examination* (September 12, 1851), before the three-year silent period—finally became the place of rest of the authorship:

> An authorship that began with *Either/Or* and advanced step by step seeks here its decisive place of rest, at the foot of the altar, where the author, personally most aware of his own imperfection and guilt, certainly does not call himself a truth-witness but only a singular kind of poet and thinker who, *without authority*, has had nothing new to bring but "has wanted once again to read through, if possible in a more inward way, the original text of individual human existence-relationships, the old familiar text handed down from the fathers"—(see my postscript to *Concluding Postscript*[15]).

THE LILY IN THE FIELD AND THE BIRD OF THE AIR (MAY 14, 1849)

These discourses are called "New Discourses on the Lilies and the Birds,"[16] inasmuch as the theme had already been developed, particularly in Part Two of *Upbuilding Discourses in Various Spirits* (March 30, 1846).[17] In substance they represent what in *Postscript* is termed Religiousness *A* as distinguished from Christianity, the

[13] See Supplement, p. 257 (*Pap.* X[2] A 148). See also p. 165.

[14] See pp. 161–88.

[15] P. 165. The reference to *Concluding Unscientific Postscript to* Philosophical Fragments is to pp. 629–30, *KW* XII.1 (*SV* VII 548–49).

[16] See Supplement, pp. 197–98 (*Pap.* VIII[1] A 643).

[17] "What We Learn from the Lilies in the Field and the Birds of the Air," *Upbuilding Discourses in Various Spirits*, pp. 155–212, *KW* XV (*SV* VIII 245–96). See also, for example, *Either/Or*, II, pp. 282–83, 344, *KW* IV (*SV* II 253, 310); *Four Upbuilding Discourses* (1843) and *Three Upbuilding Discourses* (1844), in *Eighteen Discourses*, pp. 154, 258, *KW* V (*SV* IV 50, 144); *Fragments*, pp. 29–30, 57, *KW* VII (*SV* IV 198, 223); *Christian Discourses*, *KW* XVII (*SV* X 13–93); *Judge for Yourself!*, pp. 179–87, *KW* XXI (*SV* XII 449–56).

paradoxical-historical Religiousness *B*.[18] (Therefore allusion is not made to the fifth petition of the Lord's Prayer, "Forgive us our trespasses," because the lily and the bird, as representatives of immanental Religiousness *A*, cannot be the teachers of Religiousness *B*.[19]) In accord with the immediacy of the lily and the bird, the style is poetic, also because the discourses present the conflict between the esthetic (poetry) and Christianity, "how in a certain sense Christianity is prose in comparison with poetry," and "when poetry in truth shall fall (not because of a preacher's dull and dismal jawing), it ought to wear its party clothes."[20] The discourses were not written as a parallel companion volume to the second edition of *Either/Or*, but symbolically they "came into being at the time—just what I needed!"[21]

TWO ETHICAL-RELIGIOUS ESSAYS (MAY 19, 1849)

Having revised "The Book on Adler" a number of times and having then set it aside, during 1847–48 Kierkegaard entertained the idea of "A Cycle of Ethical-Religious Essays."[22] Five of the essays, including the second of the only two that were published (*Two Ethical-Religious Essays*), were drawn from the manuscript of "The Book on Adler." The first of the two published essays had been contemplated under variants of the title "How Was It Possible That Jesus Christ Could Be Deprived of His Life?"[23] The draft, indebted to earlier reflection and journal entries,[24] was written in eight hours[25] in 1847; the second essay, on the genius and the apostle, had been planned as an addendum in the third

[18] See *Postscript*, pp. 555–61, *KW* XII.1 (*SV* VII 484–90).

[19] See Supplement, p. 201 (*Pap*. X^1 A 252).

[20] See Supplement, pp. 197–98 (*Pap*. VIII^1 A 643).

[21] *JP* VI 6383 (*Pap*. X^1 A 250). See also Supplement, pp. 237–38 (*Pap*. X^1 A 351).

[22] See Supplement, pp. 208, 212–19 (*Pap*. VIII^1 A 264, 562; IX B 1–6, 22, 12; X^1 A 79, 263, 318).

[23] See Supplement, p. 212 (*Pap*. VIII^1 A 562).

[24] See Supplement, pp. 207–11 (*Pap*. VIII^1 A 145, 271–73, 275–76, 307).

[25] See Supplement, p. 220 (*Pap*. VIII^2 B 135).

version of "The Book on Adler."[26] The persistent question of attribution of *Two Essays* arose again; were they to be published as a signed, as a pseudonymous, or even as an anonymous work?[27] The manuscript was sent to the printer on Kierkegaard's thirty-sixth birthday, May 5, 1849,[28] under the initials H. H. In commenting on the two series of the right hand and the left, Kierkegaard wrote: "'Two Ethical-Religious Essays' does not belong to the authorship in the same way; it is not an element in it but a point of view."[29]

THREE DISCOURSES AT THE COMMUNION ON FRIDAYS (NOVEMBER 14, 1849)

The title used in *Kierkegaard's Writings* (*KW*) is the alternative title that Kierkegaard considered for the collection, with "The High Priest," "The Tax Collector," and "The Woman Who Was a Sinner" as individual discourse titles.[30] Although the order was eventually reversed, the early form has been used in this edition in order more readily to indicate the nature of the writings and their place in the authorship as a whole. Originally the volume was regarded as the companion volume to *Sickness unto Death* (July 30, 1849),[31] but, although the discourses were published within a few weeks, they were followed later by two additional signed works (*An Upbuilding Discourse* and *Two Discourses at the Communion on Fridays*), lest the pseudonymous work seem to be "the place of rest of the authorship."[32] The relation of the *Three Discourses* to the theme of *Sickness unto Death* is most apparent in the substance of the first of the three discourses.[33] The text (Hebrews 4:15) of the first discourse is one that impressed Kier-

[26] See Supplement, pp. 226–27 (*Pap*. VIII² B 9:17).

[27] See Supplement, pp. 213, 217–19 (*Pap*. VIII¹ A 563; X¹ A 263, 302).

[28] See Supplement, p. 218 (*Pap*. X¹ A 302).

[29] See Supplement, p. 238 (*Pap*. X¹ A 351).

[30] See Supplement, p. 254 (*Pap*. X⁵ B 25:1).

[31] See Supplement, p. 256 (*Pap*. X² A 126); *On My Work*, in *Point of View*, *KW* XXII (*SV* XIII 494). See also p. 165.

[32] See Supplement, p. 257 (*Pap*. X² A 148).

[33] See, for example, pp. 116–21.

kegaard so much that he almost substituted it at the last minute for one that he had developed for the Communion service at Vor Frue Church on September 1, 1848.[34] The text (Luke 18:13) of the second discourse he had pondered frequently.[35] The text (Luke 7:47) of the third discourse was used again in *An Upbuilding Discourse* and in *Two Discourses at the Communion on Fridays*. The first discourse was written mid-1849[36] just after the publication of *Sickness unto Death*; the theme of the second had been under consideration as early as 1839,[37] and the theme of the third appeared as early as 1844 in *Fragments*.[38] The date of the preface was originally September 10, the date of Regine Olsen's acceptance of Kierkegaard's marriage proposal in 1840, and was changed to September 8,[39] the date of his proposal. The published volume is dated "Early September 1849."[40]

AN UPBUILDING DISCOURSE
(DECEMBER 20, 1850)

This discourse was written during the three months after the publication of *Sickness unto Death* (July 30, 1849). In the final copy the title was changed from "'The Woman Who Was a Sinner' / A Christian Discourse" to its present form,[41] which is more in keeping with the titles of Kierkegaard's other discourses. The preface is dated December 12, 1850.[42] The text is a further consideration of the theme (Luke 7:37–47) treated earlier in *Three Discourses* (1843) and again later in *Two Discourses on Fridays* (1851).

[34] See Supplement, p. 252 (*Pap*. IX A 266).

[35] See, for example, Supplement, pp. 251, 253–54 (*Pap*. VIII^1 A 635; IX A 272; X^1 A 428); see also *JP* IV 3937 (*Pap*. X^2 A 51).

[36] See Supplement, p. 255 (*Pap*. X^5 B 25:3).

[37] See *JP* I 867 (*Pap*. II A 322).

[38] See *Fragments*, p. 33, *KW* VII (*SV* IV 201).

[39] See Supplement, p. 254 (*Pap*. X^5 B 25:2).

[40] P. 111.

[41] See Supplement, p. 261 (*Pap*. X^5 B 116:1).

[42] P. 147.

TWO DISCOURSES AT THE COMMUNION ON FRIDAYS (AUGUST 7, 1851)

This pair of discourses, together with *For Self-Examination* (September 12, 1851) and the posthumously published "Judge for Yourself!" and "Point of View," constitutes the close of the second authorship prior to the three-year silence before the articles in *Fædrelandet* and *The Moment. On My Work as an Author* was published on the same day, and the reviewer in *Flyveposten* was not entirely off the mark in saying "that he hereby seems to have concluded his work proper as an author appears not only from the various utterances in the above-named work but also from the preface to the work simultaneously issued by the same publisher, *Two Discourses at the Communion on Fridays*."[43] The two discourses, written in late 1849,[44] and *The Changelessness of God*,[45] which was prepared for presentation in the Citadel church on May 10, 1851 but was published four years later on September 3, 1855, are the last of the series of discourses that began in 1843.

In two specific ways, *Two Discourses* does represent the close of the authorship (yet with more to come eventually). The preface itself declares that here is the "place of rest" of an authorship that "began with *Either/Or*" and quotes the end of the "First and Last Explanation" appended to *Postscript*.[46] In addition, the preface to the two discourses movingly summarizes "the content of my life, . . . the thought of humanity and of human equality."[47] The dedication in another way rounds off the entire authorship "as it was from the beginning."[48] That Kierkegaard had Regine in mind is clear from the alternative dedications in the *Papirer*.[49] A

[43] Anon., *Flyveposten*, 181, August 7, 1851.

[44] P. 162.

[45] *The Changelessness of God*, in The Moment *and Late Writings*, *KW* XXIII (*SV* XIV 277–94).

[46] See p. 165; *Postscript*, pp. 629–30, *KW* XII.1 (*SV* VII 548–49).

[47] P. 165.

[48] P. 163.

[49] See Supplement, pp. 270–71 (*Pap*. X^5 B 261, 263–64). See also *Pap*. X^5 B 262.

significant movement in the authorship is epitomized in the shift of the meaning of the expression "that single individual [*hiin Enkelte*]," used for Regine in the preface of the first discourses (1843) as "*my* reader,"[50] to the wider meaning of "the single individual [*den Enkelte*]" in the sense of the universal singular:

> On the whole, the very mark of my genius is that Governance broadens and radicalizes whatever concerns me personally. I remember what a pseudonymous writer said about Socrates: "His whole life was personal preoccupation with himself, and then Governance comes and adds world-historical significance to it."[51] To take another example—I am polemical by nature, and I understood the concept of "that single individual [*hiin Enkelte*]" early. However, when I wrote it for the first time (in *Two Upbuilding Discourses* [1843]), I was thinking particularly of *my* reader, for this book contained a little hint to her, and until later it was for me very true personally that I sought only one single reader. Gradually this thought was taken over. But here again Governance's part is so infinite.[52]

> The subject of the single individual [*den Enkelte*] appears in every book by the pseudonymous writers, but the price put upon being a single individual, a single individual in the eminent sense, rises. The subject of the single individual appears in every one of my upbuilding books, but there the single individual is what every human being is. This is precisely the dialectic of "the single individual" [*changed from:* the particular]. The single individual can mean the most unique one of all, and it can mean everyone. . . . The point of departure of the pseudonymous writers is continually in the differences—the point of departure in the upbuilding discourses is in the universally human.[53]

[50] See, for example, *Two Discourses* (1843), *Three Discourses* (1843), in *Eighteen Discourses*, pp. 5, 53, *KW* V (*SV* III 11, 271).

[51] Freely quoted from *Postscript*, p. 147, fn., *KW* XII.1 (*SV* VII 120–21).

[52] *JP* VI 6388 (*Pap*. X[1] A 266, p. 177).

[53] "A Word about the Relation of My Work as an Author to 'that single individual [*hiin Enkelte*],'" *Pap*. VIII[2] B 191–92, p. 299. See also *JP* II 2004 (*Pap*. VIII[1] A 482); *Pap*. VIII[2] B 193–95.

Editions (usually 525 copies) of Kierkegaard's later works were published in the ordinary way by a publisher who paid a modest one-time honorarium for each work. Even though Kierkegaard was by this time a well-known author, only two of the five works, *The Lily and the Bird* and *Two Discourses*, were printed in second editions within the six-year period before his death. Three works received little more than announcements in journals and newspapers. The other two, *Three Discourses* and *An Upbuilding Discourse*, fell unnoticed from the press.

Of *The Lily and the Bird*, Ludwig N. Helweg wrote anonymously: "*The Lily in the Field and the Bird of the Air* has no doubt found its readers. The author continues his variations on the theme he treated earlier in *Upbuilding Discourses in Various Spirits*; we meet here the same subtlety of structure, clear profundity of thought development, the same flowing poetic language."[54] A similar anonymous semi-announcement of *Two Ethical-Religious Essays* appeared, in which the writer chided "the very young author" for borrowing from Kierkegaard. "In the first essay one notes throughout that the author has his thoughts at second hand."[55] This view of H. H. as a more or less plagiarizing writer was echoed by the reviewer in *Nyt Theologisk Tidsskrift*.[56] An anonymous announcement of *Two Discourses at the Communion on Fridays* tersely states that the volume "can only be regarded as a model of spiritual eloquence."[57]

[54] *Dansk Kirketidende*, IV, 48, September 2, 1849, col. 799.

[55] Ibid., IV, 43, July 22, 1849, col. 718–19. For Kierkegaard's response in the *Papirer*, see Supplement, pp. 239–40 (*Pap.* X[1] A 551).

[56] *Nyt Theologisk Tidsskrift*, I, 1850, p. 384. For Kierkegaard's response in the *Papirer*, see Supplement, pp. 243–45 (*Pap.* X[5] B 11). For brother Peter's views on H. H.'s work, see Supplement, pp. 242–43 (*Pap.* X[2] A 280, 285).

[57] *Flyveposten*, 181, August 7, 1851. For Kierkegaard's response in the *Papirer*, see Supplement, pp. 276–77 (*Pap.* X[4] A 380).

THE LILY IN THE FIELD AND THE BIRD OF THE AIR

THREE DEVOTIONAL DISCOURSES

by S. Kierkegaard

PREFACE XI 5

This little book (which with regard to the circumstances[1] of its appearance reminds me of my first, and more particularly of my first to my first, the preface to the two upbuilding discourses of 1843, which came out immediately after *Either/Or*) will, I hope, bring the same recollection to "that single individual whom I with joy and gratitude call *my* reader": "It desires to remain in hiding, just as it came into existence in concealment—a little flower under the cover of the great forest."[2] My reader will be reminded of that by the circumstances and in turn, I hope, will be reminded, as I am reminded, of the preface to the two upbuilding discourses of 1844: "It is offered with the right hand"[3]—in contrast to the pseudonyms, which were held out and are held out with the left hand.[4]

May 5, 1849

S. K.

PRAYER XI 8

Father in heaven, what we in company with people, especially in a crowd of people, come to know with difficulty, and what we, if we have come to know it somewhere else, so easily forget in company with people, especially in a crowd of people—what it is to be a human being and what religiously is the requirement for being a human being—would that we might learn it or, if it is forgotten, that we might learn it again from the lily and the bird; would that we might learn it, if not all at once, then at least some of it, and little by little; would that from the lily and the bird we might this time learn silence, obedience, joy!

The Gospel for the Fifteenth Sunday after Trinity[5]

XI 9

No one can serve two masters, for he must either hate the one and love the other or be devoted to the one and despise the other. You cannot serve God and mammon. Therefore I say to you, do not worry about your life, what you will eat and what you will drink, nor about your body, what you will wear. Is not life more than food, and the body more than clothing? Look at the birds of the air; they sow not and reap not and gather not into barns, and your heavenly Father feeds them. Are you not much more than they? But who among you can add one foot to his growth even though he worries about it? And why do you worry about clothing? Look at the lilies in the field, how they grow; they do not work, do not spin. But I say to you that not even Solomon in all his glory was so clothed as one of them. If, then, God so clothes the grass of the field, which today is and tomorrow is cast into the stove, would he not much more clothe you, you of little faith? Therefore you should not worry and say, "What shall we eat?" or "What shall we drink?" or "What shall we wear?" The pagans seek all these things; your heavenly Father knows that you need all these things. But seek first God's kingdom and his righteousness; then all these things will be added to you. Therefore do not worry about tomorrow: tomorrow will worry about itself. Each day has enough trouble of its own.

I XI 11

"Look at the Birds of the Air; Look at the Lily in the Field."

[6]But you perhaps say with "the poet," and you like to hear the poet talk this way, "Oh, I wish I were a bird, or I wish I were like a bird, like the free bird that, delighting in travel, flies far, far away over land and sea, high in the sky, to lands far, far off—I, alas, who only feel bound and fettered and nailed to the spot, where daily worries and sufferings and adversities manifest to me that I live there—and for all my life! Oh, I wish I were a bird, or I wish I were like a bird, which lighter than all earthly gravity rises in the air, lighter than the air. Oh, I wish I were like the light bird that, when it seeks a foothold, builds its nest even upon the surface of the sea[7]—I, alas, who even at every slightest movement, if I merely move, must feel what a weight rests upon me! Oh, I wish I were a bird, or I wish I were like a bird, free from all considerations, like the little songbird that humbly sings even though no one is listening or proudly sings even though no one is listening—alas, I who have no moment and nothing for myself but am parceled out in having to serve thousands of considerations! Oh, I wish I were a flower, or I wish I were like a flower in the meadow, happily in love with myself, and with that, period—I, alas, who feel this cleft of the human heart also in my heart, neither able selfishly to break with everything nor able lovingly to sacrifice everything!"

So speaks the poet. If one listens casually, it sounds almost as if he were saying what the Gospel says—after all, he does extol the happiness of the bird and the lily in the strongest terms. But
now hear more. "For this reason it borders on cruelty for the XI 12
Gospel to praise the lily and the bird and say, 'You shall be like that'—I, alas, in whom that wish is so genuine, so genuine, so

genuine; oh, I wish that I were like a bird of the air, like a lily in the field. But it is, of course, an impossibility that I would be able to become like them, and for this very reason the wish to be like them is so heartfelt, so sad, and yet so ardent within me. How cruel, then, of the Gospel to talk this way to me—indeed, it seems as if it wanted to make me lose my mind—that I *shall* be what I all too deeply feel, just as the wish for it is deep within me, that I am not and cannot be. I cannot understand the Gospel; there is a language difference between us that, if I were to understand it, would kill me."

This is always the way it is with the poet in relation to the Gospel; for him it is just the same as with what the Gospel says about being a child.[8] "Oh, I wish I were a child," says the poet, "or I wish I were like a child, 'alas, a child, innocent and happy' —I, alas, who prematurely became old and guilty and sad!"

How strange, since we quite properly say that the poet is a child. Yet the poet cannot come to an understanding with the Gospel. Underlying the poet's life there is really the despair of being able to become what is wished, and this despair feeds *the wish*. But the wish is the invention of disconsolateness. To be sure, the wish consoles for a moment, but on closer inspection it is evident that it does not console, and therefore we say that the wish is the consolation that disconsolateness invents. What a strange self-contradiction! Yes, but the poet is also this self-contradiction. The poet is the child of pain whom the father nevertheless calls the son of joy.[9] In the poet the wish comes into existence in pain, and this wish, this burning wish, rejoices the human heart more than wine cheers it, more than the earliest bud of spring, more than the first star that one, weary of the day, gladly greets in longing for the night, more than the last star in the sky that one bids farewell as the day dawns. The poet is the child of eternity but lacks the earnestness of eternity. When the poet thinks about the bird and the lily, he weeps. Meanwhile, as he weeps, he finds relief; the wish comes into existence, and with it the eloquence of the wish, "Oh, I wish I were a bird, the bird that as a child I read about in my picture book. Oh, I wish I were a flower in the field, the flower that stood in my mother's garden." But if, with the Gospel, one were to say to him, "This is

earnestness, precisely this is the earnestness, that the bird is the teacher in earnest," then the poet would laugh—and he makes fun of the bird and the lily, so witty that he gets us all, even the most earnest person who ever lived, to laugh; but he does not XI
move the Gospel in that way. So earnest is the Gospel that all the 13
poet's sadness does not change it as this changes even the most earnest person, so that he momentarily yields, succumbs to the poet's thoughts, sighs with him and says, "My dear fellow, is it actually impossible for you! Well, then I do not dare to say, *You shall.*" But the Gospel dares to command the poet, dares to order that he *shall* be like the bird. And so earnest is the Gospel that the poet's most irresistible invention does not make it smile.

You shall become a child again, and therefore, or to that end, you shall begin by being able and willing to understand the phrase that seems to be intended for children and that any child understands; you shall understand the phrase as a child understands it: *You shall.* A child never asks about reasons. A child does not dare to; neither does a child need to—and the one corresponds to the other: just because the child does not dare to, it therefore does not need to ask about reasons, since for the child it is reason enough that it shall. Yes, all the reasons together would not to such a degree be reason enough for the child. And the child never says: I cannot. The child does not dare to, and neither is it true—the one corresponds completely to the other: just because the child does not dare to say, "I cannot," it is not therefore true that it cannot, and it is therefore manifest that the truth is that it can, since not to be able is impossible if one does not dare something else; nothing is more certain—the point is simply that it is certain that one does not dare something else. And the child never looks for an evasion or excuse, because the child understands with frightful truthfulness that there is no evasion or excuse for it, that there is no such hiding place, neither in heaven nor on earth, neither in the parlor nor in the garden, where it could hide from this *You shall.* When one is altogether certain that there is no such hiding place, then there is no evasion or excuse either. When one knows with frightful truthfulness that there is no evasion or excuse—yes, then naturally enough one ceases to find it, since what does not exist is not to be

found—but one also ceases to look for it, and then one does what one shall. The child never needs long deliberation, because when it shall, and perhaps immediately, then there is no opportunity for deliberation. Even if this were not the case, when it shall nevertheless—well, even if it were given an eternity for deliberation, the child would not need it; the child would say: Why all this time when I nevertheless shall? If the child were to take the time, it would certainly use the time in some other way, for play, for fun, and the like. What the child shall, that the child shall; that
XI stands fast and has nothing at all to do with deliberation.

14 So, then, following the instruction of the Gospel, let us in earnest look at the lily and the bird as the teachers. In earnest, since the Gospel is not so extravagantly spiritual that it cannot use the lily and the bird, but neither is it so earthly that it can look at the lily and the bird only with sadness or with a smile.

From the lily and the bird as teachers, let us learn

silence*, or learn to* ***be silent****.*

Surely it is speech that distinguishes humanity above the animal and then, if you like, far above the lily. But because the ability to speak is an advantage, it does not follow that the ability to be silent would not be an art or would be an inferior art. On the contrary, because the human being is able to speak, the ability to be silent is an art, and a great art precisely because this advantage of his so easily tempts him. But this he can learn from the silent teachers, the lily and the bird.

"Seek first God's kingdom and his righteousness."[10]

But what does this mean, what am I to do, or what is the effort that can be said to seek, to aspire to God's kingdom? Shall I see about getting a position commensurate with my talents and abilities in order to be effective in it? No, you shall *first* seek God's kingdom.[11] Shall I give all my possessions to the poor?[12] No, you shall *first* seek God's kingdom. Shall I then go out and proclaim this doctrine to the world? No, you shall *first* seek God's kingdom. But then in a certain sense it is nothing I shall do? Yes, quite true, in a certain sense it is nothing. In the deepest sense you shall make yourself nothing, become nothing before God, learn to be silent. In this silence is the beginning, which is to seek *first* God's kingdom.

Thus in a certain sense one devoutly comes backward to the beginning. The beginning is not that with which one begins but that to which one comes, and one comes to it backward. The beginning is this art of *becoming* silent, since to be silent as nature is silent is no art. In the deepest sense, to become silent in this
way, silent before God, is the beginning of the fear of God, be- XI
cause just as the fear of God is the beginning of wisdom,[13] so 15
silence is the beginning of the fear of God. And just as the fear of God is more than the beginning of wisdom, is wisdom, so silence is more than the beginning of the fear of God, is the fear of God. In this silence the many thoughts of wishes and desires God-fearingly fall silent; in this silence the verbosity of thanksgiving God-fearingly becomes silent.

The advantage of the human being over the animal is the ability to speak, but, in relation to God, wanting to speak can easily become the corruption of the human being, who is able to speak. God is in heaven and the human being is on earth and therefore they can hardly converse. God is infinite wisdom; what the human being knows is idle chatter; therefore they can hardly converse. God is love and the human being, as we say to a child, is a little ninny even in regard to his own welfare, and therefore they can hardly converse. Only in much fear and trembling is a human being able to speak with God, in much fear and trembling. But to speak in much fear and trembling is difficult for another reason, because just as anxiety makes the voice fail physically, so also much fear and trembling[14] make speech fall into silence. The one who prays aright knows this, and the one who did not pray aright perhaps learned this through prayer. There was something that lay very heavily on his mind, a matter that was very important to him; it was very urgent for him to make himself rightly understood by God; he was afraid he had forgotten something in the prayer, and, alas, if he had forgotten it, he was afraid that God by himself would not remember it—therefore he wanted to concentrate his mind on praying with all his heart. Then what happened to him if he did really pray with all his heart? Something amazing happened to him. Gradually, as he became more and more fervent in prayer, he had less and less to say, and finally he became completely silent. He became silent. Indeed, he became what is, if possible, even more opposite to speaking than silence; he became a listener. He thought that to pray is to speak; he learned that to pray is not only to be silent but is to listen. And so it is; to pray is not to listen to oneself speak but is to become silent and to remain silent, to wait until the one praying hears God.

This is why the words of the Gospel, seek *first* God's kingdom, upbringingly muzzle a person's mouth, as it were, by answering every single question he asks, whether this is what he shall do—
XI 16 No, you shall *first* seek God's kingdom. Therefore one can paraphrase the Gospel's words in this way: You shall begin by praying, not as if (which we have shown) prayer always began with silence, but because when prayer has really become prayer it has become silence. Seek first God's kingdom, that is: Pray! If you ask, yes, if you mention every single possibility and ask: Is this what I shall do, and if I do it is this seeking God's kingdom, the answer must be: No, you shall first seek God's kingdom. But to pray, that is, to pray aright, is to become silent, and that is to seek first God's kingdom.

This silence you can learn with the lily and the bird. That is, their silence is no art, but when *you* become silent like the lily and the bird, you are at the beginning, which is to seek *first* God's kingdom.

How solemn it is out there under God's heaven with the lily and the bird, and why? Ask the poet. He answers: Because there is silence. And his longing goes out to that solemn silence, away from the worldliness in the human world, where there is so much talking, away from all the worldly human life that only in a sad way demonstrates that speech distinguishes human beings above the animals. "Because," says the poet, "if this is the distinguishing characteristic—no, then I much, much prefer the silence out there. I prefer it—no, there is no comparison; it is a distinguishing characteristic infinitely above that of human beings, who are able to speak." That is, in nature's silence the poet thinks that he is aware of the divine voice. In humanity's busy talking he thinks that he not only is not aware of the divine voice but is not even aware that the human being has kinship with the divine. The poet says: Speech is the human being's advantage over the animal—yes, quite true, if he is able *to be silent.*

But to be able to be silent, that you can learn out there with the lily and the bird, where there is silence and also something divine in this silence. There is silence out there, and not only when everything is silent in the silent night, but there nevertheless is silence out there also when day vibrates with a thousand strings and everything is like a sea of sound. Each one separately does it so well that not one of them, nor all of them together, will break the solemn silence. There is silence out there. The forest is silent; even when it whispers it nevertheless is silent. The trees, even where they stand in the thickest growth, keep their word, something human beings rarely do despite a promise given: This will remain between us. The sea is silent; even when it rages uproariously it is silent. At first you perhaps listen in the wrong
way and hear it roar. If you hurry off and report this, you do the XI
sea an injustice. If, however, you take time and listen more care- 17
fully, you hear—how amazing!—you hear silence, because uniformity is nevertheless also silence. In the evening, when silence rests over the land and you hear the distant bellowing from the meadow, or from the farmer's house in the distance you hear the familiar voice of the dog, you cannot say that this bellowing or this voice disturbs the silence. No, this belongs to the silence, is in a mysterious and thus in turn silent harmony with the silence; this increases it.

Let us now look more closely at the lily and the bird from whom we are to learn. The bird is *silent and waits.* It knows, or rather it fully and firmly believes, that everything takes place in its time; therefore the bird waits. But it knows that it is not entitled to know the time or day;[15] therefore it is silent. "It will surely take place in due season," says the bird. Yet, no, the bird does not say this; it is silent, but its silence is expressive and its silence says that it believes it, and because it believes it the bird is silent and waits. When the moment comes, the silent bird understands that this is the moment; it uses it and is never disappointed.

So it is also with the lily; it is silent and waits. It does not impatiently ask, "When will spring come?" because it knows that spring will come in due season, knows that it would be least useful to itself if it were allowed to determine the seasons of the year. It does not ask, "When will we get rain?" or "When will we get sunshine?" or say, "Now we have had too much rain," or "Now it is too hot." It does not ask in advance what kind of a summer it will be this year, how long or how short. No, it is silent and waits—that is how simple it is. But still it is never deceived, something that can happen only to sagacity, not to simplicity, which does not deceive and is not deceived. Then comes the moment, and when the moment comes, the silent lily understands that now is the moment, and it makes use of it.

O you profound teachers of simplicity, should it not also be possible to find *the moment* when one is speaking? No, only by being silent does one find the moment. When one speaks, if one says merely a single word, one misses the moment—the moment *is* only in silence. Because a person cannot keep silent, it rarely happens that he really comes to understand when the moment is and to use the moment properly. He cannot be silent and wait, which perhaps explains why the moment never comes for him at all. He cannot be silent, which perhaps explains why he was not aware of the moment when it did come for him. Although pregnant with its rich meaning, the moment does not have any mes-
XI sage sent in advance to announce its coming; it comes too swiftly
18 for that when it comes, and there is not a moment's time beforehand. Nor does the moment, no matter how significant it is in itself, come with noise or with shouting. No, it comes softly, with a lighter step than the lightest footfall of any creature, since it comes with the light step of the sudden; it comes stealthily—therefore one must be absolutely silent if one is to be aware that "now it is here." At the next moment it is gone, and for that reason one must have been absolutely silent if one is to succeed in making use of it. Yet everything depends on the moment. Indeed, the misfortune in the lives of the great majority of human beings is this, that they were never aware of the moment, that in their lives the eternal and the temporal are exclusively separated. And why? Because they could not be silent.

The bird is *silent and suffers.* However heartbroken it is, it is silent. Even the mournful elegist of the desert or of solitude is silent. It sighs three times and then is silent; once again it sighs three times, but essentially it is silent. What it is, it does not say; it does not complain, does not accuse anyone; it sighs, only to fall into silence again. It seems as if the silence would burst it; therefore it must sigh in order to be silent. The bird is not exempt from suffering, but the silent bird exempts itself from what makes the suffering harder, the mistaken sympathy of others, from what prolongs the suffering, all the talk about the suffering, from what makes the suffering into what is worse than suffering, into the sin of impatience and sadness. Do not think that it is just a bit of duplicity on the part of the bird that it is silent when it suffers, that it is not silent in its innermost being however silent it is with others, that it complains over its fate, accuses God and humanity, and lets "the heart in sorrow sin."[16] No, the bird is silent and suffers. Alas, the human being does not do that. But why is it that human suffering, compared with the bird's suffering, seems so frightful? Is it not because the human being can speak? No, not for that reason, since that, after all, is an advantage, but because the human being cannot be silent. It is, namely, not as the impatient person, or even more intensely, the despairing person, thinks he understands it when he says or cries (and this is already a misunderstanding of speech and voice), "Would that I had a voice like the voice of the storm so that I could voice all my suffering as I feel it!" Ah, that would be only a foolish remedy; to XI
the same degree he will only feel his suffering the more intensely. 19
No, but if you could be silent, if you had the silence of the bird, then the suffering would certainly become less.

Like the bird, so also the lily—it is silent. Even though it stands and suffers as it withers, it is silent. This innocent child cannot dissemble, nor is it asked to, and its good fortune is that it cannot, because the art of being able to dissemble is indeed purchased at a high price. It cannot dissemble, cannot do anything about its changing color, and thereby betrays what one of course recognizes by this paling color-change, that it is suffering—but it remains silent. It would like to stand erect in order to hide what it is suffering, but for that it does not have the strength, this mastery over itself. Its head droops, feeble and bowed. The passerby—if any passerby has so much sympathy that he notices it!—the passerby understands what this means; it is sufficiently eloquent. But the lily is silent.

So it is with the lily. But why is it that human suffering, compared with the lily's suffering, seems so frightful? Is it not because it cannot speak? If the lily could speak and if, alas, like the human being, it had not learned the art of being silent, would not also its suffering become frightful? But the lily is silent. For the lily, to suffer is to suffer, neither more nor less. Yet when to suffer is neither more nor less than to suffer, the suffering is simplified and particularized as much as possible and made as small as possible. The suffering cannot become less, since it indeed *is* and therefore is what it is. But, on the other hand, the suffering can become immensely greater when it does not remain exactly what it is, neither more nor less. When the suffering is neither more nor less, that is, when it is only the definite suffering that it is, it is, even if it were the greatest suffering, the least it can be. But when it becomes indefinite how great the suffering actually is, the suffering becomes greater; this indefiniteness increases the suffering immensely. This indefiniteness appears just because of this dubious advantage of the human being, the ability to speak. On the other hand, one arrives at the definiteness of suffering, that it is neither more nor less than what it is, only by being able to be silent, and this silence you can learn from the bird and the lily.

Out there with the lily and the bird there is silence. But what
does this silence express? It expresses respect for God, that it is he
who rules and he alone to whom wisdom and understanding are
due. And just because this silence is veneration for God, is wor-
XI ship, as it can be in nature, this silence is so solemn. And because
20 this silence is solemn in this way, one is aware of God in nature—
what wonder, then, when everything is silent out of respect for
him! Even if *he* does not speak, the fact that everything is silent
out of respect for him affects one as if he spoke.

What you can learn, however, from the silence out there with the lily and the bird without the help of any poet, what only the Gospel can teach you, is that it is earnestness, that there must be earnestness, that the bird and the lily *shall* be the teacher, that you shall imitate them, learn from them in all earnestness, that you shall become as silent as the lily and the bird.

Indeed, this is already earnestness—if it is understood properly, not as the dreaming poet or as the poet who lets nature dream about him understands it—this, that out there with the lily and the bird you are aware *that you are before God*, something that usually is entirely forgotten in speaking and conversing with other human beings. When just we two are speaking together, even more so when we are ten or more, it is very easily forgotten that you and I, we two, or we ten, are before God. But the lily, who is the teacher, is profound. It does not become involved with you at all; it is silent, and by being silent it wants to be a sign to you that you are before God, so that you remember that you are before God—so that you also in earnestness and truth might become silent before God.

Silent before God, like the lily and the bird, you *shall* become. You are not to say, "The lily and the bird can easily be silent—after all, they cannot speak." You are not to say that. You are not to say anything at all, not make even the slightest attempt to frustrate the lesson in silence by, instead of being silent in earnest, foolishly and meaninglessly jumbling silence in with speaking, perhaps as the subject of speaking, so that the silence amounts to nothing, but a speech comes into existence instead, a speech about being silent. Before God you are not to become more important to yourself than a lily or a bird—yet when it becomes earnestness and truth that you are before God, this latter will be a consequence of the first. Even if what you want in the world would be the most astounding feat, you are to acknowledge the lily and the bird as your teachers and before God you are not to become more important to yourself than the lily and the bird. And even if the whole world were not large enough to hold your plans when you unfold them, you are to learn from the lily and the bird as teachers to be able before God simply to fold up all your plans into less space than a period and with less noise than the most negligible trifle—in silence. And if what you suffered in the world were as agonizing as anything ever experienced, you

XI 21 are to acknowledge the lily and the bird as your teachers and not become more important to yourself than the lily and the bird are to themselves in their minor cares.

So it is when the Gospel makes it a matter of earnestness that the bird and the lily shall be the teacher. Not so with the poet, or with the person who, just because earnestness is lacking, does not become completely silent in the silence with the lily and the bird—but becomes a poet. To be sure, poet-talk is very different from ordinary human speech, is so solemn that, compared with ordinary talk, it is almost like silence, but silence it nevertheless is not. Nor does the poet seek silence in order to become silent but, the opposite, in order to get to speak—as a poet speaks.[17] In the silence out there the poet daydreams about the exploit that he will never carry out—because the poet is certainly not a hero; and he becomes eloquent—perhaps he becomes eloquent simply because he is an unhappy lover of the exploit, whereas the hero is its happy lover, consequently because the deficiency makes him eloquent, just as deficiency essentially makes the poet—he becomes eloquent; this, his eloquence, is the poem. Out there in the silence, he devises great plans to transform and beatify the whole world, great plans that never become actuality—no, they become the poem. Out there in the silence, he broods over his pain, makes everything—yes, even the teachers, the bird and the lily, must serve him instead of teach him—he makes everything echo his pain. This echo of his pain is the poem, because a scream is not a poem at all, but the interminable echoing of the scream in himself is the poem.

Therefore, in the silence with the lily and the bird, the poet does not become silent, and why not? Simply because he reverses the relation, makes himself more important in comparison with the lily and the bird, fancies that he even has the merit, as we say, of lending the lily and the bird words and speech, whereas the task was rather that he himself learn silence from the lily and the bird.

Oh, but would that the Gospel, with the help of the lily and the bird, might teach you, my listener, earnestness, and teach me to make you completely silent before God! Would that you in silence might forget yourself, what you yourself are called, your

own name, the famous name, the wretched name, the insignificant name, in order in silence to pray to God: "Hallowed be *your* name!" Would that in silence you might forget yourself, your plans, the great, all-encompassing plans, or the limited plans for your life and its future, in order in silence to pray to God: "Your kingdom come!" Would that in silence you might forget your will, your self-will, in order in silence to pray to God: "*Your* will
be done!" Yes, if you could learn from the lily and the bird to XI
become completely silent before God, in what then would the 22
Gospel not be able to help you! Then nothing would be impossible for you. But if the Gospel, with the help of the lily and the bird, has only taught you silence, what help it has already given you! Just as the fear of God, as stated, is the beginning of wisdom, so also is silence the beginning of the fear of God. Go to the ant and become wise, says Solomon;[18] go to the bird and the lily and learn silence, says the Gospel.

"Seek *first* God's kingdom and his righteousness." But the expression for one's seeking first God's kingdom is precisely silence, the silence of the lily and the bird. The lily and the bird seek God's kingdom, nothing else whatever; all the rest will be added unto them. But then are they not seeking God's kingdom first if they seek nothing else whatever? Why, then, does the Gospel say, "Seek *first* God's kingdom," and seem to imply that there is something else to seek next, although it is still obvious that the meaning of the Gospel is that God's kingdom is the only thing that shall be sought? This surely is because it is undeniable that God's kingdom can be sought only if it is sought first; the person who does not seek God's kingdom first is not seeking it at all. Furthermore, this is because in itself the capacity to seek contains a possibility of being able to seek something else, and therefore the Gospel, which for the time being stands outside the individual, who consequently can also seek something else, says, "You shall seek first God's kingdom." Finally, this is because the Gospel gently and lovingly stoops down to the individual and whispers to him in order to attract him to the good. If the Gospel were immediately to say, "You shall simply and solely seek God's kingdom," the individual might think that too much was required and half impatiently and half anxiously and fearfully would draw back. But now the Gospel adapts itself somewhat to him. There stands the individual looking at the many things he wishes to seek—then the Gospel addresses him and says, "Seek first God's kingdom." Then he thinks, "Well, if I later am allowed to seek something else, then let me begin with seeking God's kingdom." If he then actually does begin with that, the Gospel knows very well what will follow—namely, that he will become so gratified and satisfied by this seeking that he entirely forgets to seek anything else, yes, that he does not even wish to seek anything else—thus it becomes literally true that he simply and solely seeks God's kingdom.

This is how the Gospel goes about it, and this, after all, is the
XI way an adult speaks to a child. Imagine a child who is very hun-
23 gry. When the mother is putting food on the table and the child gets to see what is offered, it is close to crying with impatience and says, "What's the good of so little? When I have eaten that, I will be just as hungry." Perhaps the child even becomes so impatient that it will not begin eating at all "because that little bit can't be of any help." But the mother, well aware that the whole thing is a misunderstanding, says, "Yes, yes, my little friend, just eat this first; then we can always see about getting a little more." So the child begins, and what happens? The child is full before the half is eaten. If the mother had promptly rebuked the child and said, "There is really more than enough," the mother would not have been wrong but she would not have exemplified by her behavior the wisdom that is really the wisdom of upbringing, which she in fact did. So also with the Gospel. For the Gospel the most important thing is not to rebuke and scold; for the Gospel the most important thing is to bring people to be guided by it. Therefore it says, "Seek first." It thereby muzzles, so to speak, all the objections a person has, silences him and gets him actually to begin first this seeking. Then this seeking so satisfies him that it literally becomes true that he simply and solely seeks God's kingdom.

Seek first God's kingdom; that is, become like the lily and the bird; that is, become completely silent before God—then all the rest will be added unto you.

II XI 24

[19]"No One Can Serve Two Masters, for He Must Either Hate the One and Love the Other or Be Devoted to the One and Despise the Other."

My listener, as you know, in the world there is frequently talk about an either/or, and this either/or creates a great stir and occupies different people in the most different ways: in hope, in fear, in busy activity, in tense inactivity, etc. You also know that in the same world there is talk about there being no either/or, and that in turn this wisdom has made just as great a stir as the most significant either/or. But out here in the silence with the lily and the bird, should it be doubtful here that there is an either/or? Or should it be doubtful here what this either/or is? Or should it be doubtful here whether this either/or is in the deepest sense the only either/or?[20]

No, here in this solemn silence not only under God's heaven, but in this solemn silence before God, there can be no doubt of that. There is an either/or: either *God*—or, well, then the rest is unimportant. Whatever else a person chooses, if he does not choose God, he has missed the either/or, or through his either/or he is in perdition. Therefore: either *God*; you see, there is no emphasis at all on the second, except by contrast to God, whereby the emphasis falls infinitely upon God. Thus it actually is God who, by being himself the object of the choice, tightens the decision of choice until it in truth becomes an either/or. If a person could light-mindedly or gloomily think that where God XI 25
is present as the one and only there are actually three things to choose among, then that person is lost, or he has lost God, and therefore there actually is no either/or for him, because with

God, that is, when the concept of God disappears or is warped, the either/or also goes out. Yet how could this happen to anyone in the silence with the lily and the bird!

So, then, either/or: either God, and as the Gospel explains it, either love God *or* hate him. Yes, when there is noise round about you or you are amid distractions, this seems to be almost an exaggeration. There seems to be much too great a distance between loving and hating for one to be able to have the right to bring them so close together, in one breath, in one single thought, in two words that, without intermediate clauses, without parenthetical phrases for closer unity, without even the slightest punctuation mark, follow immediately upon each other. But just as a body falls with exceedingly great speed in a vacuum, so also does the silence out there with the lily and the bird, the solemn silence before God, make these two opposites repellingly touch each other in one and the same instant, indeed, come into existence in the same instant: either to love or to hate. Just as there is no third factor in the vacuum that delays the falling body, so there is in this solemn silence before God no third factor that could keep loving and hating at a delaying distance from each other.

Either God, and as the Gospel explains it, either be devoted to him *or* despise him. In company with people, in business, in association with the multitude, there seems to be a great distance between being devoted to someone and despising him. "I do not need to associate with that person," one says, "but that certainly does not mean that I despise him, not at all." It is the same in association with the multitude with whom one associates sociably-diffusely without essential inwardness and with more or less indifference. But the smaller the number becomes, the less social, in the diffused sense, the association becomes, that is, the more inward it becomes, the more an either/or begins to become the law for the relationship; and in the deepest sense the association with God is unconditionally unsociable. Take just two lovers, a relationship that also is unsociable simply because it is so inward—for them and for their relationship the law applies: either be devoted to each other or despise each other. And now in the silence before God with the lily and the bird, where no one else

at all is present, where accordingly there is for you no other association than with God—yes, there the law applies: either be devoted to him or despise him. There is no excuse, since no one XI
else is present, and in any case no one else is present in such a way 26
that you can be devoted to him without despising God, since in this very silence it is clear how close God is to you. The two lovers are so close to each other that as long as the other is alive the one cannot be devoted to someone else without *despising* the other; therein lies what there is of an either/or in this relationship. Whether this either/or (either be devoted to or despise) exists depends on how close the two are to each other. But God, who certainly does not die, is even closer to you, infinitely closer than the two lovers are to each other, he, your Creator and Sustainer, he in whom you live, move, and have your being,[21] he by whose grace you have everything. So it is no exaggeration, this either be devoted to God or despise him; it is not as when a person applies either/or to a trifling matter, a person whom we may justifiably call short-tempered. Not so here. For one thing, God is indeed still God. For another, he does not apply it to trivialities; he does not say: Either a rose or a tulip. But he applies it to himself and says: Either *me* . . . . . either you are devoted to me and unconditionally in everything—or you despise me. Surely God could not speak in any other way about himself. If God were to speak or were able to speak of himself as if he were not unconditionally No. 1, as if he were not the one and only, unconditionally all, but merely also a something of sorts, one who cherished a hope of perhaps still entering into consideration also—then God would have lost himself, lost the idea of himself, and would not be God.

So, then, in the silence with the lily and the bird there is an either/or, either God . . . . . and understood in this way: either love him—or hate him; either be devoted to him—or despise him.

What, then, does this either/or mean; what does God require? Either/or is a requirement, just as the lovers require love when the one says to the other, either/or. But God does not relate himself to you as a lover; neither do you relate yourself to him as a lover. It is a different relationship, that of the creature to the

Creator. What, then, does he require with this either/or? He requires obedience, unconditional obedience. If you are not unconditionally obedient in everything, then you do not love him, and if you do not love him, then—you hate him. If you are not unconditionally obedient in everything, then you are not
XI 27 devoted to him, or, if you are not devoted to him unconditionally and in everything, then you are not devoted to him, and if you are not devoted to him, then—you despise him.

This unconditional obedience—that if one does not love God one hates him, that if one is not unconditionally and in everything devoted to him one despises him—this unconditional obedience you can learn from the teachers to whom the Gospel refers, from the lily and the bird. It is said that by learning to obey one learns to rule, but it is even more certain that by being obedient oneself one can teach obedience.[22]

So it is with the lily and the bird. They have no power with which to compel the learner; they have only their own obedience as the compelling power. The lily and the bird are "the obedient teachers." Is this not a strange expression? "Obedient," after all, is usually the word one uses about the learner; it is required of him that he shall be obedient. But here it is the teacher himself who is obedient! In what does he give instruction?—in obedience. And by what means does he give instruction?—by obedience. If you could become obedient in the same way as the lily and the bird, you would also by means of obedience be able to teach obedience. But since neither of us is obedient in this way, let us from the lily and the bird learn:

Obedience.

Out there with the lily and the bird, we said, there is silence. But this silence, or what we endeavored to learn from it, to become silent, is the first condition for truly being able to obey. When everything around you is solemn silence, as out there, and when there is silence within you, then you are aware and with the emphasis of the infinite are aware of the truth of this: You shall love the Lord your God and serve only him.[23] And you are aware that it is *you*, you who shall love God in this way, you alone in the whole world, you who are indeed alone in the surroundings of solemn silence, alone in such a way that also every doubt, and

every objection, and every excuse, and every evasion, and every question, in short, every voice, is silenced in your own inner being—every voice, that is, every voice other than that of God, who around you and within you speaks to you through the silence. If silence has never been around you and within you in this
way, then you never learned and never will learn obedience. But XI
if you have learned silence, learning obedience will surely come. 28

Pay attention, then, to nature around you. In nature everything is obedience, unconditional obedience. Here "God's will is done, as in heaven so also on earth";[24] or if anyone quotes the sacred words in another way, they still fit: here in nature "God's will is done on earth as it is in heaven." In nature everything is unconditional obedience. Here it is not only the case—as it is also in the human world—that because God is the Omnipotent nothing happens, not the least little thing, without his will—no, here it is also because everything is unconditional obedience. There is, however, an infinite difference here, because it is one thing that the most cowardly, the most defiant human disobedience, the disobedience of a single person and of the whole human race, is not capable of doing the least thing without his will, the will of the Omnipotent; it is something else again that his will is done because everything obeys him unconditionally, because there is no other will than his in heaven and on earth—and this is the case in nature. In nature it is true, as Scripture says, that "not one sparrow falls to the ground without his will."[25] This is not only because he is the Omnipotent but because everything is unconditional obedience and his will is the only will. There is not even the least little protest there; not a word, not a sigh is heard; the unconditionally obedient sparrow falls in unconditional obedience to the ground if it is God's will. In nature everything is unconditional obedience. The sighing of the wind, the echoing of the forest, the murmuring of the brook, the humming of the summer, the whispering of the leaves, the rustling of the grass,[26] every sound [*Lyd*], every sound you hear is all compliance [*Adlyd*], unconditional obedience [*Lydighed*]. Thus you can hear God in it just as you hear him in the harmony that is the movement of the celestial bodies in obedience. The vehemence of the rushing winds, the buoyant flexibility of the clouds, the droplet fluidity of the sea and its cohesion, the speed of light and

the even greater of sound[27]—it is all obedience. The rising of the sun on the hour and its setting on the hour, the shifting of the wind in a flash, the ebb and flow of the tide at specific times, and the agreement among the seasons in their precise alternating—all, all, all of it is obedience. Yes, if there were a star in the sky that wanted to have its own will, or a speck of dust on earth—they are wiped out at the same moment and with equal ease. In nature everything is nothing, understood in this way: it is noth-
XI ing but God's unconditional will; the moment it is not uncondi-
29 tionally God's will, it ceases to exist.

Let us, then, look more closely, and humanly, at the lily and the bird in order to learn obedience. The lily and the bird are unconditionally obedient to God. In this they are masters [*Mestere*]. As befits teachers [*Laeremestere*], they know how in a masterly way to find something the majority of human beings miss and mistake—the unconditioned. There is one thing of which the lily and the bird know unconditionally nothing—something the majority of human beings, alas, know best—half-measures. That a little disobedience, that this would not be unconditional disobedience—that the lily and the bird are unable, that they do not wish to understand. The lily and the bird are unable and do not wish to understand that the least little disobedience would in truth have any other name than—contempt for God. The lily and the bird cannot and do not want to understand that there would be anything else or anyone else that one, divided, could *also* serve to some extent besides serving God and how this also would not be despising God. What marvelous security in finding the unconditioned and in having one's life in it! And yet—O you profound teachers—would it indeed be possible to find security anywhere else than in the unconditioned, since, after all, in itself the conditioned is insecurity! Then I would rather speak differently; I would not admire the security with which they find the unconditioned but rather say that it is precisely the unconditioned that gives them the admirable security that makes them teachers of obedience. The lily and the bird are unconditionally obedient to God; in obedience they are so simple or so sublime *that they believe that everything that happens is unconditionally God's will, and that they have nothing whatever to do in the world other than either to do God's will in unconditional obedience or to submit to God's will in unconditional obedience.*

If the place assigned to the lily is as unfortunate as possible, so that it is easy to foresee that it will be utterly superfluous all its life and not be noticed by a single one who could find joy in it, if the place and the surroundings are so "desperately" (yes, out there I have forgotten that it is the lily I am talking about) unfortunate that it is not only unsought but is avoided—the obedient lily obediently submits to its conditions and blossoms in all its beauty. We human beings, or a human being in the lily's place, would say, "It is hard, it is too much to endure. To be a lily and as lovely as a lily, and then to be assigned a spot in such a place, to have to flower there in surroundings as unfavorable as possible, as if the XI
intention were to destroy the impression of one's loveliness—no, 30
this is too much to endure; indeed, it is a self-contradiction on the part of the Creator!" This is how a human being or we human beings would probably think and talk if we were in the lily's place, and thereupon we would wither with grief. But the lily thinks differently, thinks something like this: "I myself, of course, have not been able to determine the place and the conditions; this is not in the remotest way my affair. That I stand where I stand is God's will." This is the way the lily thinks, and that this is actually as it thinks, that this is God's will, can be seen on it, because it is lovely—Solomon in all his glory was not arrayed like this. Oh, if there were a difference in beauty between one lily and another, this lily would have to be awarded the prize—it has one additional beauty, since if one is a lily it is actually no art to be beautiful, but to be beautiful under these conditions, in such surroundings that do everything to hinder it, in such surroundings to be fully oneself and to preserve oneself, to mock the whole power of the surroundings—but no, not mock, the lily does not do this—but to be completely free of care in all its beauty! Despite its surroundings, the lily is itself because it is unconditionally obedient to God; and because it is unconditionally obedient to God it is unconditionally free of care, something only the unconditionally obedient, especially under such circumstances, can be. Because it is fully and completely itself and unconditionally free of care—the two correspond to each other

directly and inversely—it is beautiful. Only by unconditional obedience can one with unconditional accuracy find *the place* where one is to stand; and if one finds it unconditionally, then one understands that it is unconditionally a matter of indifference if the place is a dunghill.

[28]If it happens as unfortunately as possible for the lily that the very moment when it is to blossom is so unfavorable that the lily can with near certainty predict that it will be snapped off at the same moment, so its coming into existence becomes its downfall—indeed, it seems as if it came into existence and became lovely merely in order to succumb—the obedient lily obediently submits to this. It knows that this is God's will, and it blossoms. If you saw it at that moment, there would not be the slightest indication that this unfolding was also its downfall, so fully developed, so rich and beautiful did it blossom, so rich and beautiful did it go—the whole thing was but a moment—go unconditionally obedient to its downfall. In the lily's place, a human being or we human beings would surely despair at the thought that coming into existence and downfall were one and then in despair would prevent ourselves from becoming what we could have
XI 31 become, if only for a moment. Not so with the lily; it was unconditionally obedient and therefore became itself in beauty, actually became its full possibility, undisturbed, unconditionally undisturbed by the thought that the same moment was its death. Oh, if there were a difference in beauty between one lily and another, this lily would have to be awarded the prize; it had one additional beauty, to be as beautiful as this despite the certainty of downfall at the same moment. Truly, to be face-to-face with its downfall and to have the courage and faith to come into existence in all its beauty—only unconditional obedience is capable of that. The certainty of downfall would, as stated, so disturb a human being that he would not fulfill his potentiality, which nevertheless was granted to him, although only the briefest existence was allotted to him. "To what purpose?" he would say. Or "Why?" he would say. Or "What's the use?" he would say. Then he would not unfold his full potentiality but would be guilty because he, stunted and ugly, would in advance succumb to the moment. Only unconditional obedience can with unconditional

accuracy find *the moment.* Only unconditional obedience can make use of the moment, unconditionally undisturbed by the next moment.

If, when the moment comes to fly away, the bird is ever so certain that its present situation is good just as it is, so that by flying away it will let go of the certain in order to grasp the uncertain—yet the obedient bird immediately starts out on its journey. Simply, with the help of unconditional obedience, it understands only one thing but understands it unconditionally—that now is the unconditional moment. —When the bird is touched by the harshness of this life, when it is tried in troubles and adversities, when every morning for several days it finds its nest disarranged, the obedient bird begins the work from the beginning every day with the same zest and carefulness as the first time. Simply, with the help of unconditional obedience, it understands the one thing but understands it unconditionally, that this is its work, that it only has to do its work. —When the bird must experience the evil of this world, when the little songbird that sings to the glory of God must put up with a naughty child's finding its amusement in mimicking it in order if possible to disturb the solemnity; or when the solitary bird has found surroundings it loves, a beloved branch on which it especially loves to sit, perhaps additionally dear to it because of the most precious memories—and then there is some person who finds his pleasure in driving it from this place by throwing stones or in some other way—a person, alas, who is just as indefatigable in evil as the bird, although dislodged and chased away, is indefatigable in finding its way back to its love and its old place—the obedient bird submits unconditionally to everything. Simply, with the help of unconditional obedience, it understands only XI 32
one thing, but understands it unconditionally, that everything that happens to it in this way does not really concern it, that is, concerns it only figuratively, or more correctly, that what really does concern it, but also unconditionally, is, unconditionally obedient to God, to submit to it.

So it is with the lily and the bird, from whom we should learn. Therefore you are not to say, "The lily and the bird, it is easy for them to be obedient; after all, they cannot do anything else, or they cannot do otherwise. To become a model of obedience in that way is, after all, to make a virtue of necessity." You are not to speak this way; you are to say nothing at all, you are to be silent and obey, so that, if it really is true that the lily and the bird make a virtue of necessity, you also might succeed in making a virtue of necessity. You, too, are indeed subject to necessity. God's will is still done anyhow; so strive to make a virtue of necessity by unconditionally obediently doing God's will. God's will is still done anyhow; so see to it that you make a virtue of necessity by unconditionally obediently submitting to God's will, so unconditionally obediently that you might with truth be able to say of yourself with regard to doing and submitting to God's will, "I cannot do anything else, I cannot do otherwise."

This you should strive for, and you should bear in mind that whatever the situation with the lily and the bird, if it actually is more difficult for a human being to be unconditionally obedient, there is also a danger for a human being, a danger that might, if I dare say so, make this less difficult for him—the danger of forfeiting God's patience. Have you ever really earnestly considered your own life or considered people's lives, the human world, which is so different from nature, where everything is unconditional obedience? Have you ever considered this, and have you then perceived without shuddering with what truth God calls himself "the God of patience,"[29] perceived that he, the God who says either/or, meaning either love me or hate me, either be devoted to me or despise me, that he has the patience to bear with you and me and all of us! If God were a human being, what then? How long, long, long ago he must—to use myself as an example—have become sick and tired of me and of having anything to do with me, and must have said, as human parents say (but with an entirely different justification), "The child is both bad and sickly, stupid and dull. If there were only something good about him, but there is so much evil in him—no human being can put up with that." No, no human being can put up with that; only the God of patience can do that.

XI Now think of the countless number of human beings who are
33 living! We human beings say that to be a schoolmaster for small
children is a work of patience—and now God, who has to be the

schoolmaster for this countless number! What patience! What makes the requirement for patience infinitely greater is that where God is the schoolmaster all the children labor more or less under the delusion that they are big, grown-up people, a delusion from which the lily and the bird are entirely free, and surely it is for this very reason that unconditional obedience comes so easily for them. "The only thing lacking," a human schoolmaster would say, "the only thing lacking is that the children would delude themselves into thinking that they are grown-up people; then one would have to lose patience and to despair, because no human being would be able to endure that." No, no human being could endure that; only the God of patience can do that. See, this is why God calls himself the God of patience. And he knows very well what he is saying. It is not in a mood that he gets the idea of calling himself this; no, he does not change in mood—that, after all, is impatience. He knew it from eternity, knew it from thousands and thousands of years of daily experience; he knew from eternity that as long as time lasts and the human race in it, he must be the God of patience, because otherwise human disobedience would be too much to endure. In relation to the lily and the bird, God is the fatherly Creator and Sustainer; only in relation to human beings is he the God of patience. Quite true, it is a comfort, a very necessary and indescribable comfort (which is why Scripture also says that God is the God of patience—and "the God of comfort"), but it is also a terribly serious matter that human disobedience is responsible for God's being the God of patience, a terribly serious matter that human beings not take this patience in vain. Human beings discovered an attribute of God that the lily and the bird, who are always unconditionally obedient, do not know; or God had such love for human beings that he let it be manifest to them that he has this attribute, that he is patience. But then in a certain sense—what a frightful responsibility [*Ansvar*]!—God's patience corresponds [*svare til*] to human disobedience. It is a comfort, but under a terrible responsibility.[30] A person may assume that even if all people were to give him up, indeed, if he is on the verge of giving himself up, God is still the God of patience. This is a priceless wealth. Oh, but use it properly; remember that it is your

savings. For God's sake, use it properly. Otherwise you will plunge yourself into even deeper misery; it will change into its
XI 34 opposite and no longer be a comfort but become the most frightful charge of all against you. If it seems to you too hard a saying (although it is still not harder than the truth) that not to be devoted unconditionally and in everything to God is *summarily* to despise him, then it certainly cannot be too hard a saying that to take his patience in vain is to despise God!

Pay careful attention, then, to the Gospel's instruction to learn obedience from the lily and the bird. Do not let yourself be scared off; do not despair as you compare your life with the life of these teachers. There is nothing to despair over, because you *shall* indeed learn from them; and the Gospel comforts you first by telling you that God is the God of patience, but then it adds: You shall learn from the lily and the bird, learn to be unconditionally obedient like the lily and the bird, learn not to serve two masters, because no one can serve two masters; one must either . . . . . or.

But if you can become unconditionally obedient like the lily and the bird, you have learned what you were supposed to learn and you have learned it from the lily and the bird (and if you have learned it thoroughly, you have become the more perfect one, so that the lily and the bird change from being the teacher to being the metaphor), you have learned to serve only one master, to love him alone, and to be unconditionally devoted to him in everything. Moreover, then the prayer that is indeed fulfilled anyhow would be fulfilled by you when you pray to God, "Your will be done, as in heaven also on earth," since by unconditional obedience your will is one with God's will and therefore God's will is done by you on earth as it is in heaven. Then when you pray, "Lead us not into temptation,"[31] your petition would be heard, because if you are unconditionally obedient to God, then there is no ambivalence in you, and if there is no ambivalence in you, then you are sheer simplicity before God. But there is one thing that all the craftiness of Satan and the snares of temptation cannot take by surprise or capture—it is simplicity. What Satan keenly watches for as his prey (but what is never found in the lily and the bird), what all temptation keeps in sight, certain of its

prey (but what is never found in the lily and the bird)—is ambivalence. Wherever there is ambivalence, there is temptation and it is all too easily the stronger there. But where there is ambivalence, there is in one way or another also disobedience underneath at the base. There is no ambivalence at all in the lily and the bird simply because the unconditional obedience is deepest and present everywhere at the base. And for that very reason, because there is no ambivalence in the lily and the bird, it is impossible to lead the lily and the bird into temptation. Where there is no ambivalence, Satan is powerless. Where there is no
ambivalence, temptation is as powerless as a bird catcher with his XI
net when there is no bird to be spotted—but just the slightest, 35
slightest glimpse of ambivalence, then Satan is powerful, and temptation is out trapping. He is sharp-sighted, the evil one whose snare is called temptation and whose prey is called the human soul. The temptation does not actually come from him, but no ambivalence, not one, can hide itself from him, and if he spots it, the temptation is in league with him.[32] But the person who by unconditional obedience hides in God is unconditionally secure; from his secure hiding place he can see the devil, but the devil cannot see him.[33] From his secure hiding place—for just as the devil is sharp-sighted in connection with ambivalence, he becomes equally blind when he looks at simplicity, becomes blind or is stricken with blindness. Yet the unconditionally obedient one does not without a shudder observe the devil—this glittering gaze that looks as if it could penetrate earth and sea and the most hidden secrets of the heart, as indeed it can—and yet with this gaze he is blind! But if he who spreads the snare of temptation is blind in relation to the person who by unconditional obedience is hidden in God, then of course there is no temptation for him, because "God tempts no one."[34] In this way his prayer is heard, "Lead us not into temptation," that is, let me never through disobedience venture outside my hiding place at any time, and insofar as I am guilty of disobedience, then do not immediately drive me out of my hiding place, outside which I am immediately led into temptation. And if by his unconditional obedience he remains in his hiding place, he is also "delivered from evil."

No one can serve two masters; he must either love the one and hate the other or be devoted to the one and despise the other. You cannot serve God and mammon, not God and the world, not good and evil. Thus there are two powers: God and the world, good and evil; and the reason a human being can serve only one master is undoubtedly that these two powers, even though the one power is the infinitely stronger, are in mortal combat with each other. This enormous danger, in which a person is by being human—which the lily and the bird in their unconditional obedience, which is happy innocence, escape, since neither God and the world nor good and evil are fighting over them—this enormous danger, that a *human being* is placed between these two enormous powers and the choice is left up to
XI him, this enormous danger is what entails that one must either
36 love or hate, that not to love is to hate. These two powers are so inimical that the slightest leaning to one side is regarded from the other side as the unconditional opposite. When a human being forgets this enormous danger in which he is, a danger of such a nature, note well, that trying to forget it is truly not a useful means against it, when a human being forgets that he is in this enormous danger, when he thinks that he is not in danger, when he even says peace and no danger[35]—then the Gospel's message must seem to him a foolish exaggeration. Alas, but that is just because he is so immersed in the danger, so lost that he has neither any idea of the love with which God loves him, and that it is just out of love that God requires unconditional obedience, nor does he have any idea of the power and cunning of evil, and also of his own weakness. [36]And from the very beginning a human being is too childish to be able or to want to understand the Gospel; what it says about either/or seems to him to be a false exaggeration—that the danger would be so great, that unconditional obedience would be necessary, that the requirement of unconditional obedience would be grounded in love—this he cannot get into his head.

What does the Gospel do then? The Gospel, which is the wisdom of upbringing, does not become involved with a human being in a dispute about ideas or words in order to *demonstrate* to him that it is so. The Gospel knows very well that the way things

go is not that a person first understands that what it says is so and then decides to obey unconditionally, but the reverse, that by unconditionally obeying he first comes to understand that it is as the Gospel says. Therefore the Gospel uses authority and says: You *shall.* But at the same time this is tempered so that it might move the hardest heart. It takes you by the hand, so to speak—and does it just as the loving father does with his child—and says, "Come, let us go out to the lily and the bird." Out there it goes on to say, "Look at the lily and the bird. Abandon yourself to this sight, lose yourself in it. Does this sight not move you?" Then when the solemn silence out there with the lily and the bird deeply moves you, the Gospel explains further and says, "But why is this silence so solemn? Because it expresses the unconditional obedience with which everything serves only one master, turns in service toward only one, joined in perfect unity, in one great divine service. So then let yourself be gripped by this great thought, because it is all only one thought, and learn from the lily and the bird." But do not forget, you *shall* learn from the lily and the bird; you shall, like the lily and the bird, become unconditionally obedient. Bear in mind that it was human sin that—by XI
being unwilling to serve one master, or by wanting to serve an- 37
other master, or by wanting to serve two, indeed, several masters—disturbed the beauty of the whole world where previously everything was so very good, human sin that created a cleft in a world of unity. Bear in mind, too, that every sin is disobedience and every disobedience is sin.

XI 38

III

"Look at the Birds of the Air; They Sow Not and Reap Not and Gather Not into Barns"—*without Worries about Tomorrow*. "Look at the Grass in the Field, *Which Today Is*."

Do this and learn:

Joy.

Let us now look at the lily and the bird, these joyful teachers. "The joyful teachers"—yes, for you do know that joy is communicable, and therefore no one teaches joy better than one who is joyful oneself. The teacher of joy actually has nothing else to do but to be joyful oneself, or to be joy. However much he may strain to communicate joy—if he himself is not joyful, the teaching is imperfect. So there is nothing easier to teach than joy—alas, all that is needed is just to be always truly joyful oneself.[37] But this "alas"—alas, it suggests that it still is not very easy, namely, not very easy to be always joyful oneself, for it is easy enough to teach joy when one is joyful—nothing is more certain.

But out there with the lily and the bird, or out there where the lily and the bird teach joy, there is always joy. The lily and the bird are never in a predicament as a human teacher sometimes is when what he is teaching is written on paper or is in his library—that is, in some other place and not always with him. No, *out there* where the lily and the bird teach joy there is always joy—after all, it is within the lily and the bird. What joy when day is dawning and the bird awakens early to the joy of the day! What joy, even
XI 39 though in another tone, when dusk is falling and the bird joyfully

hurries home to its nest! What joy the long summer day! What joy when the bird—which not only sings at its work like a joyful worker but whose essential work is to sing—joyfully begins its song! What new joy when its neighbor also begins to sing, and then its neighbor on the other side, and then the whole chorus joins in, what joy! And finally when there is a sea of sounds that make the forest and valley, sky and earth echo, a sea of sounds in which the bird that struck the first note now frolics on high out of joy—what joy, what joy! And so it is throughout the bird's whole life. Everywhere and at all times it finds something or, rather, enough to rejoice over. It does not waste a single moment, but it would regard any moment wasted in which it was not joyful.

What joy when the dew falls and refreshes the lily, which, now cooled, composes itself for rest! What joy when after its bath the lily voluptuously dries itself in the first rays of the sun! What joy the long summer day! Oh, do look at them! Look at the lily, look at the bird, look at them together! What joy when the bird hides by the lily, where it has its nest and where it is so indescribably cozy, while for diversion it jests and banters with the lily! What joy when high up from the branch, or higher up, high up from the sky, the bird blissfully keeps its eye on its nest or on the lily, which smiling turns its eye up toward it! Blissful, happy existence, so rich in joy!

Or is the joy perhaps less because, small-mindedly understood, it is little that makes them so joyful? No, this, this small-minded understanding, is certainly a misunderstanding, alas, an extremely sad and deplorable misunderstanding, since the very fact that it is little that makes them so joyful is evidence that they themselves are joy and joy itself. Is it not indeed so? If it was nothing at all that one rejoiced over and yet one was indeed indescribably joyful, then this would be the best evidence that one is joy and joy itself—which the lily and the bird are, the joyful teachers of joy, who just because they are *unconditionally joyful* are joy itself. That is, the one whose joy is dependent on certain conditions is not joy itself; his joy, after all, is that of the conditions and is conditional in relation to them. But one who is joy itself is unconditionally joyful, just as, inversely, one who

is unconditionally joyful is joy itself. Oh, how much trouble and worry the conditions for our becoming joyful cause us human beings—even if we procured all the conditions, we perhaps would not become unconditionally joyful anyway. Yet is it not true, you profound teachers of joy, that it cannot be otherwise,
XI because with the help of conditions, even of all the conditions, it
40 is still not possible to become more than or anything other than conditionally joyful; the conditions and the conditionality are indeed equivalent. No, only the one who is joy itself is unconditionally joyful, and only by being unconditionally joyful is one joy itself.

But could one not state very briefly how joy is the content of the lily's and the bird's teaching or what is the content of their teaching of joy—that is, could one not very briefly state the thought-categories of this teaching of theirs? Yes, that can be done easily, because however simple the lily and the bird in fact are, they certainly are not thoughtless. So it can be done easily, and let us not forget that in this regard it is already an extraordinary foreshortening that the lily and the bird themselves are what they teach, themselves express what they as teachers are teaching. This—unlike the direct and first originality, that the lily and the bird in the strictest sense possess at first hand what they teach—is the acquired originality. This acquired originality in the lily and the bird is in turn simplicity, since whether a teaching is simple does not depend so much on using simple, everyday terms or grandiloquent, learned terms—no, the simplicity is that the teacher himself is what he is teaching. This is the case with the lily and the bird. But their teaching of joy, which their lives in turn express, is quite briefly as follows: There is a today; it *is*—indeed, an infinite emphasis falls upon this *is*. There is a today—and there is no worry, none whatever, about tomorrow or about the day after tomorrow. This is not light-mindedness on the part of the lily and the bird but is the joy of silence and obedience. When you are silent in the solemn silence that is nature, tomorrow does not exist. When you obey as the creation obeys, tomorrow does not exist, that unblessed day invented by garrulousness and disobedience. But when, because of silence and obedience, tomorrow does not exist, then in the silence and obedience today is, it *is*—and then the joy is as it is in the lily and the bird.

What is joy, or what is it to be joyful? It is truly to be present
to oneself; but truly to be present to oneself is this *today*, this *to be*
today, truly *to be today*. The more true it is that you are today, the
more completely present you are to yourself today, the less the
day of trouble, tomorrow, exists for you. Joy is the present time
with the whole emphasis on: *the present time*. Therefore God is XI
blessed, he who eternally says: Today, he who eternally and infi- 41
nitely is present to himself in being today. And therefore the lily
and the bird are joy, because by silence and unconditional obedience they are completely present to themselves in being today.

"But," you say, "the lily and the bird, they have it easy." Answer: Do not come with any "but"—but learn from the lily and the bird to become completely present to yourself in being today; then you, too, are joy. But as stated, no "but"; because this is earnestness, you *shall* learn joy from the lily and the bird. Even less may you become self-important, so that you, because the lily and the bird are simple, perhaps in order to feel that you are a human being, become witty and, speaking of a particular tomorrow, say: The lily and the bird, they have it easy, they who do not even have tomorrow to be plagued by; "but a human being, after all, not only has worry about tomorrow and what he is going to eat but also has worry about yesterday with regard to what he has eaten—and not paid for!"[38] No, no witticism, which rudely disturbs the lesson.[39] But learn, at least begin to learn from the lily and the bird. Surely no one would seriously think that what the lily and the bird rejoice over and comparable things are nothing to rejoice over! Therefore, that you came into existence, that you exist, that *today* you receive what is necessary for life; that you came into existence, that you became a human being; that you can see, bear in mind that you can see, that you can hear, that you can smell, that you can taste, that you can feel; that the sun shines for you and for your sake, that when it becomes weary the moon begins to shine and the stars are lit; that winter comes, that all nature disguises itself, plays the game of

stranger, and in order to delight you; that spring comes, that the birds return in great flocks, and in order to give you joy; that the leaves bud, the forest adorns itself and stands like a bride, and in order to give you joy; that autumn comes, that the bird flies away, not to make itself scarce and valuable, oh, no, but so that you will not become bored with it; that the forest hides its adornment for the sake of next time, that is, so that it can give you joy next time—and all this is supposed to be nothing to rejoice over! Oh, if I dared to chide, but out of respect for the lily and the bird
XI I dare not, and therefore, instead of saying that this is nothing to
42 rejoice over, I will say instead: If this does not give joy, then there is nothing to rejoice over. Bear in mind that the lily and the bird are joy, and yet they—to follow this vein of thought—have much less to rejoice over than you, you who have also the lily and the bird to give you joy. Therefore learn from the lily and learn from the bird, who are the teachers, who exist, *are today*, and *are* joy. If you cannot find joy in looking at the lily and the bird, who are joy itself, if you cannot find joy in looking at them so that you become willing to learn from them, then you are like the child of whom the teacher says, "It is not a lack of ability. Furthermore, the subject is so easy that it cannot be a question of a lack of ability. It must be something else, perhaps only a little indisposition, which one does not immediately deal with too severely and treat as if it were unwillingness or perhaps even obstinacy."

This is the way the lily and the bird are teachers of joy. Yet the lily and the bird do have sorrow also, just as all nature has sorrow. Does not all creation groan under the perishability under whose dominion it was placed against its will?[40] It is all under the dominion of perishability! The star, however firmly fixed it is in the sky, indeed, the most firmly fixed star, will nevertheless change its place in the fall, and the one that never changed its position will nevertheless at some time change its position as it plunges into the abyss. This whole world with everything in it will be changed as one changes a garment[41] when it is discarded, the prey of perishability! The lily, even if it escapes the fate of being cast immediately into the stove, must nevertheless wither after having already suffered this and that. The bird, even if it is allowed to die of old age, still must die at some time, be separated from its beloved after having already suffered this and that. Oh, it is all perishability, and everything at some time will become what it is, the prey of perishability. Perishability, perishability, that is the *groan*—because to be under the dominion of perishability is to be what a groan signifies: confinement, restraint, imprisonment; and the content of the groan is: perishability, perishability!

Yet the lily and the bird are unconditionally joyful; and here you really see how true it is when the Gospel says: You *shall* learn joy from the lily and the bird. Indeed, you cannot ask for a better
teacher than the one who, despite bearing extremely deep sor- XI
row, is still unconditionally joyful and joy itself. 43

How do the lily and the bird go about this, about something that looks almost like a miracle: in deepest sorrow to be unconditionally joyful; when there is such a frightful tomorrow, then *to be*, that is, to be unconditionally joyful today—how do they go about this? They go about this quite plainly and simply—the lily and the bird always do that—and yet get rid of this tomorrow as if it did not exist. The lily and the bird have taken to heart the apostle Peter's words and, simple as they are, have taken them to heart altogether literally—ah, and precisely this, that they take them altogether literally, it is precisely this that helps them. These words have enormous power when they are taken altogether literally; when not taken literally, strictly according to the letter, they are more or less without power, finally only a meaningless platitude. But it requires unconditional simplicity to take them unconditionally altogether literally. "Cast **all** your sorrow **upon God**."[42] See, the lily and the bird do this unconditionally. By means of the unconditional silence and the unconditional obedience, they cast—indeed, just as the most powerful catapult casts something from itself, and with a passion like that with which one casts away what one most detests—**all** their sorrow away, and cast it—with the sureness of one who with the most dependable gun hits the mark and with the faith and confidence of the most expert marksman—**upon God**. In the same instant—and this same instant is from the very first moment, is today, is contemporaneous with the first moment one exists—in the same instant they are unconditionally joyful. What marvelous deftness! To be able to take hold of all one's sorrow in this way and all at once and then to be able to cast it deftly away and so surely hit the mark! Yet the lily and the bird do this, and therefore they are unconditionally joyful in the same instant. This is entirely as it should be, since God the Omnipotent One carries the whole world and all its sorrow—also the lily's and the bird's—with extreme lightness. What indescribable joy! Joy, namely, over God the Omnipotent One.

Learn, then, from the lily and the bird, learn this deftness of the unconditioned. It is, to be sure, an amazing feat, but for that very reason you must pay all the closer attention to the lily and the bird. It is an amazing feat, and, just like the "feat of meekness,"
XI 44 it contains a contradiction, or it is a feat that solves a contradiction. The word "cast" leads one's thoughts to an application of strength, as if one should gather all one's strength and with an enormous effort of strength—mightily cast the sorrow away—and yet, yet *might* is precisely what must not be used. What must be used—and used unconditionally—is *compliance*; and yet one is to cast away sorrow! And one is to cast away *all* sorrow; if one does not cast away *all* sorrow, then one keeps much, some, a little of the rest, one does not become joyful, to say nothing of unconditionally joyful. If one does not cast it unconditionally *upon God* but somewhere else, then one does not become unconditionally rid of it; it returns in one way or another, often in the form of even greater and more grievous sorrow. To cast sorrow away—but not upon God—is a *scattering*. But scattering is a dubious and ambiguous remedy against sorrow. Unconditionally to cast all sorrow upon God is, however, a *gathering*, yet—how amazing this feat of contradiction!—a *gathering* by means of which you unconditionally *get rid of* all sorrow.

Learn, then, from the lily and the bird. Cast all your sorrow upon God! But joy you shall not cast away; on the contrary, you are to hold on to it with all your might, with all your life force. If you do that, then the reckoning is easy—that you always retain some joy, because if you cast all sorrow away you of course retain only whatever joy you have. But this will scarcely be sufficient. Therefore learn something more from the lily and the bird. Cast all your sorrow upon God, totally, unconditionally, just as the lily and the bird do—then you will become unconditionally joyful like the lily and the bird. This, namely, is the unconditional joy: to worship the omnipotence with which God the Omnipotent One bears all your sorrow lightly as nothing. And the next (the apostle does add this) is also unconditional joy: worshipfully to dare to believe "that God cares for you." The unconditional joy is simply joy over God, over whom and in whom you can always unconditionally rejoice. If you do not become unconditionally joyful in this relationship, then the fault lies unconditionally in you, in your ineptitude in casting all your sorrow upon him, in your unwillingness to do so, in your conceitedness, in your self-willfulness—in short, it lies in your not being like the lily and the bird. There is only one sorrow concerning which the lily and the bird cannot be your teacher and which we therefore will not discuss here: the sorrow of sin. With regard to all other sorrow, it holds true that if you do not become unconditionally joyful, then the fault is yours, that you will not learn from the lily and the bird to become unconditionally joyful over God through unconditional silence and obedience.

Yet one more thing. Perhaps you say with the poet, "Yes, if XI
only one could build and live with the bird, privately in the 45
solitude of the forest where the bird and its mate are a pair, but where there otherwise is no society, or if only one could live together with the lily in the peacefulness of the field where every lily shifts for itself and where there is no society—then one could easily cast all one's sorrow upon God and be or become unconditionally joyful. 'Society,' society itself is the trouble, the fact that a human being is the only creature who torments himself and others with the confounded delusion about society and the bliss of society, and all the more so as society, to his and its corruption, becomes greater." But you must not talk this way. No, look more closely at the matter and shamefully admit that, despite the sorrow, it is actually an unspeakable love-joy with which the birds, male and female, are a pair, and, despite the sorrow, it is the self-sufficient joy of the single state by which the lily is solitary—it is really because of this joy that society does not disturb them, since society is still there. Look at it even more closely, and

shamefully admit that it actually is the unconditional silence and the unconditional obedience with which the bird and the lily are unconditionally joyful over God—that it is actually this that makes the lily and the bird just as joyful and unconditionally just as joyful in solitude as in society. So, then, learn from the lily and the bird.

If you could learn to become just like the lily and the bird, and if I, alas, could learn it, then the prayer would be truth in you as in me, the last petition in *the prayer*, which (a model for all true prayer, which indeed prays itself joyful and more joyful and unconditionally joyful) finally has nothing, nothing more to pray and ask for, but, unconditionally joyful, ends in praise and worship, in the prayer, "Yours is the kingdom and the power and the glory." Yes, *his* is the kingdom, and therefore *you* have to be unconditionally silent lest you disturbingly make your presence known, yet by the solemnity of the unconditional silence express that the kingdom is his. And *his* is the power, and therefore you have to obey unconditionally and, unconditionally obedient, to submit to everything, because the power is his. And *his* is the glory, and therefore in everything you do and in everything you suffer you have unconditionally one thing left to do, to give him the glory, because the glory is his.

Oh, what unconditional joy: his is the kingdom and the power and the glory—forever. *Forever*, behold, this day, the day of eternity, never ends. Therefore only hold unconditionally fast to this, that his is the kingdom and the power and the glory forever; then there is for you a today that never ends, a today in which you eternally can become present to yourself. Let the sky collapse and
XI 46 the stars change their positions in the upheaval of everything, let the bird die and the lily wither—your joy in worship and you in your joy survive every destruction *this very day*. Bear in mind what pertains to you, if not as a human being then as a Christian, that Christianly even the danger of death is so unimportant for you that it is said, "*This very day* you are in paradise."[43] Hence the transition from temporality to eternity—the greatest possible distance—is so swift, and even if it should happen through the destruction of everything is yet so swift that *this very day* you are in paradise, because Christianly you *remain* in God. If you remain in

God, then whether you live or die, whether life treats you well or badly, whether you die today or not for seventy years, whether you find your death at the bottom of the ocean where it is deepest or you are blown to fragments in the air—you still will not find yourself outside God, you *remain*. Hence you are present to yourself in God and therefore on the day of your death are this very day in paradise. The bird and the lily live only one day, but a very short day, and yet are joy, because, as was explained, they rightly are *today, are present to themselves* in this today. And you, to whom the longest day is granted—to live today, and this very day to be in paradise—should you not be unconditionally joyful, you who even should, since you could, far, far exceed the bird in joy, something you are convinced of every time you pray this prayer, and something to which you also draw near every time you fervently pray this prayer of joy: "Yours is the kingdom and the power and the glory, for ever. Amen."

TWO ETHICAL-RELIGIOUS ESSAYS XI 49

by H. H.

PREFACE XI 51

These two essays probably will essentially be able to interest only theologians.

H. H.

[1]*Does a Human Being Have the Right to Let Himself Be Put to Death for the Truth?* XI 55

A Posthumous Work of a Solitary Human Being

A Poetical Venture

by H. H.

PREFACE XI 57

[2]This preface contains nothing more than an entreaty that the reader will first practice laying aside part of his customary mode of thinking. Otherwise the issue as it is presented here will not exist for him at all—and, strangely enough, precisely because long ago he was already finished with it, but in the reversed position.

The end of 1847

[3]Once upon a time there was a man. As a child he had been strictly brought up in the Christian religion. He had not heard much of what children ordinarily hear about the little baby Jesus, about angels and the like. On the other hand, the Crucified One had been all the more frequently depicted to him; therefore this picture was the one and only impression he had of the Savior. Although a child, he was already old like an old man.[4] This picture followed him throughout his life; he never became young again, and he never lost sight of this picture. Just as in the story of an artist who in anguish of conscience could not stop looking back at the picture of the murdered man who was pursuing him, so he, too, motivated by love, could not for one moment look away from this picture that drew him to itself. What he as a child had devoutly believed, that the sin of the world called for this sacrifice, what he as a child had simply understood, that the ungodliness of the Jews in the hand of Governance was the condition that could cause this horror to take place, this he believed unchanged and he understood this unchanged.

But gradually, as he grew older, this picture acquired even more power over him. It seemed to him as if it continually required something of him. He had always considered it ungodly that one would undertake to paint this picture and equally ungodly to look artistically at such a painted picture to see if it resembled him [the Crucified One]—instead of becoming himself the picture that resembled him[5]—and he was driven by an inexplicable power to want to resemble him insofar as a human being can resemble him. He was aware that there was nothing presumptuous in his desire, as if he could ever forget himself to
the degree that he could presumptuously forget that this Cruci- XI
fied One was God, the Holy One—he a sinner. But to want to 60
suffer for the same cause, unto death, there was indeed nothing presumptuous in that.

In this way he secretly attended to this picture; he never spoke of it to anyone. But the picture steadily came closer and closer to

him, and he felt its claim on him ever more deeply.[6] Yet to speak of it to anyone was an impossibility for him. But precisely this was evidence of how deeply this matter occupied him, evidence that it would not have been impossible for him to have acted accordingly at some time. Silence and the capacity to act correspond to each other completely; silence is the measure of the capacity to act; a person never has more capacity to act than he has silence. Everyone is well aware that to act is far greater than to talk about it. If, therefore, he is sure of himself, sure that he can do something and has resolved to do it, he does not talk about it. In connection with acting, what a person talks about is the very thing about which he is not sure. A man who easily persuades himself to give ten dollars to the poor, so that it occurs to him quite naturally—then he does not feel (yes, here we have it) that it is something to talk about—he never talks about it. But if you perhaps hear him talk about intending to give a thousand dollars to the poor at some time—alas, then the poor must certainly be satisfied with the ten. A girl who has sufficient inwardness to grieve, silently but deeply, for a lifetime over an unhappy love affair does not talk about it. But if in the first moment of pain you perhaps hear her say that she will commit suicide—remain calm; just because she talked about it, she will not do it; it was an empty thought. The inner conviction that one can and will satisfies in a way quite different from all chatter. This is why the subject of people's chatter is only something about which they do not have this inner conviction. One never speaks about the feeling one truly has; one chatters only about the feeling one does not have, or the degree of feeling one does not have. The law is very simple; with regard to evil it is this: If you suspect that someone dear to you is secretly harboring some terrible thought, just get him to tell it, preferably in such a way that you lure it out of him as if it were a trifle, so that even in the moment of communication there is not the pathos of a confidence. If you yourself are in the situation of being on the verge of becoming inclosed with a terrible thought, then speak to someone else about it, but preferably in the pathos-filled form of a confidence, because if you were to tell it to him in jest, it just might be a crafty device on the
XI 61 part of your inclosing reserve, which would be all the worse for

you. But the law is also the same with regard to the good. If you are honest and earnest in your resolution—above all never say one word about it to anyone. Yet all this really does not need to be said, nor is anyone helped by its being said, because the person who is truly resolved is *eo ipso* [precisely thereby] silent. To be resolved is not one thing and to be silent something else; to be resolved is simply to be silent—as was he, the subject of the discourse.

He lived on year after year. He attended only to himself and God and this picture—but he did not understand himself. Yet he by no means lacked willingness or *πληροφορία* [firm conviction]; on the contrary, he felt an almost irresistible urge to become like it. Finally there awoke a doubt in his soul, a doubt in which he did not understand himself: [7]whether a **human being** has the right to let himself be put to death for the truth.

He pondered this doubt early and late. His many thoughts are in brief summary the content of this little essay.

XI 62

A[8]

1. The doctrine about Jesus Christ's death and sacrifice has, of course, for centuries since the beginning of Christianity been the subject of consideration and deliberation by thousands and thousands. My soul rests entirely in faith, understands itself entirely in believing. Only one doubt has troubled me for some time, a doubt that I have never seen stated by a doubter and never answered by a believer. This doubt goes like this: *This I can indeed comprehend, that he, the Loving One, could be willing to sacrifice his life* **out of love; but this I cannot comprehend, that he, the Loving One, could let human beings become guilty of putting him to death,** *could allow this to happen. It seems to me that* **out of love** *he was bound to have prevented them from that.* Now, however, I have succeeded in removing this doubt; I shall here discuss how, since it is closely bound up with the answer to my question.

2. What the *philosophers* say about Christ's death and sacrifice is not worth reflecting on. In this regard the philosophers do not know what they are talking about—this I know; they do what they know not and know not what they do.[9]

3. With the *dogmaticians* it is another matter. Their point of departure is faith. In that they do well; otherwise there is nothing whatever to talk about, to ponder—except *philosophice* in the air. They try then to comprehend [10]how God's righteousness and
XI 63 human sin are concentrated: the mystery of the Atonement. Yet all that can be said about this contains nothing in answer to this doubt of mine. [11]Dogmatics ponders the eternal significance of this historical fact and raises no objections with regard to any element of its historical genesis.

4. But as dogma the death and sacrifice of Jesus Christ is indeed a historical event. Thus we can ask: How did it happen? How in the world was it still possible that Christ could be crucified? Here *theology* answers that it was the ungodliness of the

Jews, yet in such a way that this, although rebellious against God and chargeable to the guilty ones, in a deeper sense was bound to serve God's purpose and, what is often forgotten, Christ's free decision. On this matter one could certainly make many more observations than are ordinarily made in order to illuminate this historical fact, in order to make it present or, what amounts to the same thing, in order to make the purely human aspect of it present—since the eternal, the divinity in it, is indeed a constant presence. To be sure, any believer can do this. But, quite appropriately, the believer is unwilling to do this, because the death of the Holy One has a totally different meaning for him; hence he is unwilling to occupy himself with it in this way but believes, because he *shall* believe, rather than,[12] as it is meaninglessly expressed, *because he can comprehend*. On the other hand, those who have a vain itch to become important to themselves and to the world by making such observations ordinarily are incapable of doing it.

a. One might ask, for example: How was it ever possible that Christ could be crucified? In answer one might try to show that as the absolute he had to burst, as it were, the relativity in which, after all, human beings live because they are only human beings. His death then, from the Greek point of view, was a dreadful kind of self-defense on the part of *suffering* humanity, which could not endure him. But this answer misses the point, indeed, is light-minded and blasphemous if it suppresses the fact that the relativity in which human beings live is sin.

b. One might ask: How was it ever possible that Christ could be put to death, he who sought nothing, nothing for himself? How is it possible that any power or any human being at all can collide with him? Answer: For that very reason he was put to death, because he sought nothing for himself. For that very reason the lower class was just as indignant with him as the upper class, since each was pursuing its own interest and wanted him to join them in self-love. He was crucified precisely because he was love, or to develop it further, because he refused to be self- XI
loving. Therefore he also lived in such a way that he was bound 64
to be an offense to the upper class as well as to the lower class, since he refused to belong to either party but wanted to be what

he was, the Truth, and wanted to be that in love of the truth. The mighty hated him because the people wanted to make him king,[13] and the people hated him because he refused to be king.

c. [14]To shed light on this historical event, one could show how his seeming at first to want to have royal power had its place specifically in order that he could be crucified. If there is really to be passion in a life situation and flame in the passion, there must be a draft. But a draft is a double movement, the crossing of two currents of air. That the Jews had focused all their attention on him and wanted to make him king, that for a moment at the beginning he himself, as it seemed, turned in that direction,[15] precisely that became the sting in their embitterment and made the rage of hate bloodthirsty when he then refused. He was extremely important to his contemporaries, who wanted nothing more than to see in him the Expected One; they wanted almost to press it upon him and to force him into the role—but that he then refused to be that! Christ was the Expected One, and yet he was crucified by the Jews and was crucified precisely because he was the Expected One. He was much too important to his contemporaries for there to be any question of allowing him to be disregarded; no, here it was a matter of either/or, either love or hate.[16] The Jews were so captivated by the idea that he must be the Expected One that they could not endure the thought that he would not accept all the offered glory. That is to say, this is the world-conflict between two different conceptions of what is meant by "the Expected One"—that of the moment and that of eternity. *In abstracto* Christ is the Expected One for all, and he is that eternally. But now comes the conflict. The self-seeking, conceited people want to make capital of him for their own self-love: Christ must be "the Expected One," but formulated by the moment. By seeming to yield for a moment, he lures their idea out into the open—and now, step by step it becomes clearer that it is in the understanding of eternity that he is the Expected One.

His contemporaries, in error as they were and furious in their error, furious over having been mistaken about him, furious
XI over having wanted to make someone king who rejects it, furi-
65 ous over having made the admission of how in their understanding they needed him—his contemporaries no doubt re-

garded Christ's life as colossal, arrogant pride. Therefore to many in their ungodly error the words, "My God, my God, why have you abandoned me?"[17] no doubt sounded like a justified nemesis. But all this is also part of the Jews' guilt and sheds light on it as ungodliness, that they had been so attentive to Christ that here there can be no question of an ordinary misunderstanding. On the contrary, they had looked up to him, wanted to call attention to him, wanted to be proud of him, and now more than ever wanted utterly to despise all other people—if only he would have served their craving for power. That is, they had comprehended his infinite superiority. Yet they did not want to submit to him, did not want to learn from him what was the truth concerning "the Expected One." Craving power, they wanted him to serve them, to give in to their desire—in order then to idolize him, an idolization that in another sense would have become self-idolization, since it flattered their craving for power, and also because he would have been its invention. That is, they had received sufficient presuppositions from their forefathers and they had understood enough to be able to understand him if they had been willing to, but they *refused* to understand him. It is one thing when an age insults and persecutes a man whom the age literally cannot understand but must regard as mad, for example, when Columbus's contemporaries insulted him, since with the best of will they could not conceive of there being another continent. It is another matter when a man's contemporaries understand his enormous superiority, are simply infatuated with him, but then brashly (even though it is by flattery) want to bully him so that he will be what they want to make him into—instead of subordinating themselves to him and learning from him.

d. To shed light on this historical event, one could show how the historical situation, humanly speaking, was bound to contribute to inciting the Jews against Christ. This nationally and religiously proud people, bound in despised slavery, groaned, ever more insanely proud,[18] because the most insane pride is the pride that oscillates between idolizing and despising oneself. The country was going to ruin. Everyone was preoccupied with the concern of nationality. Everything was politics to the point of despair. And now he, he who could have helped them, he whom XI 66 they had wanted to make king, he from whom they had hoped everything, he who himself for a moment seemed to give the misunderstanding a foothold! And now, just now at this moment to express, and to express with such dreadful decisiveness, that he had nothing to do with politics, that his kingdom was not of this world![19] Indeed, humanly speaking, his contemporaries, blinded as they were, were bound to see this as the most terrible treason against the nation. It seemed as if Christ had picked the most glaring contrast, the most offensive contrast, in order effectively to attest to the eternal, God's kingdom—in contrast to the earthly. When earthly misery, the existence of a whole nation, of God's chosen people, is at stake, so that it is a matter of to be or not to be,[20] then it seems that, humanly, this question should come under consideration first and foremost. The contrast cannot be more chasmic. In a happy land in times of peace, the contrast of the eternal to the earthly is not as strong. To say to a rich man, "You shall first seek God's kingdom"[21] is mild speech compared with this hard, this humanly shocking speech, to say to a starving person, "You shall first seek God's kingdom." Thus it was indeed, humanly, akin to treason against his contemporaries, against the nation, against the nation's cause. This again was why the double-edged sarcasm of that proud Roman, Pilate, was so deeply offensive: to place on the cross this inscription, "The King of the Jews." Ah, this was what in its pride that despairing nation had wished, a king—and he could have been that. But now the mockery was doubly aimed at him, the Crucified One, calling him "King," and at the Jews, calling him "The King of the Jews,"[22] as if to show the Jewish nation how wretched and weak it was.

e. To shed light on this historical event, one could show how the circumstance that the whole thing takes place in the course of three years contributes, humanly speaking, to motivating Christ's death. With the speed of the first impression of the extraordinary (wanting to make Christ king), the generation rushes straight to the opposite extreme, wanting to kill him—that is, from the *direct* expression for the extraordinary the generation rushes to the opposite expression for the extraordinary. But then, too, in a certain sense time was so meagerly rationed to his con-

temporaries that as a result they were brought into an overexcited and confused state. Humanly speaking, a pause was lacking in which the contemporaries could take a breather, a pause XI 67
between the *misunderstanding* that Christ was the earthly Expected One and the *understanding* that he was Spirit and Truth. If Christ had not been the Truth, if consequently he had been able to be lenient with his contemporaries, to cool them down a bit with the aid of illusions, had withdrawn from them at appropriate intervals, had distributed his life over ten years instead of concentrating it in three—and if he had been a human being, he surely would have been constrained to do this for another reason—then perhaps, humanly speaking, he would not have been killed. But in this frightful strain of having the divine present every blessed day, in this frightful strain of having to experience the greatest possible human contrasts from elevation to abasement in such a short time, in this frightful strain of having to be kept in the greatest possible tension without the slightest interval for three years in a row, the generation is as if beside itself—and now shouts, "Crucify, crucify."[23]

f. But what is the use of all such reflections, which perhaps lead the attention of my mind away from the main issue: he declared himself to be God.[24] That is enough; here, if anywhere at all, the either/or holds and absolutely: either to fall down worshiping or to join in killing him—or to be an inhuman wretch, devoid of humanity, who is not even capable of being incensed when a human being gives himself out to be God.

But with all this I still have not come to that doubt of mine.

5. My doubt goes like this: How could the Loving One have the heart to let human beings become so guilty that they got his murder on their consciences? Would he not as the Loving One have had to do everything to prevent it and then rather to have yielded a little, he who at any moment could easily have won them for himself? That a confused person fights with other human beings in such a way that he regards them as stronger, which in truth they are, and therefore does not think about them at all but only about defending himself—this I understand. But even a mere *human being*, if he has the truth on his side and is conscious of it, must indeed feel strong to such a degree, stronger

vis-à-vis the thousands and thousands to such a degree, that he fights with them only figuratively, that all their opposition only makes him sad; then what preoccupies him especially is concern for them, so that he lovingly looks to their best interest in every respect. And now he, the Eternal Strong One—what can all the opposition and attacks of human beings have meant to him? Can XI 68 he at any moment have been concerned for himself; must he not have been solely concerned for them, he, the Loving One? Surely an element in this loving concern must have been this: whether it was too severe toward them, whether it might still be possible to spare them the dreadful extreme of putting him to death.

6. I find, however, no difficulty for my faith. He was not only the Loving One, he was the Truth. And for him, the Holy One, the world was evil, sinful, ungodly. Thus any yielding here is eternally out of the question without its being *eo ipso* untruth. Furthermore, his death was indeed the Atonement and consequently also atones for the guilt of crucifying him. His death has retroactive power; yes, in a certain sense one may say that for killing an innocent person no one is let off as easily as those very Jews. O Eternal Love—his death is the Atonement for his death! Finally, he was not just some particular individual; he relates himself totally to the race. His death is the Atonement for the whole race. Here the category of the race suddenly intervenes in the relation between him and the Jews.

This is how I understand it, and this is how I understand myself in believing. There is something of a collision; it certainly must have been part of his soul-suffering. In love he wills to die the death of Atonement, but in order for him to die, the contemporary generation must become guilty of a murder—which he, the Loving One, with all his heart would very much have wanted to prevent, but if it was prevented, then the Atonement would become impossible. With every step, alas, he drew nearer to the goal of his life: to suffer death; with every step this terrible situation comes closer, that the contemporary generation must in this way become guilty. Yet the generation did not become more guilty than it was—for he was the Truth; but the generation became just as guilty as it was—for he was indeed the Truth; the

generation's guilt only became truly manifest. One may certainly apply to the contemporary generation Christ's words, "Do you think that those Galileans were more guilty?"[25] The contemporary generation is not more guilty than any other generation; it is the guilt of *the race* that becomes manifest. Thus he wills his death; yet he is not guilty of his death, because it is the Jews who put him to death—and yet he does indeed will to die the death of Atonement, and he came to the world with that *intention*. At every moment he has had it in his power to prevent his death, XI 69
not only divinely (with the help of the thirty legions of angels[26]) but humanly, because the Jews much preferred to see in him the Expected One; even at the last moment he has had the possibility before him—but he is the Truth. He *wills* his death; yet here it is not a matter—which humanly it is—of tempting God. His free decision to will to die is in eternal agreement with the Father's will. When a human being wills his death, this is tempting God, because no human being dares to presume such an agreement with God.[27]

7. This is how I understand myself in believing. Before him I kneel in worship, as a human being, or as a sparrow, or as less than nothing. I am well aware of what I do, and I know that I have never kneeled before any human being. But I understand myself in believing. If a little girl who saw me as the epitome of all wisdom and profundity were to ask me, "Can you *comprehend* it, or at least some of it, or at least glimpse a tiny bit of it?" I would answer, "No, my girl, no more than a sparrow can comprehend me." To *believe* is to believe the divine and the human together in Christ. To *comprehend* him is to comprehend his life humanly. But to comprehend his life *humanly* is so far from being more than believing that it means to lose him if there is not believing in addition, since his life is what it is for faith, the *divine*-human. I can understand *myself* in *believing*. I can understand myself in believing, although in addition I can in a relative misunderstanding comprehend the human aspect of this life: but comprehend faith or comprehend Christ, I cannot. On the contrary, I can understand that to be able to comprehend his life in every respect is the most absolute and also the most blasphemous misunderstanding. See, if it depended on physical strength, I would ask

God to give it to me. Since this is not the case, I will ask God (I also dare to promise him that it will be entrusted to an honest person) that he will give me the spiritual power to crush all the conceitedness that presumably wants to comprehend, to crush it or drop it down into ignorance, there where I myself am—in adoration.

B XI 70

1. The pastor, collectively understood, does indeed preach about those glorious ones who sacrificed their lives for the truth. Ordinarily the pastor no doubt assumes that no one is present in the church to whom it could occur to venture anything like that. When sufficiently convinced of this through his private acquaintance with the congregation as its spiritual adviser, he preaches briskly away; he properly declaims and wipes off the sweat. If the next day there came to the pastor at home one of those resolute people who do not declaim, a quiet, modest, perhaps nondescript man, who announced himself as one whom the pastor had carried away with his eloquence, so that he had now resolved to sacrifice his life for the truth—what then? Probably the pastor would good-naturedly speak in this way: Oh, God help us! How does such a thing occur to you! Travel, find some diversion, take a laxative. Then if this nondescript man, quiet as usual, humbly fixed his gaze on the pastor and with this gaze fixed on him went on speaking about his resolve, but in the most modest words, as a man of resolve usually does, the pastor would no doubt think: Would that this man were far away! —Or if the one to whom the man came was a more competent pastor, he would probably speak earnestly with him, try to find out what kind of person he had before him, and if he found truth in the man, would then honor his courage.

But my question would not be discussed at all: **Does a human being have the right** *to let himself be put to death for the truth?* It is of course one thing to ask: *Do I have the courage to do it?* It is something else entirely to ask: *Do I have the right to do it?* Just as on a thermometer there are a plus scale and a minus scale, so also in the dialectical there are a direct scale and an inverse scale. But one seldom or never sees the dialectical used inversely this XI 71
way in people's reflection on acting in life. One never comes to the real question. For the most part, people know only the

directly dialectical. I have frequently read big philosophical works and have listened to lectures from beginning to end; all the time during the reading and during the lectures, it has seemed to me that I understood the development—but now and then it occurred to me: That was an enormously long introduction; how will the author or lecturer finish? But what happens? The book ends, the lecture is over—and what is more, the subject also is now supposed to be fully explained and exhausted. And I, who thought that we now were about to begin, I of course cannot understand the least bit of what I thought I understood. So it is in this case. One talks about what courage it takes to sacrifice one's life in the service of the truth; one describes all the dangers; one makes most people shrink in horror from them. Only he, the person of courage, enters into them, finally into the danger of death, and he is admired—Amen!

Just here is where I begin, not with the man's death—that would be too late—but with the assumption that with regard to courage everything is in due order and correct. Now I begin: Does a human being have the right to let himself be put to death for the truth?

2. When a man is put to death for the truth, there must of course be some people who killed him—that is certainly sufficiently clear. My assumption, it must not be forgotten, is that it is actually for the sake of the truth that he is put to death. At certain times it may be a government, ecclesiastical or secular, that does it; at other times, the crowd. It may also at times happen according to law and sentence, but if it is certain, which I assume, that it is for the truth that he is put to death, then law and sentence are of only little help, because what are law and sentence without truth! Therefore those who put him to death get a murder on their consciences. —Do I then have the right to do this, or does a human being have the right for the sake of the truth to allow others to become guilty of a murder? *Is my duty to the truth* of such a nature, or *does not my duty to my fellow beings* rather bid me to yield a little? How far does my duty to the truth reach, and how far my duty toward others?

Most people probably do not understand what I am speaking about. With reference to a contemporary, they speak of the rash-

ness of venturing to come to grips with powers that could put one to death; they admire the dead person who has had this courage. But I am not speaking about that at all. I assume that this is quite in order, that the hypothetical character lacks anything but courage. Nor am I speaking about the rashness of venturing to come to grips with powers that could put one to death. I am XI 72
speaking about a completely different power that, if it puts to death, puts to death for eternity. I am speaking of a completely different power with which someone may have rashly ventured to come to grips—I am speaking of *responsibility*: Does a **human being** have the right to go that far? Does he, even if he is in the right and has the truth on his side, does he have the right to make others guilty in this way, does he have the right to bring such a punishment upon others? It surely is easy enough to see that he, at the very moment they think that they are punishing him by putting him to death, is punishing them dreadfully by letting them become guilty by putting him to death. There is almost no connection between the minor suffering of being put to death innocent—and the crime of having put to death an innocent person who suffered for the truth.

Most people think like this: It takes strength, it is being strong, to have the courage to let oneself be put to death; leave it to those who do it, to those who put him to death, to consider what they are doing. Even the one who sees somewhat more deeply than most people, even an essential ironist, with bold wittiness probably thinks like this: Of what concern is it to me that I am put to death—*actually* it concerns only those who do it. But I am not speaking of that or in that way; I am speaking of something else entirely, something that perhaps requires even more strength and marks the strong person in a completely different way: with the courage to let oneself be put to death, with the ataraxia to grasp that profound irony, lovingly to *be concerned for the others*, for those who, if one is to be put to death, must become guilty of putting one to death. I am speaking of: with the courage to let oneself be put to death, in fear and trembling[28] to be concerned about one's responsibility. If, namely, in comparison with others a person really decisively has the truth on his side (and this he must have if there is to be any question of his being put to death for the truth), then he is also decisively the superior. And what is superiority? It is responsibility increased more and more to the same degree to which the superiority is greater and greater. Truly to be the superior one is not exactly something comfortable, that is, truly to be that and, what that implies, truly to understand oneself in being that.

So, then, do I have the right to let myself, does a **human being** have the right to let himself, be put to death for the truth?

3. Probably it seldom occurs to a person to occupy himself with this thought: to be willing to sacrifice his life for the truth. Everyone, however, has frequently heard and read about those glorious ones who, so it is said, did it. Consequently, we look only at the past, and this no doubt accounts for our backward way of thinking. It very likely is generally assumed that it hap-
XI pens in this way. A man has boldly and courageously expressed
73 some truth. He himself has thought least of all that his words would lead to his death. But then, well, we do not know how it actually happened, then suddenly he stands there and is condemned to death—and then he dies for the truth. Thus the whole thing is an event, only an event. Here there is no room at all for (something that corresponds to *responsibility*) *the voluntary collaboration in one's own death*, which is the real self-sacrifice for the truth. He, the person put to death, is the sufferer, not the voluntary sufferer who, at every moment from the very beginning and then step-by-step, voluntarily acquiesces in willing to suffer, although at every moment he has the power to prevent it, and by scaling down the truth a little has it in his power even to become the object of admiration. But most people have no idea of what superiority is and of what superiority it must take to have the truth on one's side, have no idea of the voluntary sufferer's freedom of self-determination by which he collaborates in his death and lets the others get on their consciences the guilt of putting him to death. Individuals are left standing face-to-face with one another in an external relation; the others put him to death. No one, however, has in this way ever been *sacrificed* for the truth. If he has been sacrificed, then he has also understood (just because freedom and self-determination are inseparable

from being sacrificed, and responsibility is inseparable from freedom and self-determination) that he had it in his power to prevent his death and consequently that he had the responsibility of letting others become guilty of his death.

That which on the whole occupies people least is precisely what occupies me most—the beginning. I do not pay much attention to the rest, especially not much to what *happens*. I cannot occupy myself with anything except as something present and thus must ask: How did the person come to begin? It is from the beginning that I will learn something. Only from what he has done and how he has done it can I learn; therefore I have to know from the beginning. I can learn nothing from what has happened to a person.

So I have in mind a person who has just as much reflection as he has courage and enthusiasm. As he begins, such a person must make clear to himself where this may lead. He must agree that if it should become his—no, not his *fate*, since it does not become that—if he is put to death for the truth, it is his *choice*. Hence he must agree to be a voluntary collaborator in his death. He must accept the responsibility he takes upon himself, which also contains what is in question, the responsibility for letting others XI
become guilty of his death. In particular, there must come a mo- 74
ment in his life when he says to himself, "If I jack up the definition of truth even higher, such as it truly is for me, then this will lead to my death; the end must be that either the government or the people (whichever of these two powers he now relates to) will put me to death."

Here is the issue: Does he have the right to do this? Most people will have difficulty in perceiving it: with regard to a contemporary, they will censure his intractability, his persisting so stubbornly; with regard to one dead, they will admire his having persisted so perseveringly. I ask: Does he have, does a **human being** have the right to let himself be put to death for the truth?

4. "He is himself responsible for his death," so say the contemporaries of someone who sacrifices his life for the truth. This is precisely what occupies me. Many a person has been put to death, many a person has dropped down from a scaffold, etc.—

but no one has *sacrificed* his life for the truth without having been personally guilty of it. Yet, if he has sacrificed his life for the truth, he has indeed been innocent in the noblest sense.

But if he is "himself responsible for his death," then here is also a consciousness of what offense he allowed others to become guilty of—and now I ask: Do I have a right to do this, does a **human being** have the right to do this for the sake of the truth, is it not a cruelty to the others? Most people have difficulty in seeing my issue. They say that it is cruel to put him, the innocent one, to death, but I ask: Was it not cruel of him or is it not cruel of him to others to let the matter come to the point where they did put or they do put him to death?

5. What does a *human being* achieve by being sacrificed for the truth, or to state it in the words of my issue, by allowing others to become guilty of putting him to death for the truth? (a) His achievement is that he remains faithful to himself and fulfills absolutely his duty to the truth. (b) Furthermore, his achievement is that by means of his innocent death he perhaps has an awakening effect and thus helps truth to be victorious. It is quite certain that when people have hardened themselves against the truth there is no means of procuring its entry that is comparable to their being allowed to put a truth-witness to death. The very moment untruth has killed him, it becomes fearful for itself, about what it has done, powerless through its victory, and precisely this is the untruth's defeat. Now that it no longer has him to fight, it becomes weak. It was precisely his opposition that gave untruth its strength; in itself it has no strength, which now
XI becomes manifest, and most strikingly, most ironically manifest
75 in this, that it was not defeated but was victorious—therefore the victory shows how powerless it is. When someone suffers defeat, we do not fully see how weak he is; we see how strong the other one is. But when someone is victorious and then, powerless, collapses, we see how weak he is and was—and how strong the other one was, he who tricked him into being victorious in that way, tricked him into being crushed as no defeat could crush him. (c) Finally, his death for the sake of truth will stand as an awakening example for later generations.

But now, regarding those who killed or kill him, can the death of the truth-witness do anything to take away their guilt, does the death of the truth-witness have *retroactive* power? No, only Christ's death had that, since he was more than human and related himself to the whole human race. Moreover, even if their becoming guilty of the death of the truth-witness did help them to become aware of the truth, their guilt remains unchanged and now must only appear greater. Do I then have the right to use so powerful and so horrible a means of awakening? —Most people have difficulty in seeing the issue. They speak of the horror of using the death penalty to compel a person to accept the truth. But I speak of the horror of allowing a person or a contemporary age to become guilty of putting me to death in order in that way to awaken him or it to accept the truth. Is not the latter a far more responsible procedure than the former?

6. Can the truth give release from all responsibility with regard to the guilt of letting others become guilty of putting one to death for the truth? Yes, why not. But (and now I give the question a turn different from that in the foregoing, where I therefore questioned this "yes") can I or can a *human being* in his relation to other human beings be assumed to be in possession of the truth to that degree? For Christ it was another matter; he was *the Truth.*

For the solitary *human being* in his relation to other *human beings*—in conflict—is there an absolute duty to the truth? Instead of replying directly, may I formulate my reply in a new question that also gives to the matter a turn different from when I asked: Does a human being, even if he is in the right and has the truth on his side, have the right to let others make themselves guilty of a murder (see 2)? The question is: Can the solitary human being in relation to other human beings be assumed to be in absolute possession of the truth? If not, then an absolute duty to something of which I do not have absolute possession involves a contradiction.

7. When, however, the truth-witness perceives that the mo- XI 76
ment has come, that it will be his death, he can indeed from that moment on *be silent.* Does he have the right to do that? Does he not have the duty to the truth to speak—whatever the cost?

Most people will no doubt understand this contrary to the way I understand it. They understand by this "whatever the cost" the willingness to sacrifice one's life; I understand by it that the cost will be to let others become guilty of a murder. Does he have the right to be silent? Suppose, now, that they force him to speak—if he knows that the truth, if he speaks it, will become his death or, more correctly, will have the effect that the others become guilty of putting him to death: does he have the right to tell a falsehood? And is he then entirely without responsibility because the others did indeed force him into this, that is, because they themselves forced him to let them become guilty of putting him to death?

8. But then of course he could—from the moment he foresees, because he has the others in his power, that their conflict must end with their putting him to death—then of course he can do something else. It is true that it is he who has the others in his power. Most people think the opposite, that it is the others, the strong ones, who have him in their power—but this is an illusion. The truth is always the stronger, and he has them in his power by being able to *compel* them to put him to death, because he is the free one and knows that the unfree are so in the power of untruth that they must kill him if he speaks the truth thus and so. Therefore he could do something else: he could say to them, "By all that is holy I beg and beseech you to yield. I cannot do that; the truth obligates, the truth compels me—the only thing that compels me. But I see that it will be my death; I see that consequently I will be responsible for the guilt, which you draw upon yourselves, of putting me to death. From this my guilt I beg, indeed, I implore, to be free, because this I fear—not death." But *if they then cannot understand him*, is he then guiltless in letting them become guilty? —Or he could say, "I lay upon you the responsibility for the guilt I in a way acquire by letting you become guilty of my death." Is he then guiltless?

9. Therefore—"if they then *cannot* understand him." Or does a human being have the right to say: They *refuse* to understand me? Christ had the right to say this. For him, the Holy One, the Truth, opposition was ungodliness. Moreover, he who was God and saw into their hearts also knew how great was their guilt. He
XI 77 for whom nothing was hidden knew that they *refused* to under-

stand him; thus what guilt they were obviously guilty of corresponded exactly to what guilt resided in them. But when it is a matter of this extremity of allowing oneself to be put to death, does a *human being* in relation to other human beings have the right to say, "They *refuse* to understand me; their misunderstanding is ungodliness"? Is a *human being* able to look into the hearts of others and see? That he certainly cannot do, but neither can he definitely know that the reason for their opposition is that they refuse to understand him. Therefore, does a *human being* dare, when the matter has reached the extremity of letting them become guilty of putting him to death, does he dare to say: They *refuse* to understand me?

Or is not the dialectical in the relation between *human beings* relative (just because no human being is the absolute) in such a way that it turns around and their wanting to kill him signifies to him that, doubting, he should turn against himself and doubt whether he actually is in the right and has the truth on his side, since the others (who, after all, *qua* human beings cannot be so absolutely different from him with respect to the truth) want to kill him? In any case, should he not stop being polemical and use every permissible means to win them for the truth? —But if this fails, just as gentleness in the heat of conflict frequently is like oil on fire, the attempt at reconciliation is the most inflammatory—what then?

Is all error merely ignorance, or is there error that is sin? But if that is the case, then is it that also in the relation between human beings; that it was so in the relation between Christ and human beings is indeed something entirely different.

The falseness in Socrates' conduct was that he was an ironist, that he naturally had no conception of Christian love, which is known specifically by the concern of responsibility, responsibility with regard to others, whereas he thought he had no responsibility on behalf of the contemporaries but only to the truth and to himself. Was not this the truth in the Socratic view of sin as ignorance[29] that he, Greek, had in mind only the relation between human beings? Christianly, the relation is between God and human beings; therefore error is sin. But does this Christian view hold in the relation between human beings? If it does not

hold, if in the relation between human beings all error is ignorance, then do I dare to let anyone become guilty of putting me
XI to death for the truth; is this not punishing ignorance too cruelly?

78 10. Christianity teaches that the world is evil; as a Christian I believe this. But is this not too lofty to use in the relation between human beings? For this purpose, I (occupied with my most cherished thought of sacrificing one's life) have very diligently striven to get to know humanity. What I have become convinced of is that every human being is good-natured when he is alone, or when one is allowed to speak with him alone. As soon as there is a "crowd," then come the abominations. [30]Oh, the worst tyrant has never, never at any time behaved as abominably as the crowd, or as—what is even more terrible—the abominably unrepentant crowd. But Christ did not relate himself as an individual human being to others but essentially to the human race.

At this point, however, there emerges a dubiousness with regard to the attribution of guilt. Indeed, it looks as if the "crowd," this phantom, this abstraction, could become guilty of what none of the individuals constituting the crowd was guilty. But to "blame" the "crowd" is ludicrousness, like declaring the wind guilty. Therefore this expedient would not help me: to consider the crowd as guilty and the individuals as innocent in the sense that I, although a human being, dared to say that the crowd *sinned* against me, but the individuals did not—they were merely in error. Nor was this the case in relation to Christ—each individual in the crowd that sinned against him, each individual sinned against him.

Do I, then, myself a human being who belongs to the evil world, dare to say that the world in relation to me is evil, is sinful, that is, that I am pure and holy? If not, then it certainly is, I almost said, something pretentious, but, to express it more accurately, it is blasphemy to act on such a grand scale: to let oneself be put to death for the truth.

11. Or may it be the case that every time a person actually is to be put to death for the truth this signifies that the truth has become dialectical? I shall now examine this, and may I take care not to speak in spoonerisms,[31] not to speak about what has hap-

pened in the past, but to speak about something in the present. So the people who are putting him or will put him to death (future tense) are following their conception of the truth and to that extent are in the right in putting him to death. But if they are in the right in putting him to death, then of course it is no murder by which they end up making themselves guilty; they get no murder on their consciences. On the other hand, the person who
is being put to death certainly must possess the truth, inasmuch XI
as according to the assumption it is for the truth that he will be 79
put to death. Which, then, is which? Then the truth itself finally becomes something indefinite, something vacillating, if not even *this* remains fixed for all time: that it is a murder to put an innocent person to death, but that there are cases where this is not so, where intentionally and deliberately putting an innocent person to death is not murder, cases where the victim is put to death for the truth while those who do it are not in untruth but also possess the truth.

And if this is the case, my question remains the same: do I have the right to let myself be put to death for the truth—that is, assuming that the others do not get a murder on their consciences, do I have the right to assume (which follows from that assumption) that with regard to the truth I stand so far removed from other people, so high above them, so far ahead of them, that there is almost no kinship between us? The mark of kinship is that they get a murder on their consciences; the other interpretation makes them almost into what a child is in relation to an adult.

12. But even if it were the case that on the grounds of their ignorance the contemporaries could put a person to death for the truth without getting a murder on their consciences, he, the victim, according to his own conception must still regard it as a murder. If perhaps the verdict, when eternity eventually judges between them, is acquittal on the grounds of their ignorance, he, the victim, according to his own conception of what truth is, must regard his death as a murder. But then he still retains the responsibility, because he must have *his* responsibility in relation to *his* conception of truth. In his concern for his responsibility, it is of only slight help to him if they, guilty of a murder according

to his conception, are possibly innocent according to their conception, even though it is a fact that it is they who put him to death. In his responsibility he must make an accounting to God according to what he understands, that is, for his having allowed them to become guilty of what he himself understands as a murder.

This means that the responsibility for letting people become guilty of a murder becomes all the greater if what makes the guilty ones innocent is that with the best of intentions they could not possibly understand him, and it almost seems as if his suicide would be the only expedient for resolving the collision. Would it not be horribly cruel to allow simple human beings to become guilty of putting someone to death because they could not understand him and thus even believed that they were doing the right thing?

XI But now if it was because they *refused* to understand him?
80 Well, I have already given myself the answer: Does a **human being**, in relation to other human beings, dare to feel so pure that in relation to himself he dares to call them sinners, rather than that he, like them, is a sinner before God? But if he does not dare to do this, then neither does he dare to let them become guilty of putting him to death for the truth.

So, then, does a human being dare to let himself be put to death for the truth?

C XI 81

1. Among the many ludicrous things in these foolish times, perhaps the most ludicrous is the comment I have frequently read, written as wisdom and admiringly heard as felicitous: that in our age one cannot even become a martyr, that our age does not even have the energy to put someone to death. *Sie irren sich* [You are mistaken]! It is not the age that is to have the energy to put someone to death or make him a martyr; it is the martyr, the prospective martyr, who is to have the energy to give the age passion, in this case the passion of indignation, to put him to death. This is the relation, and it is also the superiority without which no one, viewed in the idea, actually was a martyr, even if he sacrificed his life or, more correctly, lost it, was put to death. True superiority always works in two places, itself produces the manifestation of power that puts it to death. When, for example, a preacher of the Law is to be put to death, it is not the age that puts him to death [*slaa ihjel*] with its own energy; it is he who, chastising, by striking forcefully, gives the age the passion to strike back [*slaa igjen*]. Be it the most lethargic of times, such a fellow will soon make it passionate. But such a preacher of the Law would surely be a rarity in the age in which everyone is alike. [32]Just as a pupil, about to get a licking, puts a towel under his jacket, unbeknownst to the teacher, so that he will not feel the blows, so a preacher of the Law in our day is for good reasons helpful to the congregation by surreptitiously slipping in another figure, who is now punished—to the edification, *contentement* [satisfaction], and enjoyment of the congregation. For good reasons, because in the case of the pupil there is no danger involved in being the teacher who is to administer the beating. But truly to be a preacher of the Law (yes, here the concept flips over [*slaa om*]!) means not so much to beat [*slaa*] as to be beaten, or to beat XI 82
so that one is beaten. The more lickings the preacher of the Law gets, the more competent he is. Therefore one does not dare to

be the true preacher of the Law, or therefore the one so called does not dare actually to administer a beating, because he knows very well and understands only all too well that those before him are not children, but that the others, the ones he is to beat, are far, by far the stronger ones, who will *actually* strike back [*slaa igjen*], perhaps put him to death [*slaa ihjel*], since to be the great preacher of the Law is to be put to death. The so-called preacher of the Law, however, beats—on the pulpit—and shadowboxes in the air,[33] which certainly does not give the age the passion to put him to death. In this way he achieves his ridiculous purpose, to be the most ridiculous of all monstrosities—a preacher of the Law who is honored and esteemed, greeted with applause.

2. If a person is a psychologist and has the courage to use the remedy, then nothing is easier than to give energy to another person, at least the energy of indignation. Of how many of Socrates' contemporaries did it not hold true that they, as he relates, could become so indignant that they really wanted to bite him every time he deprived them of a foolish notion?[34] One can give even the silliest female such energy of indignation that she would like to kill one. Thus in any age one can in fact become a martyr in the sense of being put to death. In a certain sense nothing is easier; the whole thing can be quite systematically arranged. But the one who is to be put to death must be able to do that; he must be able to give the age the energy of indignation. If, therefore, I were to see a person, until now totally unknown to his contemporaries, rush forth with the declaration that he wants to sacrifice his life, wants to be put to death, I would calmly (since I am so accustomed to associating with such thoughts that I am never more calm than with them), as calmly as a money changer calmly examines the markings on a bill to see if it is genuine—I would calmly reject him. Such a person would never manage to be put to death by his contemporaries, even if in other respects it were the case that he actually had the courage and was willing to die. He does not know the secret. He obviously thinks that the age as the stronger one is to do it, rather than that he should be so superior to the age that he does not passively allow the age to do it to him or commission it with the age but
XI 83 in freedom compels the age to do it. Jurists, after all, have the

custom of not using capital punishment when someone out of life-weariness wants to die.[35] A contemporary age is also just as sagacious—what pleasure would it have from putting him to death!

3. Such a person, then, does not compel the age to kill him. No, if that is what you want you must go about it in a different way. First learn to know your age intimately, especially its error, its desire, its craving, what it actually wanted if it might have its way. If you are well informed in this regard, then fervently, eloquently, stirringly, glowingly give expression to what darkly lurks in the age. For that you must have energy and qualifications. What happens? Well, it is quite simple; it happens that the age falls for this talk completely—you become the object of the age's admiration. Now you stand at the beginning of being put to death. Now the thing to do is this, turn aside, equally decisively, equally repellingly, and you will see the contemporaries acquire a passion that will inflame them, and very quickly.

For someone to be able to become a martyr, he must first and foremost have been the object of the age's admiration; otherwise he does not get the age along with him. He must have been so situated that he has had it in his power to bask in admiration—but he has declined. Spurned admiration is at the same moment an absolute passion of indignation. The one whom a contemporary age has wanted to idolize—if he proudly, yes, or God-fearingly and sincerely declines, this becomes his death.

The whole thing can be determined quite simply by calculating the dialectical relation. "The sacrifice" must dialectically relate to one's contemporaries in this way: he must be able to be what the age in the sense of the moment craves, must be *the demand of the times*.[36] By falsifying his mission he is *eo ipso* the idol of the age. From the point of view of the truth, however, he is *what the age needs* in the sense of eternity. If he remains true to himself in being that, then he is *eo ipso* dedicated to death. He must relate himself to the age in such a way that he can lift the whole age and carry it along while it gives him jubilant applause: no one else, no one else can woo it thus and be so sure of its love. And just when he has won it, he must with even greater energy
thrust it away, lest the falsehood appear that he is a product of XI 84

the age. That is what the age wants; it wants to admire itself in admiring him. But his task is specifically to make the age understand that truth is not the invention of the age.

4. This I can easily understand. I can also see that, besides the terrible possibility that such a thing could to a certain degree be daimonically imitated, there could be a dreadful, deliberate intractability on the part of a person who had the presumptuousness to want to play a game with a whole age, and the terrible game of being put to death, only more horrible if he blasphemously tried to fool himself and them into thinking that it was for the truth. But I can also see that in the strictest sense it can be the truth and that acting in this way can be in the service of the truth.

So, then, it can be done. But now comes the question: Does a **human being** have the right to let himself be put to death for the truth?

D XI 85

1. The answer to the question will depend on the relation between human beings with regard to the truth. Everything revolves around this: what heterogeneity can there be between human beings with regard to the truth? How heterogeneous from others can the solitary human being be assumed to be in this regard? But first of all a difficulty must be brought up here. The less the heterogeneity is assumed to be, the greater the possibility seems that the two antagonists actually are able to understand each other. But then in turn does not this version come closer to saying about the others: They refuse to understand me; they certainly could? Yet, as has been shown (B 9, 10, 11, 12), this is the supreme expression for heterogeneity in relation to others, something only God can actually say: They refuse; this is ungodliness. Amazing! Yet should there not be a second version also? If the heterogeneity is no greater than it is assumed to be, then it is callousness on my part to be so rigid about my own.

So, then, what is the heterogeneity? Can a *human being* be justified in regarding a contemporary age as evil? Or is not a human being, simply as a human being, so relative in relation to other human beings that at most there can be a question only of their weakness and mediocrity?

Therefore, either yield a little or let others become guilty of a murder. Which guilt is the greater? *In the one case the guilt is* that a human being by yielding a little somewhat modifies or accommodates XI 86 the truth he has understood. Now, if it were possible for a human being to be in absolute possession of the truth, this would be absolutely indefensible, an infinite guilt, because the one who is the truth cannot yield in the least thing. But surely no human being is in this situation, least of all in relation to other human beings. Every human being is himself a sinner. Thus he does not relate himself as a pure one to sinners but as a sinner to sinners, because this is the common fundamental relation of all human beings to Christ. So here it is even. In the equality of this fundamental relationship he is different from the others in that he has understood the truth more truly or possesses it more inwardly.

In the second case the guilt is this: to let others become guilty of a murder. Now, which guilt is greater? The strongest expression of absolute superiority over others still is and remains: to let them become guilty of one's death—for the truth. This, namely, is not merely saying that in relation to oneself the others are weak, blind, erring, and mediocre, but that in relation to oneself they are sinners. Probably most people do not agree with me on what is to be seen there. They perhaps think that with regard to being in possession of the truth this heterogeneity is the greatest pretension: to think one has the truth and then to want to put another human being to death in order to compel him, if possible, to accept the truth. No, an even greater pretension is this: to think that one possesses the truth in such a way that one is put to death for the truth, that one lets others become guilty of putting one to death for the truth.

2. I think, then, that a **human being** does not have the right to let himself be put to death for the truth. And yet, yet this conclusion makes me very sad. It is very sad to have to be separated, as from a recollection that will never come again, from the thought that a human being could have a conviction to the degree that it would seem natural to him that he then would also dare to venture to let himself be put to death for it, to venture what is the conviction's need, to gesticulate in a way corresponding to the degree of his conviction.

And there is something disconsolate for me about this conclusion. Humanity becomes more and more apathetic because it becomes more and more commonsensical. It becomes busier and busier because it becomes more and more worldly. The absolute goes more and more out of use. Awakening will become more and more necessary. But where is the awakening to come from if one does not dare to use the only true means of awakening, to let oneself be put to death for the truth, not rushing blindly ahead but calculating this step with more calm levelheadedness than
XI 87 any financier calculates the state of the market. And yet is it not

an *absolute* difference, the difference between apathy, lack of spirit—and zeal, enthusiasm! But no, I think that a *human being* does not have the right to do it.

3.[37] In other respects, it is remarkable enough to consider psychologically-dialectically that it would not be at all inconceivable that a person could be put to death simply because he championed the view that a human being does not have the right to let himself be put to death for the truth. For example, if he were contemporary with a tyrant (whether an individual or the crowd), the tyrant would perhaps mistakenly consider this as a satire on himself and become so incensed that he would put him to death, the very one who defended the view that a human being does not have the right to let himself be put to death for the truth.

XI 88

E

1. But with regard to my issue (whether a *human being* has the right to let himself be put to death for the truth), has not Christianity essentially changed the relationship? With *Christ* it is, as stated, once and for all another matter. He was not a *human being*, he was the Truth; therefore he could not do anything else than to let the sinful world become guilty of his death.

Consequently, then, the derived relationship to Christ: if one is a Christian and relates oneself to pagans, is one not then in relation to them in absolute truth? If in relation to others a person is so situated that he dares truthfully to claim to have the absolute truth, then he is in the right if he lets himself be put to death for the truth. The difference between them is absolute, and being put to death is also the absolute expression for the absolute difference.

According to my concept, this cannot be denied. [38]Otherwise my theory would also be in the predicament of passing judgment on the apostles and all who were placed in the same situation. This would be a huge error. Letting oneself be put to death for the truth is actually a product of Christianity precisely because it is the truth, since Christianity, by being the truth, discovered the infinite distance between truth and untruth. Yes, only in the relation between Christianity and non-Christianity can being put to death for the truth take place in truth. Socrates, therefore, will certainly not claim that in the strictest sense he was put to death—for the truth. As an ironist, consistent to the end, he was
XI 89 put to death for his ignorance, which, in light of Greek culture, certainly contained much truth but yet was not the truth.

2. But in the relation between Christian and Christian my theory again holds true. As a Christian in relation to other Christians, I dare not pretend to be in the possession of the truth to that degree. I dare not by way of contrast to them pretend to be in absolute possession of truth (and in relation to the pagans, the

pretension is to be in possession of the absolute truth)—ergo, neither do I dare to use the absolute expression for having an absolute duty to the truth in contrast to them; I do not dare to let them become guilty of putting me to death. Just as in the relation between individuals, in the relation between Christian and Christian there can be only a relative difference. Therefore a Christian would dare to let them become guilty of ridiculing, mocking, insulting him. It certainly is also a guilt to let them be guilty of this, but to that extent he can relatively have a duty to the truth, that is, up to that point he can be superior to them in perceiving what is true. And then it can be a beneficial awakening, but it does not reach the point of committing the kind of crime that cannot possibly be made good again. If it would, however, be permissible in Christendom to let oneself be put to death for the truth, then it must first of all be assumed that so-called Christendom is not Christian at all, that just like "spiritlessness"[39] it is far more pagan than paganism was. The one who, face-to-face with persons who claim to be Christians, does not dare to deny that they are (and if anyone dares to do that, does this not take something that only the Omniscient One has, knowledge of the human heart?), does not dare either to let himself be put to death or to let the others become guilty of putting him to death.

3. For most people, what I write here, even if I submitted it to them, would probably be as if it were unwritten, nonexistent. Their thinking, as has been shown, ends just where mine begins.[40]

4. With regard to the truth, the simplest and most natural relation between human beings is this, that "the individual" assumes that "the others" have more truth than he has. Therefore he subordinates himself to them, adapts his opinions to them, and considers their approval a criterion of truth.

Even Socratically, and still more according to the teaching of Christianity, truth is in the minority and "the many" is the criterion of untruth; the triumphant informer is the one who makes manifest the falsehood. But if truth is in the minority, then the
distinguishing mark that someone exists in the truth must be- XI
come polemical, inverse: the distinguishing mark is not jubila- 90
tion and applause, but disapproval.

Yet in relation to other human beings, or as a Christian to other Christians, no individual human being or no individual Christian dares to think he is in absolute possession of the truth: ergo, does not dare to let others become guilty of putting him to death for the truth. In other words, if one does so, then it is not actually *for the truth*; there is, on the contrary, something *untrue* in it.

The untruth consists in this, that the one struggling in this way relates himself to the others only polemically, thinking only of himself, not lovingly considering their cause. But in that case he is very far from being truly superior to them or superior in truth, because superiority is to be the counsel for the defense of one's enemy and as such to be concerned and, with more insight than he has, to keep watch so that he does not falsely become more guilty than he deserves. Oh, for the supposedly strong it looks so easy to put a person to death, as if they could easily do it—alas, the one who has a conception of the guilt of killing an innocent person will certainly examine himself before he allows anyone to become guilty in this way. In this self-examination, he will understand that he does not have the right to do it. Thus love will prevent him. It is this love, which in its eternal, divine perfection was in him who, as the Truth, had to express absolutely that he was the Truth and therefore let the ungodly world become guilty in this way—it is this love in him that prayed for his enemies.[41] He could not prevent his death; it was indeed for this that he came to the world. But, since he sacrificed himself out of love, he also lovingly bore in mind his enemies' cause (and this again is why he is called *the Sacrifice*). This is the unity of *truth* and *love*.

XI 91 [42]This is, as stated, "this man's many thoughts in a brief summary." Since the whole thing is fiction, "a poetical venture," but, note well, by a thinker, the thoughtful reader will surely find it appropriate that I say nothing about this man's character; just because it is fiction I can, indeed, just as well say one thing as another, can say exactly what I wish. In another respect also, I can, inasmuch as the whole thing is fiction, say exactly what I wish with regard to his life, how he fared, what he became in the world, etc. etc. But just because I *qua* poet have a poet's absolute power to say what I wish, I will in all these respects say nothing, in order not to contribute, by speaking about the novelistic aspects, to drawing the reader's attention away from what is essential, the thought content.[43]

The Difference between a Genius and an Apostle XI 93

1847

[44]WHAT is it that the erroneous* exegesis and speculative XI 95
thought have done to confuse the essentially Christian, or by what means have they confused the essentially Christian? Quite briefly and with categorical accuracy, it is the following: they have shifted the sphere of the paradoxical-religious back into the esthetic and thereby have achieved the result that every Christian term, which by remaining in its sphere is a qualitative category, can now, in a reduced state, serve as a brilliant expression that means all sorts of things.[45] When the sphere of the paradoxical-religious is now abolished or is explained back into the esthetic, an apostle becomes neither more nor less than a genius, and then good night to Christianity. Brilliance [*Aandrighed*] and spirit [*Aand*], revelation and originality, the call from God and genius, an apostle and a genius—all this ends up being just about one and the same.

In this way an erroneous scholarship has confused Christianity, and from the scholarship the confusion has in turn sneaked into the religious address, so that one not infrequently hears pastors who in all scholarly naiveté *bona fide* [in good faith] prostitute Christianity. They speak in lofty tones about the Apostle Paul's brilliance, profundity, about his beautiful metaphors etc.—sheer esthetics. If Paul is to be regarded as a genius, then it looks bad for him; only pastoral ignorance can hit upon the idea of praising him esthetically, because pastoral ignorance has no criterion but thinks like this: If only one says something good about Paul, then it is all right. Such good-natured and well-meaning thoughtlessness is due to the person's not having been disciplined by the qualitative dialectic that would teach him that an apostle XI 96
is simply not served by having something good said about him when it is wrong; then he becomes recognized and admired for being what is unimportant and for what he essentially is not, and then, because of that, it is forgotten what he is. Such thoughtless eloquence could equally well hit upon the idea of praising Paul as a stylist and an artist with words or, even better, since it is well

* Furthermore, the error is not only that of heterodoxy but also of ultra-orthodoxy and of thoughtlessness generally.

known that Paul also carried on a trade, claim that his work as tent maker must have been such perfect masterwork that no tapestry maker, either before or later, has been able to make anything so perfect—since, if only one says something good about Paul, everything is all right. As a genius, Paul cannot stand comparison with either Plato or Shakespeare; as an author of beautiful metaphors, he ranks rather low; as a stylist, he is a totally unknown name—and as a tapestry maker, well, I must say that I do not know how high he can rank in this regard. See, it is always best to turn obtuse earnestness into a jest, and then comes the earnestness, the earnestness—that Paul is an apostle. And as an apostle he again has no affinity, none whatever, with either Plato or Shakespeare or stylists or tapestry makers; they all (Plato as well as Shakespeare and tapestry maker Hansen) are without any comparison to Paul.

A genius and an apostle are qualitatively different, are qualifications that belong each in its qualitative sphere: **of immanence and of transcendence. (1) Therefore the genius can very well have something new to bring, but this in turn vanishes in the human race's general assimilation, just as the difference "genius" vanishes as soon as one thinks of eternity. The apostle has something paradoxically new to bring, the newness of which, just because it is essentially paradoxical and not an anticipation pertaining to the development of the human race, continually remains, just as an apostle remains for all eternity an apostle, and no immanence of eternity places him essentially on the same line with all human beings, since essentially he is paradoxically different. (2) The genius is what he is by himself, that is, by what he is in himself; an apostle is what he is by his divine authority. (3) The genius has only immanent teleology; the apostle is absolutely teleologically positioned paradoxically**.

1. All thinking draws its breath in immanence, whereas the paradox and faith constitute a separate qualitative sphere. Immanently, in the relation between persons *qua* human beings, every difference is for essential and eternal thinking something vanishing, a factor that surely has its validity momentarily but

essentially vanishes in the essential equality of eternity. Genius, as XI 97
the word itself says (*ingenium*, the innate, primitivity [*primus*], originality [*origo*], pristineness, etc.), is immediacy, natural qualifications; the genius *is born*. Long before there can be any question of whether the genius will or will not assign his rare endowment to God, the genius already is and is a genius even if he does not do that. With the genius there can occur the change of developing into being what he κατὰ δύναμιν [potentially] is, of coming into conscious possession of himself. Insofar as the expression "paradox" is used to designate the new that a genius may have to bring, it is still used only in the inessential sense of the transitory paradox, of the anticipation that condenses into something paradoxical, which, however, in turn vanishes. A genius may be paradoxical in his first communication, but the more he comes to himself the more the paradoxical vanishes. Perhaps a genius can be a century ahead of his time and therefore stand as a paradox, but ultimately the human race will assimilate the one-time paradoxical in such a way that it is no longer paradoxical.

It is different with an apostle. The word[46] itself indicates the difference. An apostle is not born; an apostle is a man who is called and appointed by God and sent by him on a mission. An apostle does not develop in such a way that he gradually becomes what he is κατὰ δύναμιν. Prior to becoming an apostle, there is no potential possibility; every human being is essentially equally close to becoming that. An apostle can never come to himself in such a way that he becomes aware of his apostolic calling as an element in his own life-development. The apostolic calling is a paradoxical fact that in the first and the last moment of his life stands paradoxically outside his personal identity as the specific person he is. Perhaps a man has long since arrived at the age of discretion; then he is called as an apostle. By this call he does not become more intelligent, he does not acquire more imagination, greater discernment, etc.—not at all; he remains himself but by the paradoxical fact is sent by God on a specific mission. By this paradoxical fact the apostle is for all eternity made paradoxically different from all other human beings. The new that he can have
to proclaim is the essentially paradoxical. However long it is XI 98

proclaimed in the world, it remains essentially just as new, just as paradoxical; no immanence can assimilate it. The apostle did not act as the person distinguished by natural gifts who was ahead of his contemporaries. Perhaps he was what we call a simple person, but by a paradoxical fact he was called to proclaim this new thing. Even if thought considered itself capable of assimilating the doctrine, it cannot assimilate the way in which the doctrine came into the world, because the essential paradox is specifically the protest against immanence. But the way in which such a doctrine entered the world is specifically what is qualitatively decisive, something that can be disregarded only through deceit or through thoughtlessness.

2. A genius is evaluated purely esthetically according to what his content, his specific gravity, is found to be; an apostle is what he is by having divine authority. *The divine authority is what is qualitatively decisive.* It is not by evaluating the content of the doctrine esthetically or philosophically that I will or can arrive at the conclusion: ergo the one who has delivered this doctrine is called by a revelation, ergo he is an apostle. The relationship is just the reverse: the one called by a revelation, to whom a doctrine is entrusted, argues on the basis that it is a revelation, on the basis that he has authority. I am not to listen to Paul because he is brilliant or matchlessly brilliant, but I am to submit to Paul because he has divine authority; and in any case it must become Paul's responsibility to see to it that he produces this impression, whether anyone submits to his authority or not. Paul must not appeal to his brilliance, since in that case he is a fool; he must not become involved in a purely esthetic or philosophic discussion of the content of the doctrine, since in that case he is absentminded. No, he must appeal to his divine authority and precisely through it, while he willingly sacrifices life and everything, *prevent* all impertinent esthetic and philosophical superficial observations against the form and content of the doctrine. Paul must not commend himself and his doctrine with the aid of the beautiful metaphors; on the contrary, he would surely say to the individual, "Whether the image is beautiful or [47]it is threadbare and obsolete makes no difference; you must consider that what I say has been entrusted to me by a revelation; so it is God himself or the Lord

Jesus Christ who is speaking, and you must not become involved presumptuously in criticizing the form. I cannot, I dare not compel you to obey, but through the relationship of your conscience to God, I make you eternally responsible for your relationship to this doctrine by my having proclaimed it as revealed to me and therefore by having proclaimed it with divine authority."

Authority is what is qualitatively decisive. Or is there not a XI
difference, even within the relativity of human life, although it 99
immanently disappears, between a royal command and the words of a poet or a thinker? And what is the difference but this, that the royal command has authority and therefore forbids all esthetic and critical impertinence with regard to form and content? The poet, the thinker, on the other hand, does not have any authority, not even within this relativity; his utterance is evaluated purely esthetically or philosophically by evaluating the content and form. But what is it that has radically confused the essentially Christian but this, that in doubt we have first become almost uncertain whether a God exists and then in rebelliousness against all authorities have forgotten what authority is and its dialectic. A king exists physically in such a way that one can physically assure oneself of it, and if it is necessary perhaps the king can very physically assure one that he exists. But God does not exist in that way. Doubt has made use of this to place God on the same level with all those who have no authority, on the same level with geniuses, poets, and thinkers, whose utterances are simply evaluated only esthetically or philosophically; and if it is said well, then the man is a genius—and if it is said exceptionally and extremely well, then it is God who has said it!!!

In this manner God is actually smuggled away. What is he to do? If God stops a person on his way, calls him by a revelation, and sends him out equipped with divine authority to the other people, they then say to him, "From whom do you come?" He answers, "From God." But see, God cannot help his emissary in such a physical way as a king can, who gives him an escort of soldiers or police, or his ring, or his signature that all recognize—in short, God cannot be of service to human beings by providing them with physical certainty that an apostle is an apostle—indeed, that would be nonsense. Even the miracle, if the apostle

has this gift,[48] provides no physical certainty, because the miracle is an object of faith. Moreover, it is nonsense to obtain *physical* certainty that an apostle is an apostle (the paradoxical qualification of a relation of spirit), just as it is nonsense to obtain *physical* certainty that God exists, since God is *spirit*. So the apostle says that he is from God. The others answer, "Well, then let us see if the content of what you teach is divine; then we will accept it, also that it has been revealed to you." In this way both God and
XI the apostle are cheated. The divine authority of the one called
100 should be specifically the sure defense that would safeguard the doctrine and keep it from impertinences at the majestic distance of the divine, but instead the content and form of the doctrine must let itself be criticized and sniffed at—so one can by that way come to a conclusion as to whether it was a revelation or not. In the meantime the apostle and God presumably must wait at the door or with the doorman until the matter has been decided by the wise ones on the second floor. According to God's stipulation, the one who is called should use his divine authority to drive away all the impertinent people who are unwilling to obey but want to be loquacious; and instead of getting people on the move, the apostle is changed into an examinee who as such comes to the market with a new doctrine.

[49]What, then, is authority? Is authority the profundity of the doctrine, its excellence, its brilliance? Not at all. If, for example, authority would only signify, to the second power or doubled, that the doctrine is profound—then there simply is no authority, because, if a learner completely and perfectly appropriated this doctrine by way of understanding, then of course there would be no difference anymore between the teacher and the learner. Authority, however, is something that remains unchanged, something that one cannot acquire by having perfectly understood the doctrine. *Authority is a specific quality that enters from somewhere else and qualitatively asserts itself precisely when the content of the statement or the act is made a matter of indifference esthetically.*

Let us take an example, as simple as possible, in which the relation is nevertheless manifest. When someone who has the authority to say it says to a person, "Go!" and when someone who does not have the authority says, "Go!" the utterance (Go!)

and its content are indeed identical; evaluated esthetically, it is, if you like, equally well spoken, but the authority makes the difference. If the authority is not the other (*το ἕτερον*[50]), if in any way it should indicate merely an intensification within the identity, then there simply is no authority. If, for example, a teacher is enthusiastically conscious that he himself, existing, expresses and has expressed, with the sacrifice of everything, the teaching he proclaims, this consciousness can indeed give him an assured and steadfast spirit,[51] but it does not give him authority. His life as evidence of the rightness of the teaching is not the other (*το ἕτερον*) but is a simple redoubling. That he lives according to the teaching does not demonstrate that it is right, but because he is XI
himself convinced of the rightness of the teaching, he lives ac- 101
cording to it. On the other hand, whether a police officer, for example, is a scoundrel or an upright man, as soon as he is on duty, he has authority.

In order to elucidate more explicitly the concept of authority, so important to the paradoxical-religious sphere, I shall follow up the dialectic of authority. *In the sphere of immanence, authority is utterly unthinkable, or it can be thought only as transitory.** Insofar as it is a matter of authority in the political, civic, social, domestic, and disciplinary realms or of the exercise of authority, authority is still only a transitory factor, something vanishing that either disappears later even in temporality or disappears inasmuch as temporality and earthly life itself are a transitory factor that vanishes with all its differences. The only basis of any relation between persons *qua* human beings that can be *thought* is the dissimilarity within the identity of immanence, that is, the essential likeness. The single human being cannot be *thought* as being different from all others by a specific quality (then all thought

[52] * Perhaps it happens here with some reader as it happens with me, that in connection with this discussion of "authority" I come to think of Magister Kierkegaard's *Upbuilding Discourses*, where it is so strongly accentuated and emphasized, by being repeated in the preface every time and word for word: "they are not *sermons*, because the author does not have *authority* to preach."[53] Authority is a specific quality either of an apostolic calling or of ordination. To preach is precisely to use authority, and that this is what it is to preach has simply been altogether forgotten in our day.

ceases, as it quite consistently does in the sphere of the paradoxical-religious and faith). All human differences between persons *qua* human beings disappear for thought as factors within the totality and quality of identity. I shall certainly respect and obey the difference in the factor, but I am permitted to be built up religiously by the certainty that in eternity the differences vanish, the one that makes me distinguished and the one that subordinates me. As a subject I am to honor and obey the king with undivided soul, but I am permitted to be built up religiously by the thought that essentially I am a citizen of heaven[54] and that if I ever meet his departed majesty there I shall not be bound in subservient obedience to him.

XI 102 This, then, is the relation between persons *qua* human beings. *But between God and a human being there is an eternal essential qualitative difference*,[55] which only presumptuous thinking can make disappear in the blasphemy that in the transitory moment of finitude God and a human being are certainly differentiated, so that here in this life a human being ought to obey and worship God, but in eternity the difference will vanish in the essential likeness, so that God and human beings become peers in eternity, just as the king and the valet.

Between God and a human being, then, there is and remains an eternal essential qualitative difference. *The paradoxical-religious relation* (which, quite rightly, cannot be thought but only be believed) *appears when God appoints a specific human being to have divine authority*—with regard, note well, to what God has entrusted to him. The person called in this way does not, in the relation between persons, relate himself *qua* human being; he does not relate himself to other people in a quantitative difference (as a genius, an exceptionally gifted person, etc.). No, he relates himself paradoxically by having a specific quality that no immanence can revoke in the likeness of eternity, because it is essentially paradoxical and *after* thought (not prior to, before thought), against thought. If such a called person has a doctrine to bring according to divine order and, let us imagine, another person has arrived at the same doctrine by himself and on his own—these two will not become alike in all eternity, because the former by his paradoxical specific quality (the divine authority) will be different from every other human being and from the qualification of the essential likeness lying immanently at the basis of all other human differences. The qualification "an apostle" belongs in the sphere of the transcendent, the paradoxical-religious sphere, which, altogether consistently, also has a qualitatively different expression for the relation of other people to an apostle—in other words, they relate themselves to him in faith, whereas all thought lies and is and breathes in immanence. But faith is not a transitory qualification any more than the apostle's paradoxical qualification was transitory.

Thus in the relation between persons *qua* human beings, no *enduring* [*bestaaende*] or *constant* [*bestandig*] difference of authority was *thinkable*; it was something vanishing. Let us, however, for a moment dwell on some examples of such so-called relations of authority between persons *qua* human beings that are true under the conditions of temporality in order to become aware of the essential view of authority. A king, of course, is assumed to have XI
authority. Why, then, do we even find it offensive that a king is 103
brilliant, is an artist etc.? It no doubt is because one essentially accentuates in him the royal authority and in comparison with this finds the more ordinary qualifications of human differences to be something vanishing, something inessential, a disturbing incidental. A government department is assumed to have authority in its stipulated domain. Why, then, would one find it offensive if in its decrees such a department was actually brilliant, witty, profound? Because one quite properly accentuates the authority qualitatively. To ask if a king is a genius, and in that case to be willing to obey him, is basically high treason, because the question contains a doubt about submission to authority. To be willing to obey a government department if it can come out with witticisms is basically making a fool of the department. To honor one's father because he is exceptionally intelligent is impiety.

Yet, as stated, in the relation between persons *qua* human beings, authority, even if it exists, is something vanishing, and eternity abolishes all earthly authority. But now in the sphere of transcendence. Let us take an example that is very simple, but for that very reason also as striking as possible. When Christ says, "There is an eternal life," and when theological graduate

Petersen says, "There is an eternal life," both are saying the same thing; there is in the first statement no more deduction, development, profundity, richness of thought than in the second; evaluated esthetically, both statements are equally good. And yet there certainly is an eternal qualitative difference! As God-man, Christ possesses the specific quality of authority; no eternity can mediate this or place Christ on the same level with the essentially human likeness. Christ, therefore, taught with authority.[56] To ask whether Christ is profound is blasphemy and is an attempt (be it conscious or unconscious) to destroy him in a subtle way, since the question contains a doubt with regard to his authority and attempts in impertinent *straightforwardness* to evaluate and grade him, as if he were up for examination and should be catechized instead of being the one to whom all power is given in heaven and on earth.[57]

Yet rarely, very rarely, does one hear or read these days a
XI 104 religious address that is entirely correct. The better ones still usually dabble a bit in what could be called unconscious or well-intentioned rebellion as they defend and uphold Christianity with all their might—in the wrong categories. Let me take an example, the first that comes along. I prefer to take a German, so I then know that no one can hit upon the idea, not the most obtuse and not the most malicious, that I am writing this about a matter that in my opinion is immensely important—in order to point a finger at some clergyman. In a homily for the fifth Sunday in Lent, Bishop Sailer* preaches on the text John 8:47–51. He selects these two verses: "*Wer von Gott ist, der höret Gottes Wort* [Whoever is of God hears the word of God]" and "*Wer mein Wort hält, der siehet den Tod nicht* [Whoever keeps my word will not see death]" and thereupon comments: "*Es sind in diesen Worten des Herrn drei grosze Räthsel gelöset, mit denen sich die Menschen von jeher den Kopf so oder anders zerbrochen haben* [In these words by the Lord three great riddles are solved, over which people have racked their brains since time immemorial]."

There we have it. The word *Räthsel* [riddle], and especially

* See *Evangelisches aus Joh. Michael Sailers religiösen Schriften*, by August Gebauer (Stuttgart: 1846 [*ASKB* 270]), pp. 34, 35.

drei grosze Räthsel [three great riddles] and then what follows, *mit denen die Menschen den Kopf sich zerbrochen haben* [over which people have *racked their brains*] promptly lead our thoughts to the profound in the intellectual sense, the cogitating, the ruminating, the speculating. But how can a simple apodictic statement be profound—an apodictic statement that is what it is only by having been said by such and such a person, a statement that by no means is to be understood or fathomed but only believed? How can a person hit upon the idea that a riddle in the nature of cogitating and ruminating profundity should be solved by a direct statement, by an assertion? The question is: Is there an eternal life? The answer is: There is an eternal life. Now, where in the world is the profundity? If Christ is not the one who has said it, and if Christ is not the one he has said that he is, then the profundity, if the statement is in itself profound, must still be ascertainable.

Let us take theological graduate Mr. Petersen; he, too, says: There is an eternal life. Who in the world would hit upon the idea of ascribing profundity to him on the basis of a direct statement? What is decisive consists not in the statement but in the fact that it is Christ who has said it; but what is confounding is that in order, as it were, to lure people into believing, one says something about profundity and the profound. A Christian pastor, if he is to speak properly, must quite simply say, "We have Christ's word that there is an eternal life, and with that the matter is decided. Here it is a matter neither of racking one's brains nor of speculating, but of its being Christ who, not in the capacity of XI 105 profundity but with his divine authority, has said it."

Let us go further, let us assume that someone believes that there is an eternal life because Christ has said it; then in faith he avoids all the deep profundity and cogitating and ruminating "with which people rack their brains." On the other hand, let us take someone who wants to rack his brains profoundly on the question of immortality—will he not be justified in denying that the direct statement is a profound answer to the question? What Plato says about immortality[58] is actually profound, attained by profound cogitating; but then poor Plato does not have any authority.

The point, however, is this. Doubt and disbelief, which make faith worthless, have, among other things, also made people ashamed of obeying, of submitting to authority. This rebelliousness even sneaks into the thought process of the better ones, perhaps unconsciously, and so begins all this extravagance, which basically is treason, about the deep and the profound and the wondrously beautiful that one can glimpse etc. If one were to describe with a single specific adjective the Christian-religious address as it is now heard and read, one would have to say that it is *affected*. Ordinarily when mention is made of a pastor's affectation, one perhaps has in mind that he decks himself out and dolls himself up, or that he speaks in a sentimental tone, or that he rolls his *r*'s like a Norwegian and wrinkles his brow,[59] or that he strains himself in energetic postures and revivalist leaps etc. Yet all such things are of minor importance, even though it is always desirable that such things not occur. But it is corrupting when the thought process of the sermon address is affected, when its orthodoxy is achieved by placing the emphasis on an entirely wrong place, when basically it exhorts believing in Christ, preaches faith in him on the basis of what cannot at all be the object of faith. If a son were to say, "I obey my father not because he is my father but because he is a genius, or because his commands are always profound and brilliant," this filial obedience is affected. The son emphasizes something altogether wrong, emphasizes the brilliance, the profundity in a *command*, whereas a command is simply indifferent to this qualification. The son is willing to obey on the basis of the father's profundity and brilliance, and on that basis he simply cannot *obey* him, because his critical attitude with
XI regard to whether the command is profound and brilliant under-
106 mines the obedience.

Similarly, it is also affectation when there is so much talk about appropriating Christianity and believing in Christ on account of the depth and profundity of the doctrine. One ascribes orthodoxy to oneself by emphasizing something altogether wrong. Thus all modern speculative thought is affected by having abolished *obedience* on the one hand and *authority* on the other, and by wanting despite that to be orthodox. A pastor who is entirely correct in his address must, when he quotes words of Christ, speak in this way: "These words are by the one to whom, according to his own statement, all power is given in heaven and on earth. You, my listener, must now in your own mind consider whether you will submit to this authority or not, accept and believe these words or not. But if you refuse, then for God's sake do not accept the words because they are brilliant or profound or wondrously beautiful—because this is blasphemy, this is wanting to criticize God." As soon, namely, as the dominance of authority, of the specifically paradoxical authority, is established, then all relations are qualitatively changed, then the kind of appropriation that is otherwise permissible and desirable is an offense and presumptuousness.

But how, then, can the apostle demonstrate that he has authority? If he could demonstrate it *physically*, he would simply be no apostle. He has no other evidence than his own statement. This is just the way it must be, since otherwise the believer would enter into a direct relation to him, not into a paradoxical relation. In the transitory relations of authority between persons *qua* human beings, authority will as a rule be physically recognizable by power. An apostle has no other evidence than his own statement, and at most his willingness to suffer everything joyfully for the sake of that statement. His speech in this regard will be brief: "I am called by God; do with me now what you will; flog me, persecute me, but my last words will be my first: I am called by God, and I make you eternally responsible for what you do to me." If in actuality it were so, let us imagine it, that an apostle had power in the worldly sense, had great influence and powerful connections, by which forces one is victorious over people's opinions and judgments—if he then used the power, he *eo ipso* [precisely thereby] would have forfeited his cause. That
is, by using the power, he would define his endeavor in essential XI
identity with the endeavor of other people, and yet an apostle is 107
what he is only by his paradoxical heterogeneity, by having divine authority, which he is able to have absolutely unchanged, even if he, as Paul says, is regarded by people as being of no more worth than the dirt on which they walk.[60]

3. *The genius has only an immanent teleology; the apostle is absolutely teleologically positioned paradoxically.*

If any human being can be said to be positioned absolutely teleologically, it is an apostle. The doctrine communicated to him is not a task given to him to cogitate about; it is not given to him for his own sake. On the contrary, he is on a mission and has to proclaim the doctrine and to use authority. Just as little as a person sent into the city with a letter has anything to do with the contents of the letter but only with delivering it, and just as little as the envoy sent to a foreign court has any responsibility for the contents of the message but only for conveying it properly, so an apostle primarily has only to be faithful in his duty, which is to carry out his mission. Even if an apostle is never persecuted, his sacrificial life consists essentially in this: "that he, himself poor, only makes others rich,"[61] that he never dares to take the time or the quiet or the freedom from care in pleasant days, in *otium* [leisure], to be enriched by that with which, through its proclamation, he enriches others. Spiritually understood, he is like the busy housewife who herself, in order to prepare food for the many mouths, scarcely has time to eat. And if he, when he began, dared to hope for a long life, his life will still remain unchanged until the end, because there will always be ever new ones to whom to proclaim the doctrine.

Although a revelation is the paradoxical fact that passes human understanding,[62] one can still understand this much, which also has manifested itself everywhere: that a person is called by a revelation to go out in the world, to proclaim the Word, to act and to suffer, is called to the unceasingly active life as the Lord's messenger. On the other hand, that a person would be called by a revelation to remain in undivided possession of the estate, in busy
XI 108 literary *far niente* [idleness], to be momentarily brilliant and subsequently a collector and publisher of the dubieties of his brilliance—this is almost a blasphemous thought.

It is different with a genius. He has only an immanent teleology, he develops himself, and as he develops himself he plans this, his self-development, as his activity. He surely acquires significance, perhaps even great significance, but he is not himself teleologically positioned in relation to the world and to others. A genius lives within himself, and he can humorously live in secluded self-satisfaction without therefore nullifying his talent if only, without regard for whether others benefit from it or not, he develops himself earnestly and diligently, following his own genius. The genius is by no means therefore inactive; within himself he perhaps works even more than ten businessmen; he perhaps accomplishes a great deal, but each of his accomplishments has no *τέλος* [end, goal] outside. This is simultaneously the humanity of the genius and his pride: the humanity consists in his not defining himself teleologically in relation to any other person, as if there were anyone who stood in need of him; the pride consists in his relating himself immanently to himself. It is modest of the nightingale not to demand that anyone must listen to it, but it is also proud of the nightingale that it does not care at all to know whether anyone listens to it or not.

The dialectic of the genius will be especially offensive in our day, when the crowd, the masses, the public, and other such abstractions seek to turn everything upside down. The honored public, the power-craving crowd, wants the genius to express that he exists for its or for their sake; the honored public, the power-craving crowd, sees only one side of the dialectic of the genius, is offended by the pride, and does not perceive that this is also humility and modesty. Therefore the honored public, the power-craving crowd, wants also to nullify an apostle's existence. It surely is true that he exists entirely for the sake of others, is sent out for the sake of others; but it is not the crowd and not humanity, not the honored public, not even the honored cultured public, that is his master or his masters—it is God—and the apostle is the one who has *divine authority* to *command* both the crowd and the public.

The humorous self-satisfaction of the genius is the unity of modest resignation in the world and proud elevation above the world, is the unity of being a useless superfluity and a costly
ornament. If the genius is an artist, he produces his work of art, XI
but neither he nor his work of art has any *τέλος* outside. Or he is 109
an author who destroys every teleological relation to the surrounding world and defines himself humorously as a lyric poet. The lyrical quite rightly has no *τέλος* outside itself. Whether someone writes one page of lyrical poetry or folios of lyrical poetry makes no difference with regard to defining the direction of

his work. The lyrical author cares only about the production, enjoys the joy of the production, perhaps often through pain and effort, but he has nothing to do with others. He does not write *in order to*, in order to enlighten people, in order to help them onto the right road, in order to accomplish something—in short, he does not write: *in order to*. And so it is with every genius. No genius has an "in order to"; the apostle *absolutely paradoxically* has an "in order to."[63]

THREE DISCOURSES AT THE COMMUNION ON FRIDAYS

THE HIGH PRIEST—THE TAX COLLECTOR—THE WOMAN WHO WAS A SINNER

by S. Kierkegaard

PREFACE XI 247

May "that single individual,[1] whom I with joy and gratitude call *my* reader," receive this gift. It is true that to give is more blessed than to receive, but if this is so, in one sense the giver is indeed the needy one, needing the blessedness of giving; and if this is so, then the greatest benefaction is indeed that of the one who receives—and thus it is really more blessed to receive than to give.

[2]May he receive it! I see again what I thought I saw the first time, when I sent forth the little book (see the preface to *Two Upbuilding Discourses* 1843[3]) that was compared to and in fact could best be compared to "a humble little flower under the cover of the great forest"—I see again "how the bird I call *my* reader suddenly notices it, flies down to it, picks it, and takes it home." Or, from the other side and in another metaphor, I see again what I saw that time, how the little book "wends its way down solitary paths or walks solitary on public roads . . . . . until it finally meets that single individual, whom I call *my* reader, that single individual it is seeking, to whom, so to speak, it stretches out its arms": that is, I saw and see that the little book is received by that single individual, whom it seeks and who seeks it.

Early September 1849

S. K.

[4]I XI 249

[The High Priest]
Hebrews 4:15

 XI 251

Where should we go[5] if not to you, Lord Jesus Christ! Where should the one who is suffering find sympathy if not with you, and where the penitent, alas, if not with you, Lord Jesus Christ!

> Hebrews 4:15. **We have not a high priest who is unable to have sympathy with our weaknesses, but one who has been tested in all things in the same way, yet without sin.**

My listener, whether you yourself have been, possibly are, one who suffers, or whether you have become acquainted with sufferers, perhaps with the beautiful aim of wanting to comfort, you no doubt have often heard this, the universal lament of sufferers: "You do not understand me, oh, you do not understand me; you are not putting yourself in my place. If you were in my place or if you could put yourself in my place, if you could put yourself completely in my place and in so doing really understand me, you would speak differently." You would speak differently; this means, according to the sufferer, that you would perceive and understand that there is no comfort.

This, then, is the lament; the one who is suffering almost always complains that the one who wants to comfort him does not put himself in his place. Surely the sufferer is always somewhat in the right, because no one has exactly the same experience as another person, and even if this were the case, each particular person has the universal and common limitation of being unable to put himself completely in another's place, of being un- XI 252
able even with the best will to perceive, feel, and think exactly as another person. But in another sense the sufferer is in the wrong insofar as he thinks that this means there is no comfort for the sufferers, because this of course could also mean that every sufferer must try to find comfort within himself, that is, with God. It certainly would not be God's will that the one person should be able to find complete comfort in the other; on the contrary, it is God's gracious will that every human being is to seek it with him, that when the grounds of comfort that others

offer become insipid for a person, he is then to look to God in accordance with the Scripture's words: Have salt in yourselves, and be at peace with one another.[6] O you suffering one, and you who perhaps honestly and with good intentions desire to comfort: do not become embroiled in this futile argument with each other! You who sympathize, show your genuine sympathy by not claiming to be able to put yourself completely in the other person's place; and you who suffer, show your genuine discretion by not claiming the impossible of the other—there is indeed still one who is able to put himself completely in your place, just as in every sufferer's place: the Lord Jesus Christ.

It is of this that the holy words just read speak. "We have not a high priest who is unable to have sympathy with our weaknesses"; that is, we have someone who is able to have sympathy with our weaknesses, and further, "we have one who has been tested in all things in the same way." This is, namely, the condition for *being able* to have true sympathy—since the sympathy of the inexperienced and the untried is a misunderstanding, most often for the sufferer a more or less irksome and wounding misunderstanding—this is the condition, to be tried in the same way. If this is the case, then one is able to put oneself completely in the sufferer's place; and if one has been tested in all things in the same way, one can put oneself completely in every sufferer's place. We have such a high priest who *is able* to have sympathy. And that he *must* have sympathy, that you see from its having been out of sympathy that he was tested in all things in the same way—it was indeed sympathy that was determinative for him in coming to the world, and it was sympathy again, it was in order to be able to have true sympathy, that he in free decision was tested in all things in the same way, he who can put himself completely in your place, in my place, in our place.

Of this we shall speak in the brief moment prescribed.

XI 253 Christ put himself completely in your place. He was God and became man—in this way he put himself in your place. This is namely what true sympathy [*Medlidenhed*] wants; it wants so very much to put itself completely in the place of the sufferer [*Lidende*] in order to be able really to comfort. But this is also what human sympathy is incapable of doing; only divine sympathy is capable of that—and God became man. He became a human being, and he became the human being who of all, unconditionally all, has suffered the most. No human being was ever born or will or can ever be born who will suffer as he suffered. Oh, what security for his sympathy, oh, what sympathy to provide such a security! In sympathy he opens his arms to all sufferers. Come here, he says, all you who suffer and are burdened.[7] Come here to me, he says, and he guarantees what he says, because he—this is the invitation the second time—he was unconditionally the one who suffered most. It is already very great if human sympathy ventures to suffer almost as much as the sufferer, but out of sympathy, in order to ensure the comfort, to suffer infinitely more than the sufferer—what sympathy! Human sympathy usually shrinks back, prefers to remain, commiserating, on the safe beach; or if it ventures out it does not want to go quite as far out as where the sufferer is—but what sympathy to go even further out! You who suffer, what do you require? You require that the one sympathizing put himself completely in your place; and he, sympathy itself, he not only put himself completely in your place, he suffered infinitely much more than you! Oh, to a sufferer this at times perhaps seems, discouragingly, to border on treachery, that sympathy is holding itself back a little; but here sympathy is behind you in the infinitely greater suffering!

You suffering one, whoever you are, he put himself, he is able to put himself, completely in your place. —Is it temporal and earthly concern, poverty, worry about the future and what that involves? He, too, has suffered hunger and thirst, and just in the most difficult moments in his life, when he also battled spiritually, in the desert and on the cross. And for everyday use he owned no more than the lily in the field and the bird of the air—even the poorest own that much! And he, who was born in a stable, wrapped in rags, and laid in a manger, throughout his life he had no place where he could lay his head[8]—even the homeless have that much shelter! Should he not then be able to put himself com- XI
pletely in your place and understand you! 254

Or is it a broken heart? He, too, once had friends, or rather, he once thought he had them, but when the decision came they all abandoned him—yet, no, not all, two remained—the one betrayed him and the other denied him! He, too, once had friends, or he once thought he had them. They attached themselves so closely to him that they even quarreled about who should occupy the place on his right and who on his left hand,[9] until the decision came and instead of being elevated to the throne he was lifted upon the cross. Then two thieves were forced against their will to occupy the empty place on his right and the empty place on his left side! Do you not think that he is able to put himself completely in your place!

Or is it sorrow over the wickedness of the world, over the opposition you and the good must suffer, if only it is otherwise altogether certain that it truly is you who wills the good and the true? Oh, in this regard you, a human being, certainly would not dare to compare yourself to him; you, a sinner, would certainly not dare to compare yourself to him, the Holy One, who experienced these sufferings first, so that you at most can suffer in likeness to him, and eternally sanctified these sufferings, yours also if you suffer at all in likeness to him—he who was scorned, persecuted, insulted, mocked, spat upon, flogged, mistreated, tortured, crucified, abandoned by God and crucified amid public exultation—whatever you have suffered, and whoever you are, do you not think that he is able to put himself completely in your place!

Or is it sorrow over the sin and ungodliness of the world, sorrow over the world's being immersed in evil, sorrow over how deeply humanity has fallen, sorrow over the fact [10]that gold is virtue, that might is right, that the crowd is truth, that only lies make progress and only evil is victorious, that only selfishness is loved and only mediocrity is blessed, that only sagacity is esteemed, that only half measures are praised and only contemptibleness succeeds? Oh, in this regard you, a human being, certainly would not dare to compare your sorrow to the sorrow that was in him—the Savior of the world—as if he would be unable to put himself completely in your place! —And so it is with regard to every suffering.

Therefore, you suffering one, whoever you are, do not in despair shut yourself up with your sufferings, as if no one, not even he, could understand you. Do not complain loudly and impatiently about your sufferings either, as if they were so frightful that not even he would be capable of putting himself completely in your place; do not have the audacity for this falsehood. Bear in mind that unconditionally and incomparably unconditionally he of all sufferers was the one who suffered the most. If you want to know who suffers the most, well then, let me tell you. It is not the smothered scream of silent despair and it is not the loud scream that terrifies others that decide the outcome—no, just the opposite. The one who unconditionally suffers most is the one of whom it is veritably true—through his doing it—that he unconditionally has no other comfort than to comfort others. This and only this is a manifestation of the truth that no one can truly put himself in his place, also that it is truth in him. So it was with him, the Lord Jesus Christ. He was not a sufferer who sought comfort from others; still less did he find it in others, still less did he complain about not finding it in others—no, he was *the* suffering one, whose only, whose unconditionally only comfort was to comfort others. See, here you have come to the highest point of suffering, but also to the border of suffering, where everything turns around, because he, he alone, is *the Comforter.* XI 255

You complain that no one can put himself in your place. I can imagine that it may never occur to you, preoccupied day and night with that thought, that you should comfort others; and he, the Comforter, he is the only one of whom it truly holds that no one could put himself in his place—how true if he had complained in that way! —He, the Comforter, in whose place no one could put himself, he can put himself completely in your place and in every sufferer's place. If it were the truth that no one at all can put himself in your place, well, then demonstrate it. There is only one thing left for you, that you yourself become the one who comforts others. This is the only evidence that can be advanced for its being the truth that no one can put himself in your place. As long as you talk about no one's being able to put himself in your place, you have not unconditionally made up your mind about it; otherwise you would at least be silent. But even if you were silent, as long as it is not conducive to your undertaking to comfort others, you have not unconditionally

made up your mind that no one can put himself in your place. You merely go on sitting in silent despair, again and again preoccupied with the thought that no one can put himself in your place—that is, you must firmly fix this thought at every moment. In other words, the thought is not firmly fixed; you have not
XI unconditionally made up your mind about it; it is not wholly
256 truth in you. Nor can it be true for any human being that no one, unconditionally no one, can put himself in his place, because he, Jesus Christ, in whose place no one either completely or even approximately can put himself, he is the very one who can put himself completely in your place.

He put himself completely in your place; whoever you are, you who are being tested in temptation and spiritual trial, he is able to put himself completely in your place, "tested in all things in the same way."

Just as with the sufferer, so also with the person in temptation and spiritual trial; he, too, usually complains that someone who wants to comfort or counsel or caution him does not understand him, cannot put himself completely in his place. "If you were in my place," he says, "or if you could put yourself in my place, you could understand with what dreadful power temptation embraces me, you could understand how frightfully spiritual trial mocks my every effort—then you would judge me differently. But you, who do not sense it yourself, you can easily talk calmly about it, can easily use the opportunity to feel yourself superior because you did not fall into temptation, did not succumb in spiritual trial—that is, because you are not being tested in either the one or the other. If you were in my place!"

O my friend, do not carry on any futile argument that only further embitters life for yourself and another. There is still one who is able to put himself completely in your place, the Lord Jesus Christ, who "because he has suffered and himself been tempted is able to help those who are tempted" (Hebrews 2:18). There is one who is able to put himself completely in your place, Jesus Christ, who truly learned to know every temptation by holding out in every temptation. If it is worry about livelihood, and quite literally and in the strictest sense worry about livelihood, so that starvation threatens—he, too, was tempted in this

way. If it is a reckless venture that tempts—he, too, was tempted in this way. If you are tempted to fall away from God—he, too, was tempted in this way. Whoever you are, he is able to put himself completely in your place. If you are tempted in solitude—so also was he, whom the evil spirit led out into solitude in order to tempt him.[11] If you are tempted in the world's confusion—so also was he, whose good spirit prevented him from withdrawing from the world before he had completed his work of love. If you are tempted in the great moment of decision, when it is a matter of renouncing everything—so also was he. Or if it is in the next moment, when you are tempted to regret that you sacrificed everything—so also was he. If, prostrated by XI 257
the possibility of danger, you are tempted to wish that the actuality would soon be at hand—so also was he; if, languishing away, you are tempted to wish your death—so also was he. If the temptation is that of being abandoned by humanity—so also was he tempted. If it is—but no, surely no human being has experienced that spiritual trial, the spiritual trial of being abandoned by God—but he was tempted in that way. And so it was in every way.

Therefore, you who are tempted, whoever you are, do not become silent in despair, as if the temptation were suprahuman and no one could understand it. Do not impatiently depict the magnitude of your temptation either, as if even he could not put himself completely in your place! If you want to know what is required for truly being able to ascertain how great a temptation truly is, then let me tell you. What is required is that you have held out in the temptation. Only then do you find out the truth about how great the temptation was; as long as you have not held out in it, you will know only the untruth, only what the temptation, simply in order to tempt, deludes you into thinking about, how frightful it is. To insist on truth from the temptation is insisting on too much; the temptation is a deceiver and liar, who certainly guards against speaking the truth, because its power is precisely untruth. If you want to get the truth out of it with regard to how great it actually is, then you must become the stronger, you must hold out in the temptation—then you will

get to know the truth, or you will get the truth out of it. Therefore there is only one who in truth knows exactly the magnitude of every temptation and can put himself completely in the place of everyone who is tempted: he who himself was tested in all things in the same way—tempted, but who held out in every temptation. Watch, then, your describing and complaining ever more passionately about the magnitude of your temptation; with every step you take along this road, you only accuse yourself more and more. A defense of your succumbing to the temptation cannot be made by describing more and more inordinately the magnitude of the temptation, because everything you say in this way is untruth, since you can find out the truth only by holding out in the temptation. Perhaps another person could help you if you would allow yourself to be helped, another person who has been tempted in the same way but held out in the temptation—because he knows the truth. But even if there is no other person who can tell you the truth, there still is one who can put himself completely in your place, he who was tested in all things in the same way, tempted, but who held out in the temptation. From him you will get to know the truth, but only on the condition that he sees that it is your honest intention to will to hold out in
XI the temptation. And when you have held out in the temptation,
258 then you will be able to understand the truth completely. As long as you have not held out in the temptation, you complain that no one can completely put himself in your place—because if you have held out in the temptation, it would of course make no difference to you, would not be anything to complain about, if it were the case that no one could put himself in your place. This complaint is an invention by the untruth that is in the temptation, and the meaning of the untruth is that if anyone is to understand you completely it must be someone who also succumbed to the temptation—hence you two would understand each other—in the untruth. Is this what it is to "understand" each other? No, here is the border where everything turns around: there is only one who can truly put himself completely in the place of anyone who is tempted—and he is able to do it because he alone held out in every temptation. But also, oh, do not forget it, he can put himself completely in your place.

He put himself completely in your place, in every respect was tested in all things in the same way—**yet without sin**. So in this respect, then, he did not put himself in your place, he cannot put himself completely in your place, he, the Holy One—how could it be possible! If the difference is infinite between God, who is in heaven, and you, who are on earth, the difference between the Holy One and the sinner is infinitely greater.

Oh, but yet, also in this respect, even though in another way, he put himself completely in your place. If he, if the Redeemer's suffering and death is the satisfaction for your sin and guilt—if it is the satisfaction, then he does indeed step into your place for you, or he, the one who makes satisfaction, steps into your place, suffering in your place the punishment of sin so that you might be saved, suffering in your place death so that you might live—did he not and does he not then put himself completely in your place? Here it is indeed even more literally true that he puts himself completely in your place than in the situation we described earlier, where we indicated that he could completely understand you, but you still remain in your place and he in his. But the satisfaction of Atonement means that you step aside and that he takes your place—does he not then put himself completely in your place?

What is the Redeemer but a substitute who puts himself completely in your place and in mine, and what is the comfort of Redemption but this, that the substitute, atoning, puts himself completely in your place and in mine! Thus when punitive justice here in the world or in judgment in the next seeks the place where I, a sinner, stand with all my guilt, with my many sins—it
does not find me. I no longer stand in that place; I have left it XI
and someone else stands in my place, someone who puts himself 259
completely in my place. I stand saved beside this other one, beside him, my Redeemer, who put himself completely in my place—for this accept my gratitude, Lord Jesus Christ!

My listener, this is the kind of high priest of sympathy we have. Whoever you are and however you are suffering, he can put himself completely in your place. Whoever you are and however you are being tempted, he can put himself completely in your place. Whoever you are, O sinner, as we all are, he puts himself completely in your place! Now you go to the Communion table; the bread is handed to you and then the wine, his holy body and blood, once again as an eternal pledge that by his suffering and death he did put himself also in your place, so that you, behind him saved, the judgment past, may enter into life, where once again he has prepared a place for you.

[12]II XI 261

[The Tax Collector]

Luke 18:13

Lord Jesus Christ, let your Holy Spirit really enlighten us and convince us of our sin so that we, humbled and with downcast gaze, acknowledge that we stand far, far off and sigh: God, be merciful to me, a sinner. But then by your grace let it happen also to us in accordance with your word about that tax collector who went to the temple to pray: he went home to his house justified.

Luke 18:13. **And the tax collector stood far off and would not even lift up his eyes to heaven, but beat his breast and said: God, be merciful to me, a sinner!**

My devout listener, as you know, the sacred words just read are from the Gospel about the Pharisee and the tax collector.[13] The Pharisee is the hypocrite who deceives himself and wants to deceive God, the tax collector the honest man whom God justifies. But there is also another kind of hypocrisy, hypocrites who resemble the Pharisee but have chosen the tax collector as their prototype, hypocrites who, according to Scripture's description of the Pharisee, "trust in themselves that they are righteous and despise others,"[14] while they nevertheless fashion their character in the likeness of the tax collector and sanctimoniously stand far
off, unlike the Pharisee, who proudly stood by himself, sancti- XI 264
moniously cast their eyes to the earth, unlike the Pharisee, who proudly lifted his eyes to heaven, sanctimoniously sigh, "God, be merciful to me, a sinner," unlike the Pharisee, who proudly thanked God that he was righteous. These are hypocrites who, just as the Pharisee blasphemously said in his prayer, "God, I thank you that I am not like this tax collector,"[15] sanctimoniously say, "God, I thank you that I am not like this Pharisee."

Yes, alas, this certainly is the way it is. Christianity came into the world and taught humility, but not everyone learned humility from Christianity; hypocrisy learned how to change its mask and remain the same or, rather, become even worse. Christianity came into the world and taught that you shall not proudly and conceitedly seek to sit at the head of the table at a dinner but shall seat yourself at the foot of the table[16]—and soon pride and conceit conceitedly sat at the foot of the table, the same pride and conceit—no, not the same, even worse.

In view of the fact that hypocrisy and pride and conceit and the worldly mind may want to reverse the relation, one might think it necessary to reverse this Gospel text and almost all the others. But what good would that do? Indeed, to want to be so sagacious as to want, by means of sagacity, to prevent misuse, can only be the idea of a sickly shrewdness, a conceited sagacity. No, there is only one thing that vanquishes and more than vanquishes, from the beginning has infinitely vanquished, all cunning—the simplicity of the Gospel, which simply lets itself be deceived, as it were, and yet simply goes on being simplicity itself. The upbuilding in the Gospel's simplicity is also this, that evil could not get the power over it to make it sagacious or get the power over it so that it would want to be sagacious. Indeed, evil would have already won one victory and a very alarming victory if it has influenced simplicity to want to be sagacious—in order to safeguard itself. Simplicity is safeguarded, eternally safeguarded, only by simply allowing itself to be deceived, however clearly it sees through the deceit.

Let us then in the brief prescribed moments simply consider the tax collector. Throughout all the ages he has been presented as the prototype of an honest and God-fearing churchgoer. Yet it seems to me that he is even more closely related to going to Communion, he who said, "God, be merciful to me, a sinner"—is it not as if he were now going to Communion, he of whom it
XI 265 is said, "He went home to his house justified"—is it not as if he now went home from Communion!

The tax collector *stood far off.* What does that mean? It means to stand by yourself, alone with yourself before God—then you are far off, far away from people, and far away from God, with whom you still are alone. In relation to a human being, you are closest to him when you are alone with him and are further away when others are present, but in relation to God it seems to you as if you are closer to God when several are present, and not until you literally are alone with him do you discover how far away you are. Oh, even if you are not such a sinner as the tax collector, whom human justice also judges guilty, if you are alone with yourself before God, then you are indeed standing far off. As soon as there is someone between God and you, you are easily deceived, as if you were not so far off. Yes, even if it was your opinion that the person or persons who before you are between you and God are better and more nearly perfect than you, you still are not as far off as when you are alone before God. As soon as anyone comes between you and God, regardless of whether it is someone you consider more nearly perfect than you, or someone you consider less perfect, you acquire a fraudulent criterion, the criterion of human comparison. It is then as if a measurement could still be made of how far off you are and thus you are not far off.

But the Pharisee, who, according to the words of Scripture, "stood by himself," did he not then stand far off? Yes, if he truly had stood by himself, then he, too, would have stood far off; but he did not truly stand by himself. The Gospel says that he stood by himself and thanked God "that he was not like other men." When one is in the company of other people, one is of course not standing by oneself. The Pharisee's pride consisted precisely in his proudly using other people to measure his distance from them, in his refusing before God to let go of the thought of other people but clinging to this thought in order to stand proudly by himself—in contrast to other people. But that, of course, is not standing by oneself, least of all standing alone by oneself before God.

The tax collector stood far off. Was it perhaps easier for him, conscious of his own guilt and offense, not to be tempted by the thought of other people, who, after all, he had to admit were better than he? We shall decide nothing about that, but this is sure—he had forgotten all the others. He was alone, alone with the consciousness of his guilt and offense; he had completely for- XI 266
gotten that there certainly were also many other tax collectors; he was as if he were the only one. He was not alone with his guilt before a righteous person; he was alone before God—oh, this is being far off. What is further away from guilt and sin than God's holiness—and then, oneself a sinner, to be alone with this holiness: is this not being infinitely far off!

And he would not even lift up his eyes to heaven; that is, he cast his eyes down. Well, no wonder! Even physically there is something in the infinite that overwhelms a person since there is nothing on which he can fix his eyes. This effect is called dizziness; then one must shut one's eyes. And the one who, alone with his guilt and his sin, knows that if he opens his eyes he will see God's holiness and nothing else, that one surely learns to cast his eyes down; or he perhaps looked up and saw God's holiness—and cast his eyes down. He looked down, saw his wretchedness; and more heavily than sleep weighs on the eyelids of the exhausted, more heavily than the sleep of death, the conception of God's holiness weighed his eyes down; like one exhausted, indeed, like one dying, he was unable to lift up his eyes.

He would not even lift up his eyes to heaven, but he, who with downcast gaze, turned *in*ward, had only *in*sight into his own wretchedness, *did not look to the side either*, like the Pharisee, who saw "this tax collector," for we read that he thanked God that he was not like this tax collector. This tax collector—yes, it is the very tax collector of whom we are speaking; there were, of course, two men who went up to the temple to pray. Scripture does not say that two men went up together to the temple to pray—well, neither would it have been fit company for the Pharisee to go up to the temple in the company of a tax collector. Moreover, in the temple they seem as far as possible from being together; the Pharisee stands by himself, and the tax collector stands far off. And yet, yet, the Pharisee saw the tax collector, this tax collector, but the tax collector—ah, how well in the sense of distinction you deserve to be called this tax collector!—the tax collector did not see the Pharisee. When the Pharisee came home, he knew very well that this tax collector had been in church, but this tax collector did not know that the Pharisee had been in church. The Pharisee proudly found satisfaction in seeing the tax collector; the tax collector humbly saw no one, did not see this Pharisee either; with downcast, with inward gaze he was in truth—before God.

And he beat his breast and said: God, be merciful to me, a sinner.
XI O my listener, when a person in the solitude of the desert is
267 attacked by a ravenous beast, his cry no doubt comes by itself,

and if on some out-of-the-way road you fall among robbers, the terror itself produces the cry. So also with something that is infinitely more terrible. When you are alone, alone in the place that is more solitary than the desert—since even in the most solitary desert it would still be possible for another person to come; alone in the place that is more solitary than the most out-of-the-way road, where it would still be possible that another person could come; alone in singleness, or as the single individual, and before God's holiness—then the cry comes by itself. And when you, alone before God's holiness, have learned that it does not help you if your cry were to call any other person for help, that *there*, where you are the single individual, there is literally no one else but you, that it is the most impossible of all that there could be anyone but you and that anyone else could come *there*—then just as need has produced the prayer, the terror produces this cry, "God, be merciful to me, a sinner." Moreover, the cry, the groan, is so sincere in you—yes, how could it not be! What hypocrisy would there possibly be in the cry of someone for whom in distress at sea the abyss opens, even though he knows that the storm mocks his frail voice and that the birds out there listen to him indifferently; he cries out nevertheless—to that degree his cry is true and truth. So also with what in an altogether different sense is infinitely more terrible, the conception of God's holiness when a person, himself a sinner, is alone before it—what hypocrisy would there be in this cry: God, be merciful to me, a sinner! If only the danger and the terror are actual, the cry is always sincere, but more than that, God be praised, it is not futile either.

The Pharisee, however, was not in danger. He stood proud, secure, and self-satisfied; from him no cry was heard. What does this mean? It also has another and totally different meaning: neither was he before God.

And now the conclusion. *The tax collector went home to his house justified*.

He went home to his house justified. What Scripture says about all tax collectors and sinners, that they kept *close* to Christ, applies to this tax collector also: simply by standing far off, he kept close to him, whereas the Pharisee in his presumptuous forwardness stood far, far off. Thus the picture turns around. It

XI begins with the Pharisee standing near, the tax collector far off;
268 it ends with the Pharisee standing far off, the tax collector near.

He went home to his house justified. He cast his eyes down, but the downcast gaze *sees* God, and the downcast gaze is the *uplifting* of the heart. Indeed, no gaze is as sharp-sighted as that of faith, and yet faith, humanly speaking, is blind; reason, understanding, is, humanly speaking, sighted, but faith is against the understanding. In the same way the downcast gaze is sighted, and what the downcast gaze signifies is humility—humility is the uplifting. The picture turns around again as the two go home from the temple. The one who was lifted up was the tax collector, and with that it ended. But the Pharisee, who began by proudly lifting up his eyes to heaven, him God opposes, and God's opposition is an annihilating pressing down. In former times an astronomer did not do as he does now, erect a building on an elevation from which he observes the stars; in former times he dug down into the earth in order to find the place from which to observe the stars. In the relationship to God no change has taken place, none takes place—to be lifted up to God is possible only by going down. No more than water changes its nature and runs up the mountains can a human being lift himself up to God—by pride.

He went home to his house justified. Self-accusation is the possibility of *justification*. The tax collector accused himself. There was no one else who accused him. It was not civic justice that seized him by the chest and said, "You are a criminal"; it was not the people whom he perhaps cheated who beat him on the breast and said, "You are a cheater"—but he beat his own breast and said, "God, be merciful to me, a sinner." He accused himself, that he was a sinner before God.

The picture turns around again. The Pharisee, who far from accusing himself proudly praised himself—as he goes away, he is accused before God. He is unaware of it, but as he goes away he accuses himself before God—the tax collector began by accusing himself. The Pharisee goes home with the new, in the strictest sense the crying-to-heaven sin, with one more sin added to his earlier sins, which he retained—the tax collector went home justified. Before God "to want to justify oneself" is to inform on oneself as guilty, but before God "to beat one's breast, saying, 'God, be merciful to me, a sinner'" is to justify oneself, or it is at least the condition for God's declaring you justified.

So it was with the tax collector. But now you, my listener! The similarity comes very close. From having made your confession, you go to Holy Communion. But to make confession is precisely *to stand far off*; the more honestly you confess, the further XI
off you stand—and it is all the more true that you kneel at 269
the Communion table, since to kneel is like a symbol of standing far off, far off from the one who is in heaven, from whom the distance is as great as possible when, kneeling, you sink down to the earth—and yet at the Communion table you are closest to God.

To make confession is precisely *to cast the eyes down*, not to want to lift the gaze to heaven, not to want to see anyone else. Indeed, the more honestly you confess, the more you will want to cast your eyes down, the less you will want to see anyone else—and all the more truly you will kneel at the Communion table, since to kneel down expresses even more powerfully what it means to cast one's eyes down, because the person who only casts his eyes down nevertheless stands even somewhat erect—and yet at the Communion table your heart is lifted up to God. —To make confession is *to beat one's breast* and, without being too disturbed by the thought of the particular sins, to gather all, most concisely and most truthfully, into one thought: *God, be merciful to me, a sinner.* The more inwardly you make confession, the more will your confession end in this silent indication, beating your breast, and in this groan: God, be merciful to me, a sinner—and the more true will be your kneeling at the Communion table, a kneeling that expresses that the kneeler, condemning himself, prays only for mercy—and yet at the Communion table is the justification.

He went home to his house justified. And you, my listener, when you go home from the Communion table to your house, devout sympathy will greet you with this wish: Joy and blessing, be assured that you found justification at the Communion table, that your going there will become a joy and a blessing to you. Now, before you go to the Communion table, the same wish:

May you find joy and blessing in it. Oh, the natural man finds greatest satisfaction in standing erect: the person who truly learned to know God, and by learning to know God learned to know himself, finds blessedness only in falling upon his knees, worshiping when he thinks about God, penitent when he thinks about himself. Offer him what you will, he desires only one thing, like that woman who chose—not the better part, ah, no, how can there be a question of a comparison!—no, who chose, according to the words of Scripture, the good part when she sat at the Savior's feet[17]—he desires only one thing: to kneel at his Communion table.

[18] III

XI 271

[The Woman Who Was a Sinner]
Luke 7:47

Lord Jesus Christ, in order to be able to pray aright to you about everything, we pray to you first about one thing: help us so that we might love you much, increase our love, inflame it, purify it. And this prayer you will hear, O Christ, you who are not, cruelly, love of such a kind that you are only the object, indifferent to whether anyone loves you or not; you who are not, in anger, love of such a kind that you are only judgment, jealous about who loves you and who does not. Oh, no, you are not like that; then you would only instill fear and anxiety. Then it would be terrifying "to come to you,"[19] frightful "to abide in you,"[20] and then you yourself would not be the perfect love that casts out fear.[21] No, mercifully, or lovingly, or in love, you are love of such a kind that you yourself love forth the love that loves you, encourages it to love you much.

Luke 7:47. **Therefore I say to you, her many sins are forgiven her, because she loved much.**

My listener, you know whom these words are about, that they are about that woman whose name is: the woman who was a sinner.[22] "When she learned that Christ was at a dinner in the XI 274
Pharisee's house, she fetched an alabaster jar of ointment, and she stood behind him at his feet, weeping, and began to wet his feet with her tears and wipe them with the hair of her head and to kiss his feet and anoint them with the ointment."[23]

Yes, she loved much. There are indeed opposites that are in mortal combat with each other, or for the one of the opposites it is like the most frightful annihilation to come near to the other. For example, when one is a sinner, man or woman, to come near to the Holy One, to become disclosed before him, that is, in the light of holiness. Ah, the night does not flee more terror-stricken before the day, which wants to annihilate it, and if there are ghosts, an apparition is not more anxiously startled when day is dawning than the sinner who shrinks from the holiness that, like the day, discloses everything. Inventive in malingering excuses and evasions and deceits and glosses, the sinner flees, avoids this death march as long as he can, this encounter with the light. But she loved much. And what is the strongest expression for loving much? It is to hate oneself—*she went in to the Holy One*. She, a sinner! Alas, a woman. In a woman, the power of the sense of shame is the strongest, stronger than life; she would rather give up her life than give up her sense of shame. True enough, this sense of shame ought to have kept her from, prevented her from sinning; but then in turn it is also true that when a woman comes to herself again her sense of shame is all the more powerful, crushing, annihilating. Perhaps that was what made the pathway to annihilation easier for her, that she was annihilated. Yet, humanly speaking, there could still be a question of leniency. Oh, even a sinner who in truth has confessed to himself, or at least is conscious that he is annihilated, would perhaps still be lenient with himself if face-to-face with the Holy One he were to become disclosed; he would be lenient with himself, that is, he would still love even himself that much. But she—is there then no leniency, none at all? No, there is no leniency! —She hated herself: she loved much.

She went in to the Holy One *in the Pharisee's house*, where the many Pharisees were assembled who would judge her, also in this way, that it was vanity, disgusting vanity, especially for a woman, to thrust herself forward with her sin, she who should hide herself from the eyes of all people in a remote corner of the world. She could have traveled the world over and been certain
XI 275 of finding nowhere such a severe judgment as the one that awaited her from the proud Pharisees in the house of the Pharisee. On the other hand, there perhaps is no suffering so designed to torture particularly a woman as the cruelty of the mockery that awaited her from the proud Pharisees in the house of the Pharisee. But she—is there no sympathy that spares her this cruelty? No, there is no sympathy! —She hated herself: she loved much.

She went in to the Holy One in the Pharisee's house—*to a dinner*. To a dinner! You shudder, you shrink from following her. You are easily convinced of how appalling it is, because you will be continually tempted to forget that this is all taking place at a dinner, that it is not a "house of mourning" but a "house of feasting."[24] At a dinner a woman enters; she brings with her an alabaster jar of ointment—well, that is appropriate at a dinner. She sits down at the feet of one of the guests—and weeps—that is not appropriate at a dinner. Indeed, she disturbs the dinner, this woman! Yes, but it did not disturb her, this woman who was a sinner, she who, surely not without shuddering, not without shrinking back, nevertheless went forward to the dinner—and to confession. She hated herself: she loved much.

Oh, sin's heavy secret weighs more heavily on a person than anything else; there is only one thing that is heavier—to have to go to confession. Oh, sin's frightful secret is more frightful than any other secret; there is only one thing even more frightful: confession. Therefore human sympathy has commiseratingly devised something that is able to alleviate and to assist this difficult birth. At the holy place where everything is quiet, earnest solemnity, and in a more hidden inclosure[25] inside where everything is silence like that of the grave and leniency like judgment on the dead—there the sinner is provided the opportunity to confess his sin. And human sympathy devised the alleviation that the one who received the confession was hidden, so that the sight of him would not make it too heavy—yes, too heavy for the sinner to lighten his conscience. The final device of human sympathy was that not even such a confession was needed or such a hidden listener. Confession should be only in secret before God, who knows everything anyway, and thus it could remain hidden in one's innermost being. But at a dinner—and a woman! A dinner—it is not some hidden, remote place, nor is the lighting dim, nor is the mood like that among graves, nor are the listeners XI silent or invisibly present. No, if concealment and semidarkness 276 and remoteness and everything connected with confessing one's sin are an alleviation, then a dinner would be the cruelest device. Who, then, is this cruel one, so that our pleas might mollify him so as to be lenient with her? No, no device of cruelty was so cruel; she alone devised such a thing, she, the sinner. She—oh, but usually the cruel person is one person and the tortured person is another! She herself devised the torture, she herself was the cruel one; she hated herself: she loved much.

Yes, she loved much. "She sat down at Christ's feet, wet them with her tears, wiped them with her hair"—she is expressing: I am capable of literally nothing at all; he is capable of unconditionally everything. But this is indeed to love much. If a person thinks he is capable of something, he certainly may love but he does not love much; and to the same degree that he thinks himself capable of something, to the same degree he loves less. She, however, loved much. She says not a word; neither does she make an assertion—oh, only all too often a deceitful expression very easily necessitates a new assertion that it actually is as one asserts. She makes no assertions; she acts: she weeps, she kisses his feet. She does not think of stopping her tears—no, weeping, after all, is her task. She weeps; it is not her eyes that she dries with her hair—no, it is his feet. She is capable of literally nothing at all; he is capable of unconditionally everything—she loved much. O eternal truth, that he is capable of unconditionally everything! O indescribable truth in this woman, O indescribable power of truth in this woman, who powerfully manifests the powerlessness that she is capable of literally nothing—she loved much.

Yes, she loved much. She sits weeping at his feet: she has forgotten herself completely, forgotten every disturbing thought in her own inner being, is perfectly calm, or is calmed like the sick baby that is calmed at its mother's breast, where it cries itself out and forgets itself. One cannot succeed in forgetting such thoughts and yet keep thinking about oneself; if one is to succeed, one must forget oneself—that is why she weeps, and as she weeps she forgets herself. O blessed tears—that in weeping there is also this blessing: forgetting! She has forgotten herself completely, forgotten the setting with all its disturbing elements. A setting like this is impossible to forget unless one forgets oneself. Indeed, it was a setting frightfully and agonizingly designed to remind
XI her of herself—but she weeps, and as she weeps she forgets her-
277 self. O blessed tears of self-forgetfulness, when her weeping does not once remind her anymore of what she is weeping over;[26] in this way she has forgotten herself completely.

But the true expression of loving much is just to forget oneself completely. If one remembers oneself, one can, to be sure, love but not love much; and the more one remembers oneself, to the same degree one loves less. She, however, has forgotten herself completely. But the greater the incitement simultaneously to remember or to think of oneself, if one nevertheless forgets oneself and thinks of the other, the more one loves. This is indeed the case in the relationship of love between individuals; although these relationships do not correspond entirely to what the discourse is about, they are still able to illuminate it. The one who forgets himself when he is most preoccupied, at the moment that to himself is the most precious, and thinks of another, that one loves much. The one who, himself hungry, forgets himself and gives the other the scanty supply that is only enough for one, that one loves much. The one who in mortal danger forgets himself and lets the other have the only life-saving plank, that one loves much. So also the one who at the moment when everything in his inner being and everything around him not only reminds him of himself but wants to compel him against his will to think about himself—if he nevertheless forgets himself, that one loves much, just as she did.

"She sits at his feet, anoints them with the ointment, wipes them with the hair of her head, kisses them—and weeps." She says nothing and therefore is not what she says, but she is what she does not say, or what she does not say is what she is. She *is* the symbol, like a picture.[27] She has forgotten speech and language and the restlessness of thoughts, has forgotten what is even greater restlessness, this self, has forgotten herself—she, the lost woman, who is now lost in her Savior, who, lost in him, rests at his feet—like a picture. It is almost as if the Savior himself momentarily looked at her and the situation that way, as if she were not an actual person but a picture. [28]Presumably in order to make the application more impressive to those present, he does not speak *to* her; he does not say, "Your many sins are forgiven you, because you loved much." He speaks *about* her; he says: Her many sins are forgiven her, because she loved much. Although she is present, it is almost as if she were absent; it is almost as if he changed her into a picture, a parable.[29] It is almost as if he said, "Simon, I have something to tell you. There was once a woman. She was a sinner. When the Son of Man was at a dinner
one day in the house of a Pharisee, she, too, came in. The Phari- XI 278
sees mocked her and judged her, that she was a sinner. But she sat at his feet, anointed them with ointment, wiped them with her

hair, kissed them, and wept. Simon, I want to tell you something: her many sins were forgiven her, because she loved much." It is almost like a story, a sacred story, a parable—and yet at the same moment the same thing was actually taking place on the spot.

But "*her many sins were indeed forgiven her*"—and how could this be expressed more strongly, more truthfully, than by this, that it is all forgotten, that she, the great sinner, is changed into a picture. When it is said, "Your sins are forgiven you"—oh, how easily the recollection of herself returns to her if she was not first strengthened by this infinite oblivion: her many sins were forgiven her. "She loved much"; therefore she forgot herself completely; she forgot herself completely—"therefore her many sins were forgiven her." Forgotten, yes, they were drowned with her, so to speak, in oblivion. She is changed into a picture; she becomes a recollection, yet not so that it reminds her of herself. No, just as she forgot it by forgetting herself, so also, not eventually but immediately, recollection forgot what she is called. Her name is: the woman who was a sinner, neither more nor less.

Now, if someone were to say: Yet there was something self-loving in this woman's love; the Pharisees indeed took exception to her coming near to Christ and from it drew an unfavorable conclusion about him, that he was no prophet—so she exposed him to that, she with her love, that is, with her self-love. If someone were to say: Yet there was something self-loving in this woman's love; after all, in her need she basically still loved herself. If someone were to talk that way, I would answer: Naturally, and then add, God help us, there is no other way, and then add, God forbid that I would ever presume to want to love my God or my Savior in any other way, because if there were literally no self-love in my love, then I would no doubt be only imagining that I could love them without standing in need of them—and from this blasphemy may God preserve me!

My listener, this woman was a sinner. The Pharisees condemned her; they even condemned Christ for being willing to become involved with her; they judged, and just because of that, that he was no prophet, not to mention the Savior of the world—whereas it was precisely by this that he manifested him-
XI 279 self as the Savior of the world. This woman was a sinner—yet she

became and is a prototype. Blessed is the one who resembles her in loving much! The forgiveness of sins that Christ offered while he lived continues from generation to generation to be offered to all in Christ. "Your sins are forgiven" is said to all, to each one individually; all, each one individually, receive at the Communion table the pledge that their sins are forgiven. Blessed is the one who resembles the woman who was a sinner in loving much! Even though it is said to all, yet it is true only when it is said to the one who, like that woman, loved much! It is true, in Christ your sins are forgiven you, but this truth, which therefore is said also to each one individually, is yet in another sense still not true; it must be made into truth by each one individually. This is how that woman is an eternal picture; by her great love she made herself, if I dare to speak this way, indispensable to the Savior. That there is forgiveness of sins, something he acquired for us, she makes into truth, she who loved much. Therefore you may turn it however you wish and still say basically the same thing. You can consider her blessed because her many sins are forgiven, and you can consider her blessed because she loved much—basically you are saying the same thing—if you note well that the one she loved much was specifically Christ, and if you also do not forget that Christ is grace and the giver of grace.

What kind of test is it in which her love is tested; what is it that she can be said to love much; what is it that she loves less? Is this the test: to love Christ more than father and mother, gold and material goods, honor and reputation? No, the test in which this woman is tested is: to love her Savior more than her sin. Oh, there perhaps was someone who loved Christ more than he loved father and mother and gold and material goods and honor and life, and yet loved his sin more than his Savior, loved it—not in the sense of wanting to remain in it, of wanting to go on sinning, but in the sense of not really wanting to confess it. It is frightful in a certain sense, yet it is true, and anyone with any knowledge of the human heart will verify it: there is nothing to which a human being so desperately firmly clings as to his sin. This is why a perfectly honest, deep, completely true, completely unsparing confession of sins is the perfect love—such a confession of sins is to love much.

Now the discourse is ended. But is it not true, my listener, even if the Pharisees have judged that this woman forced herself into a dinner in a most unseemly way, that today she has not come to the wrong place, between the confessional and the Communion table! Oh, forget the speaker who has spoken here, XI 280 forget his art if he has shown any at all, forget his flaws, which perhaps were many, forget the discourse about her—but do not forget her. On this path she is a guide, she who loved much and to whom therefore the many sins were forgiven. She is far from being a forbidding picture; on the contrary, she is more inciting than all rhetorical incitements when it is a matter of accepting that invitation that leads to the Communion table: "Come here, all you who labor and are burdened," because she walks there in the lead, she who loved much, she who therefore also found rest for her soul in loving much—yes, or in the forgiveness of her many sins—yes, or she who, because she loved much, found rest in this, that her many sins were forgiven her.

AN UPBUILDING DISCOURSE

---

by S. Kierkegaard

TO THE MEMORY OF THE LATE

Michael Pedersen Kierkegaard

MY FATHER

THIS LITTLE WORK IS DEDICATED

PREFACE[1] XII 247

See the preface to *Two Upbuilding Discourses* 1843.[2]

December 12, 1850[3]

The Woman Who Was a Sinner XII 249

LUKE 7:37ff.[4]

That a woman is presented as a teacher, as a prototype of piety, cannot amaze anyone who knows that piety or godliness is fundamentally womanliness. Even if "the woman should keep silence in the congregation"[5] and to that extent not teach—well, being silent before God does indeed belong essentially to true godliness and therefore you may be able to learn that from the woman.

From a woman, therefore, you also learn the humble faith in relation to the extraordinary, the humble faith that does not incredulously, doubtingly ask, "Why? What for? How is this possible?"—but as Mary humbly believes and says, "Behold, I am the handmaid of the Lord."[6] She *says* this, but note that to say this is actually to be silent. From a woman you learn the proper hearing of the Word, from Mary, who although she "did not understand the words that were spoken" yet "kept them in her heart."[7] Thus she did not first demand to understand, but silent she hid the Word in the right place, since it is, of course, the right place when the Word, the good seed, "is kept in a devout and beautiful heart."[8] From a woman you learn the quiet, deep, God-fearing sorrow that is silent before God, from Mary; it indeed happened, as was prophesied, that a sword did pierce her heart,[9] but she did not despair—either over the prophecy or when it was fulfilled. XII 250
From a woman you learn concern for the one thing needful, from Mary, sister of Lazarus, who sat silent at Christ's feet with her heart's choice: the one thing needful.[10]

In the same way you can also learn from a woman the proper sorrow over one's sin, from the woman who was a sinner, from her whose many sins long, long ago did not remain but were forgotten, but who herself became eternally unforgettable. How would it be otherwise than that in this regard one may be able to learn from a woman! To be sure, compared with the woman the man has many thoughts—if ordinarily that is unconditionally an advantage, especially in this regard, since in addition he also has many half-thoughts. To be sure, the man is stronger than the weak one, the woman, has far more expedients, knows how to get along much better, but then in turn the woman has one thing, one—indeed, precisely that, namely, that her element is: one. One wish, not many wishes—no, only one wish, but then, too, her whole soul is in it. One thought, not many thoughts—no, only one thought, but by the power of passion an enormous power. One sorrow, not many sorrows—no, one sorrow, but so deep in the heart that one sorrow certainly is immensely much more than the many. One sorrow, yes, only one sorrow, but that sorrow is also very deep—sorrow over her sin, as the woman who was a sinner. What, then, is earnestness? With regard to thought, let the man have more earnestness; with regard to feeling, passion, decision, with regard to not thwarting oneself and the decision by thoughts, intentions, resolutions, with regard to not deceiving oneself by coming very close to a decision but without its becoming a decision—in this regard, the woman has more earnestness. But decision (especially in the godly sense and, again, especially in relation to sorrow over her sin) is precisely earnestness:

So let us then pay attention to the woman who was a sinner and to what we can learn from her.

First of all, we can learn: to become like her, indifferent to everything else, in unconditional sorrow over our sins, yet in such a way that one thing is important to us and unconditionally important: to find forgiveness.

My listener, concerned people are a familiar sight in this life,
concerned people who now have one thing, now another, about
which to be concerned, and sometimes all sorts of different things
at once; concerned people, who themselves do not really know
XII why they are concerned—but it is rare to see someone who is
251 concerned about only one thing and so unconditionally about
this one thing that everything else becomes unconditionally unimportant.

Yet one does see this, even though not ordinarily. I, and you also, no doubt, have seen the one who has become unhappy in love and for whom everything forever or for a long time has then become of no importance; but this, after all, was not sorrow over one's sin. The one whose bold plans were in an instant all wrecked on an unexpected obstacle, and for whom then everything for a long time or forever became of no importance; but this is not sorrow over his sin.[11] The one who fought with the duration of time and fought long, who held out, still held out, even yesterday, and then today the renewed life within failed to come, he collapsed, everything became of no importance to him; but this is not sorrow over his sin. The one who by nature is depressed—how the depressed person looks upon everything as alien and unimportant, how in a certain sense, just as the air can be too light to breathe—for him everything is too light because his mind is so heavy; but this is not sorrow over his sin.[12] The one who year after year with dreadful zest for life piled crime upon crime, most of whose time was spent in sinning—until he stood there annihilated and everything became unimportant to him; but sorrow over his sin this truly was not—there were sins enough, but sorrow over his sin there was not. On the whole, there is one thing that is altogether common; you can find it in all and in everyone, in yourself just as I find it in myself: sin and sins; there is one thing that is more rare: sorrow over one's sin.

Yet I have seen, and perhaps you also, the one who unconditionally sorrowed over only one thing, over his sin. It followed him everywhere, yes, or it pursued him by day and in his dreams at night, during work and when he futilely sought rest after work, in solitude and when he futilely sought diversion in the company of others. It wounded him from behind when he turned toward the future and in front when he turned toward the past; it taught him to wish for death and to fear life, and then in turn to fear death and to wish for life, so that without killing him it nevertheless somewhat took life from him, afraid of himself as of a ghost; it made everything extremely unimportant to him—but, see, this sorrow was despair.

On the whole, there is one thing that is very common; you can find it in each and in everyone, in yourself just as I find it in myself: sin and sins. There is one thing that is very rare: true sorrow over one's sin, which no doubt is why it is made necessary every holy day to pray in the opening prayer in the church ser-
XII vice "that we might learn to sorrow over our sins." Happy is the
252 one in whom there is this true sorrow over his sin, so that the extreme unimportance to him of everything else is only the negative expression of the confirmation that one thing is unconditionally important to him, so that the unconditional unimportance to him of everything else is a deadly sickness that still is very far from being a sickness unto death[13] but is precisely unto life, because the life is in this, that one thing is unconditionally important to him: to find forgiveness. Happy is he; he is very rarely seen. My listener, this is seen often enough in the world, a person for whom the unimportant has become important, even more often people for whom all sorts of things have become important, but rarely a person for whom only one thing is important, and even more rarely a person of whom it is true that the one single thing that is unconditionally important to him is in truth the one and only important thing.

Pay attention, then, to the woman who was a sinner, so that you may learn from her.

For her everything else had become unimportant. She had no concern except over her sin, or every other concern was as if it did not exist, because that sorrow was for her unconditional. This, if you like, is the blessing bound to having only one sorrow—freedom from care with regard to everything else, and this is the distinctive mark of having only one sorrow.

So it was with the woman who was a sinner. But how different this is from what usually happens in life! When a person, not free of sin and guilt—which no human being is!—has other concerns also and then is concerned, weighed down, he perhaps then mistakenly confuses this dejection with concern over his sin, as if all that is required is that a person shall be concerned, rather than that the requirement is that he *shall* be concerned over his *sin*,

and that he shall *not* be concerned over *anything else*; but he mistakenly confuses things and does not perceive that if it was his sin that he sorrowed over, not to mention if he sorrowed over this alone, he would feel the other concerns less or not at all and would use the opportunity to express true sorrow over his sin by bearing these other concerns more lightly. Possibly he does not understand it this way but rather wishes that he might be relieved of his other concerns so that he could sorrow only over his sin. Alas, he scarcely understands what he is asking for, that then the matter surely would instead become all too rigorous for him. When God in rigorous judgment will impress a person's sin upon him, he sometimes goes about it in the following way: he says, "I will relieve this person of every other concern; everything will XII
smile upon him, everything will comply with his wishes, every- 253
thing he touches will be successful—but all the less will he succeed in forgetting, all the more powerfully will he sense, what is gnawing in him." So the excuse that is often heard is not true, that because of other concerns one cannot really begin to sorrow over one's sin. No, "other concerns" are the very opportunity to express genuine sorrow over one's sin by bearing the other concerns more lightly; and "other concerns" are not an intensification but rather an alleviation, since no latitude remains for thoughts to go astray, but there is promptly a task with regard to expressing sorrow over one's sin by bearing the other concerns more patiently, more humbly, and more lightly.

To the woman who was a sinner everything else had become unimportant: everything temporal, earthly, and worldly, honors, esteem, prosperity, the future, relatives, friends, people's opinion. All concerns, whatever their name might be, she had borne lightly, almost as if they were nothing, because in concern she was preoccupied unconditionally with only one thing: her sin. She sorrowed over this and not over its consequences: shame, disgrace, humiliation. No, she did not confuse the sickness with the remedy. Alas, how rarely a person who, provided he could receive the forgiveness of his sins, would be willing to suffer the punishment of becoming totally disclosed to people, so that they could look into his soul and see every secret guilt! Alas, how rarely one becomes unconditionally indifferent in this way; the same sin for which he himself condemns himself and for which he prays to God for forgiveness, the same sin is perhaps hidden with a miser's exceedingly anxious solicitude about anyone's getting to see it.

On the other hand, to the woman who was a sinner everything had become unimportant: the opposition of those around her, the objection about the dinner invitation, the cold superiority or cruel mockery of the Pharisees—yes, the place was like an impregnable fortress, fortified in just such a way that it was bound to make her entrance impossible if everything else had not become unimportant to her. She, to whom everything else had become unimportant, dared to do what perhaps no other woman who was unaware of being a sinner, therefore with less danger, would have dared to do.

But no, this is not exactly the case; she dared to do it because one thing was unconditionally important to her: to find forgiveness. And it was to be found in there—that is why she dared; it was that which moved her from the spot and urged her forward. But that everything else had become unimportant to her, it was that which made her scarcely notice the opposition. "That is the
XII courage of despair," you will say. Yes, but truly she is far from
254 being a despairing person, or would *the one* for whom one thing is unconditionally important be a despairing person if this one thing is what is unconditionally important! She has the energy of despair. It is this that makes her indifferent to everything else and stronger than all the opposition of those around her, so strong that she does not sink under the shame, does not flee from the mockery. But she, who has this energy, is not in despair, she is a believer. And so she enters, indifferent to everything else. Yet this unconditional indifference of hers does not create any sensation, any uproar, because she is a believer and therefore so quiet, modest, and humble, so unnoticeable in her infinite indifference to everything, that she does not draw any attention to herself by her entrance. Nor was it of the least importance to her to express her indifference to everything; but one thing was infinitely important to her: to find forgiveness. Yet if this one thing had not been important to her to the degree that everything else had

become unconditionally unimportant to her, she would not have found her way into that Pharisee's house—where she then found forgiveness.

The next thing you can learn from the woman who was a sinner, something she herself understood, is that with regard to finding forgiveness she herself is able to do nothing at all.

If we are to describe her whole behavior from beginning to end, we must say: She does nothing at all.

She did not wait to go to that house where she would find the Savior and salvation, she did not wait until she felt worthy. No, then she would have stayed away for a long time, perhaps would never have gone there or entered; she decides to go immediately, in her unworthiness. The very feeling of her unworthiness impels her; therefore her decision is to go immediately—in this way she herself does nothing, or she understands that she herself is able to do nothing. Can this be expressed more powerfully than when it is the very feeling of unworthiness that is determinative for her!

So she prepares to go—but does not prepare what she is going to say or other such things. Oh no, she buys an alabaster jar of ointment to take with her. Thus she complies with the words of
Scripture: "When you fast, anoint your head and wash your face, XII
so that people will not see you fasting, but your Father, who is in 255
secret."[14] Then she goes festively to the dinner—indeed, who would have guessed what her errand was or what her entrance into that house meant to her! She, however, fully understands that she herself is able to do nothing. Instead of perhaps abandoning herself to self-torment, as if she would thereby become more pleasing to God and she would come closer to God, instead of that she *squanders*—yes, that was Judas's opinion[15]—she *rashly* squanders—yes, that is the self-tormentor's opinion—she squanders on something that in a worldly way goes along with festiveness; she takes along an alabaster jar of ointment, festively appropriate to the dinner.

She enters. She fully understands that she herself is able to do nothing. She does not for that reason abandon herself to expressions of passionate self-accusation, as if that would bring her closer to salvation or make her more pleasing to God. She does not exaggerate—indeed, no one can charge her with that. No, she does nothing at all, she is silent—she weeps.

She weeps. Perhaps someone will say: Then she did do something after all. Well, yes, she could not hold back her tears. But if it had occurred to her that these tears themselves would be doing something, she would also have been able to hold them back.

So, then, she weeps. She has seated herself at Christ's feet, and there she sits weeping. Yet let us not forget the festiveness, just as she herself did not forget it, simply because she fully understood that with regard to finding forgiveness she herself is able to do nothing at all. Let us not forget the festiveness—and the ointment she has brought along. She does not forget it, quite properly perceives this as her task: she anoints Christ's feet with ointment, dries them with her hair, and weeps.

Can you, if you do not know already, can you guess what this picture means? Indeed, since she says nothing it is of course in a certain sense impossible; and for her it all seems to merge, this anointing of his feet, which is appropriate to festiveness, and this weeping, which is appropriate to something entirely different. Yet what it means is not the business of anyone but her, she who fully understands that she is capable of nothing at all with regard to finding forgiveness, and him, who she fully understands is unconditionally capable of everything.

Then she listens to him speak with those present at the dinner. She understands very well that he is speaking about her when he tells about the difference between the debtors, that the one owes
XII five hundred denarii and the other fifty, but that it is also reason-
256 able, when both are forgiven, that the former loves more than
the latter.[16] She certainly understands how, alas, the one, and how, God be praised, also the other apply to her. But she also fully understands that she herself is able to do nothing. Therefore she does not enter into the conversation; she is silent, keeps her eyes to herself or on the task she is doing; she anoints his feet, dries them with her hair, weeps. Oh, what a powerful and true expression for: doing nothing, for being in this way like one

absent although present—yes, although the one present, the one talked about.

Then she hears him say, "Her many sins are forgiven her" . . . . . that she does hear. He says still more, he adds, "*because* she loved much." I assume that she did not even hear this; it might have disturbed her that there was a "because"—which referred to her. Perhaps it would also have made her love uneasy that it was praised in this way. Therefore I assume that she did not hear it, or perhaps she did hear it but heard it wrong and believed that he said: because he loved much, and therefore the talk was about his infinite love, that *because* it was so infinite, her many sins were therefore forgiven her, something she could so very well understand—indeed, it seemed as if she herself could have said it.

Then she goes home—a silent character in this whole scene. Who would guess what this going meant to her, this going when she went there with her sin and sorrow, and when she went away from there with forgiveness and joy.

So what does she do, then, this woman from whom we are to learn? Answer: Nothing, she does nothing at all. She practices the sublime, rare, exceedingly difficult, true feminine art: to do nothing at all, or to understand that in regard to finding forgiveness we are able to do nothing ourselves. "How easy!" Yes, if the very easiness were not the difficulty. How true it is that the one who conquers himself is greater than someone who captures a city.[17] Greater than the one who sets everything in motion in order at least to do something himself is the one who, in relation to God and to receiving the forgiveness of sins, is able to become altogether still in order devoutly to let God do everything, fully understanding that in this regard he himself is able to do nothing at all, and that everything, everything a person is able to do himself, be it even the most glorious, the most amazing, still in this XII
regard is infinitely nothing, is (if in other respects, humanly 257
speaking, it was something really good and not a deplorable self-deception of the deceitful heart) so far from contributing even the slightest in the most remote way to gaining the forgiveness of sins for him that it places him much more in a new debt, a debt of gratitude for the infinite mercy that in addition permitted this

to succeed for him. No, what a deplorable aberration, or what frightful presumptuousness, for a human being to get such an idea even in the most remote way! No, with regard to gaining the forgiveness of sins, or *before* God, a person is capable of nothing at all. How would it even be possible, since, after all, even in connection with the slightest thing of which a person is capable, humanly speaking, he is capable of nothing except *through* God!

Finally, we learn from the woman who was a sinner—certainly not directly from her but by considering our own situation compared with hers—*that we have one comfort that she did not have.*

Someone may say: Yes, but it was easy for her to believe in the forgiveness of her sins; after all, she heard it from Christ's own mouth. What thousands and thousands have experienced over the centuries, what has been handed down as experience from generation to generation, "that one word from him heals for eternity"—how she must have sensed and experienced this, she who heard these healing words from his own mouth!

On this point there is, to be sure, a rather common misunderstanding, so that, deceived by one's imagination, one does not really make this matter present to oneself and therefore forgets that in one sense contemporaneity with Christ is just what makes believing most difficult of all. But, of course, for the one who, despite all difficulties and dangers, actually believed, for him there was also one advantage over anyone who came later—to hear the words from Christ's own mouth, not as we read it and ordinarily read about there being forgiveness of sins in Christ, but to hear it said to him by Christ. Thus there cannot possibly be any doubt that it is I who is meant, that it is true for me that I have the gracious forgiveness of my sins, any more than there can be any doubt that these are Christ's words.

But then in turn this matter has another side. There is a com-
XII fort that had not yet come into existence while Christ lived,
258 which he therefore could not offer to anyone: the comfort of his
death as the Atonement, as the pledge that the sins are forgiven. In his lifetime Christ is for his contemporaries primarily the prototype, even though he is the Savior and even though his life is suffering, so that even in his lifetime he can be said to bear the

sins of the world;[18] but the salient point is that he is the prototype. And since Christianity is not like a teaching that is the same whoever the proclaimer is but is related to the proclaimer, to how truthfully the proclaimer's life expresses the teaching, so it also became manifest that when Christ proclaims Christianity and as the prototype, no human being can hold out with him entirely; they all fall away, even the apostles.

But then he dies. And his death infinitely changes everything. It is not as if his death abolished the importance of his also being the prototype. No, but his death becomes the infinite comfort, the infinite headstart with which the striver begins, that satisfaction has been made infinitely, that the doubter, the discouraged one is offered the ultimate pledge—it is impossible to find anything more reliable!—that Christ died to save him, that Christ's death is the Atonement, is the satisfaction. This comfort the woman who was a sinner did not have. It is true that she heard from his own mouth that her many sins were forgiven her, but she did not have his death as a comfort, as the later one has. If you imagine that sometime later in spiritual trial the woman who was a sinner doubted whether her many sins also were now actually forgiven her, then she would, since she could not again hear it directly from Christ himself, find rest in hearing, as it were, Christ say: Just believe it; after all, you have heard it from my own mouth. On the other hand, when in spiritual trial the one who lives many centuries after Christ doubts whether his sins also are forgiven, he will surely find comfort in hearing, as it were, Christ say to him: Just believe it; I have laid down my life in order to gain for you the forgiveness of your sins; so just believe it, a stronger assurance is impossible. To the contemporary, Christ can only say: I will offer myself as a sacrifice for the sins of the world and for yours also. Is this easier to believe now than when he has done it, has offered himself? Or is the comfort greater because of his saying that he will do it than it is because of his having done it? There is no greater love than this, that
someone lays down his life for another,[19] but when is it easier to XII
believe, and when is the comfort derived greater: when the lov- 259
ing one says he will do it—or when he has done it? No, not until

he has done it, not until then is doubt made impossible, as impossible as it is possible to be. And not until Christ has been offered as the sacrifice of Atonement, not until then does the comfort come into existence that makes doubting of the forgiveness of sins impossible—yes, as impossible as it is possible to be, because this comfort is only for faith.

TWO DISCOURSES
AT THE COMMUNION ON FRIDAYS

by S. Kierkegaard

The end of 1849.

TO ONE UNNAMED,

WHOSE NAME WILL ONE DAY BE NAMED,

IS DEDICATED,

WITH THIS LITTLE WORK, THE ENTIRE AUTHORSHIP,

AS IT WAS FROM THE BEGINNING.

PREFACE[1] XII 267

An authorship that began with *Either/Or* and advanced step by step seeks here its decisive place of rest, at the foot of the altar, where the author, personally most aware of his own imperfection and guilt, certainly does not call himself a truth-witness but only a singular kind of poet and thinker who, *without authority*, has had nothing new to bring but "has wanted once again to read through, if possible in a more inward way, the original text of individual human existence-relationships, the old familiar text handed down from the fathers"—(see my postscript to *Concluding Postscript*[2]).

Turned this way,[3] I have nothing further to add. Allow me, however, to express only this, which in a way is my life, the content of my life, its fullness, its bliss, its peace and satisfaction—this, or this view of life, which is the thought of humanity [*Menneskelighed*] and of human equality [*Menneske-Liighed*]: Christianly, every human being (the single individual), unconditionally every human being, once again, unconditionally every human being, is equally close to God—how close and equally close?—is loved by him.

Thus there is equality, infinite equality, between human beings. If there is any difference—ah, this difference, if it does exist, is like peaceableness itself. Undisturbed, the difference does not in the remotest way disturb the equality. The difference is: that one person bears in mind that he is loved—keeps it in mind perhaps day in and day out, perhaps day in and day out for seventy years, perhaps with only one longing, for eternity, so that he can really grasp this thought and go forth, employed in this blessed occupation of keeping in mind that he—alas, not because of his virtue!—is loved.

Another person perhaps does not think about his being loved, perhaps goes on year after year, day after day, without thinking about his being loved; or perhaps he is happy and grateful to be loved by his wife, his children, by his friends and contemporaries, but he does not think about his being loved by God; or he may bemoan not being loved by anyone, and he does not think about his being loved by God.

"Yet," the first person might say, "I am innocent; after all, I cannot help it if someone else ignores or disdains the love that is lavished just as richly upon him as upon me." Infinite, divine love, which makes no distinctions! Alas, human ingratitude! —What if the equality between us human beings, in which we completely resemble one another, were that none of us really thinks about his being loved!

As I turn to the other side, I would wish and would permit myself (in gratitude for the sympathy and good will that may have been shown to me) to present, as it were, and to commend these writings to the people whose language I with filial devotion and with almost feminine infatuation am proud to have the honor to write, yet also with the consolation that it will not be to their discredit that I have written it.

Copenhagen, late summer 1851

S. K.

I[4] XII 269

[But One Who Is Forgiven Little Loves Little] Luke 7:47

 XII 271

Lord Jesus Christ, you who certainly did not come to the world in order to judge,[5] yet by being love that was not loved you were a judgment upon the world. We call ourselves Christians; we say that we know of no one to go to but you—alas, to whom then shall we go[6] when, precisely by your love, the judgment falls also upon us, that we love little? To whom, what hopelessness, if not to you! To whom, what despair, if you actually would not receive us mercifully, forgiving us our great sin against you and against love,[7] we who sinned much by loving little!

Luke 7:47. **But one who is forgiven little loves little.**

Devout listener, at the Communion table the invitation is indeed given, "Come here, all you who labor and are burdened, and I will give you rest."[8] The single individual then responds to the invitation and goes to the Communion table. After that he turns back and leaves the Communion table. Then there are other words—they could be the inscription over the door of the church, on the inside, not to be read by those who are entering the church but only by those who are leaving the church—the words: One who is forgiven little loves little. The former words are the Holy Communion's invitation; the latter words are the Holy Communion's justification, as if it were said: If at the Communion table you are not aware of the forgiveness of your sins, of your every sin, this is due to yourself. Holy Communion is XII 272 without fault; the fault is yours, because you love only little. [9]Just as in praying aright it is difficult to be able to reach the Amen—for the one who has never prayed it seems easy enough, easy to finish quickly, but for the one who felt the need to pray and began to pray it surely happens that he continually seemed to have something more upon his heart, as if he could neither get everything said nor get it all said as he wished it said, and thus he does not reach the Amen—in the very same way it is also difficult to receive aright the forgiveness of sins at the Communion table. There the gracious forgiveness of all your sins is pronounced to you. Hear it aright, take it altogether literally, the forgiveness of all your sins. You will be able to go away from the Communion table as light of heart, divinely understood, as a newborn child, upon whom nothing, nothing weighs heavily, therefore even lighter of heart, insofar as much has weighed upon your heart. There is no one at the Communion table who retains against you even the least of your sins,[10] no one—unless you yourself do it. So cast them all away from yourself, and the recollection of them, lest in it you retain them; and cast away the recollection of your having cast your sins away, lest in it you retain them. Cast it all away from yourself; you have nothing at all to do except, believing, to cast away from yourself and to cast away from yourself what weighs heavily and burdens. What can be easier! Usually the heaviness is to have to shoulder burdens, but to dare, to have to cast away from oneself! And yet how difficult! Yes, even more rare than a person who shouldered every burden, even more rare is a person who accomplished the apparently very easy task, after having received the assurance of the gracious forgiveness of his sins and the pledge thereof, of feeling completely unburdened of every sin, even the least, or relieved of every sin, also even the greatest! If you could look into the hearts, you would surely see how many go to Holy Communion burdened, groaning under the heavy burden; and when they go away from the Communion table, if you could look into the hearts, you would possibly see that basically there was not a single one who left it completely unburdened, and at times you might see someone who went away even more burdened, burdened by the thought that he probably had not been a worthy guest at the Communion table because he found no alleviation.

That this is the case we shall not conceal from one another. We shall not speak in such a way that the discourse leaves you ignorant of how things go in actuality, shall not depict everything as so perfect that it does not fit us actual human beings. Ah, no, what good would the discourse be then! If, however, the dis-
XII course makes us as imperfect as we are, then it helps us to be kept
273 in a continuous striving, neither makes us, intoxicated in dreams, imagine that everything was decided by this one time, nor, in

quiet despondency, give up because this time we did not succeed according to our wish, because things did not turn out as we had prayed and desired.

In the brief moments prescribed, let us consider these words: One who is forgiven little loves little—*words of judgment*, but also *words of comfort*.

And you, my listener, do not be disturbed by my speaking this way at this moment before you go up to the Communion table, perhaps thinking and insisting that the one who is to speak at this time ought to speak in a different way and devote everything to reassuring the single individual and making him feel secure. If the speaker later learned that the holy act had not been entirely a joy and blessing to an individual, he could then, of course, speak to him in a different way. O my friend, for one thing, it is truly not the case that it is only for a rare individual that the perfect does not succeed—no, it is only for a rare individual that the perfect does succeed. For another, there is a concern, a heartfelt concern, that perhaps better assists so that a person succeeds in the highest, better than too much trust and a too carefree bold confidence. There is a longing for God, a trust in God, a reliance upon, a hope in God, a love, a bold confidence—but what most surely finds him may still be a sorrowing for God. Sorrowing for God—this is no fugitive mood that promptly disappears as one draws close to God; on the contrary, it may be deepest just when one draws close to God, just as the person sorrowing in this way is most fearful for himself the closer he comes to God.

One who is forgiven little loves little. These are words of judgment.

Usually it is presented this way: justice, this is the severe judgment; love is leniency, which does not judge, and if it does judge, love's judgment is the lenient judgment. No, no, love's judgment is the most severe judgment. Was not the most severe judgment passed upon the world, more severe than the flood,[11] more severe than the confusion of tongues at the Tower of Babel,[12] more severe than the destruction of Sodom and Gomorrah,[13] was it not Christ's innocent death, which still was love's

sacrifice? And what was the judgment? Surely it was this: *love* was not loved. So also here. The words of the judgment do not say: One who is forgiven little sinned much; hence his sins were too
XII great and too many to be able to be forgiven. No, the judgment
274 says: He loves little. Thus it is not justice that severely denies the forgiveness and pardon of sins. It is love that leniently and mercifully says: *I* forgive you everything—if you are forgiven only little, then it is because you love only little. Justice severely sets the boundary and says: No further! This is the limit. For you there is no forgiveness, and there is nothing more to be said. Love says: You are forgiven everything—if you are forgiven only little, it is because you love only little. Thus there comes a new sin, a new guilt, the guilt of being forgiven only little, a guilt incurred not by the sins committed, but by the lack of love. If you want to learn to fear, then learn to fear—not the severity of justice, but the leniency of love!

Justice looks judgingly at a person, and the sinner cannot endure its gaze; but love, when it looks at him—yes, even if he avoids its gaze, looks down, he nevertheless does perceive that it is looking at him, because love penetrates far more inwardly into life, deep inside life, in there whence life emanates, than justice does, which repellingly establishes a chasmic abyss between the sinner and itself, whereas love is on his side, does not accuse, does not judge, but pardons and forgives. [14]The sinner cannot endure the judging voice of justice; he tries, if possible, to shut his ears to it. But even if he wanted to, it is impossible for him not to hear love, whose judgment—and what frightful judgment!—is: Your sins are forgiven! What frightful judgment, even though the words in themselves are anything but terrifying; and this is the very reason that the sinner cannot help but hear what is nevertheless the judgment. Whither shall I flee from justice? If I take the wings of the morning and fly to the furthest sea, it is there. And if I hide myself in the abyss, it is there, and thus it is everywhere.[15] Yet, no, there is one place to which I can flee—to love. But when love judges you, and the judgment is—what horror!—the judgment is: Your sins are forgiven! Your sins are forgiven—and yet there is something (yes, this something is within you; where else in all the world would it find an abode when love

forgives everything!), there is something within you that makes you perceive that they are not forgiven. What is the horror of the most severe judgment compared with this horror! What, then, is anger's severe judgment, the curse, compared with this judgment: Your sins are forgiven! Thus it is indeed almost leniency
on the part of justice to say as you say: No, they are not forgiven! XII
What is the suffering of the "brother-murderer" when he, fugi- 275
tive and unsteady, fears that everyone will recognize him by the mark of justice that condemned him[16]—what is this suffering compared with the anguish of the unhappy person for whom the words "Your sins are forgiven" become the judgment, not salvation! What frightful severity! That love, that it is love, the forgiving love, which, not judging, no, alas, itself suffering, is nevertheless changed into the judgment! That love, the forgiving love, which does not want, like justice, to make the guilt manifest but on the contrary wants to hide it by forgiving and pardoning, that it nevertheless is this which, itself suffering, makes the guilt more frightfully manifest than justice does!

Ponder that thought: "self-inflicted." It is self-inflicted, says justice, that there is no forgiveness for a person. Justice is thinking of his many sins, since it can forget nothing. Love says: It is self-inflicted—it is not thereby thinking of his many sins—ah, no, it is willing to forget them all, it has forgotten them all; and yet it is self-inflicted, says love. Which is the more terrible? Surely the latter, which sounds almost like insane talk, because the charge is not his sins, no, the charge is: he is forgiven, he is forgiven everything. Think of a sinner who is sinking in the abyss; listen to his cry of anguish when with his last groan he vindicates the justice his life has mocked and says: It is self-inflicted. How terrible! There is only one thing more terrible, if it is not to justice that he speaks but to love and says: It is self-inflicted. Justice is not mocked,[17] indeed, love even less. More severe than justice's most severe judgment of the greatest sinner is love's: He is forgiven little—because he loves little.

One who is forgiven little loves little. These are words of judgment, but they are also words of *comfort*.

I do not know, my listener, what your crime, your guilt, your sins are, but surely we are all more or less guilty of the guilt of

loving only little. Take comfort, then, in these words just as I take comfort in them. And how do I take comfort? I take comfort because the words say nothing about divine love but only
XII 276 something about mine. The words do not say that divine love has now become weary of being love, that it has now changed, weary of the wasting, as it were, of indescribable mercy on the ungrateful race of human beings or on me, the ungrateful one. The words do not say that divine love has now become something else, a lesser love, its warmth cooled because love became cold in the ungrateful race of human beings or in me, the ungrateful one. No, the words do not speak of that at all. Take comfort as I take comfort—from what? From this, that the reason the words do not say it is that the sacred words do not lie; so, then, it has not accidentally or cruelly been suppressed in the words while in actuality it is true that God's love has become weary of loving. No, if the words do not say it, then it is not so; and if the words did say it—no, the words could not say it, because the words cannot lie. Oh, what blessed comfort in the deepest sorrow!

Suppose God's love had in truth changed, suppose you had heard nothing about it but were concerned about yourself, that until now you had loved only little, with devout purpose you had striven to make the fire of love in you flame up and you fed the flame in the same way as you had made it flame up—and now, even though you felt ashamed of how imperfect your love still was, you now wanted to draw close to God in order, according to the words of Scripture,[18] to be reconciled to him—but he had changed! Imagine a girl in love; in concern she confesses to herself how little she has loved until now—but now, she says to herself, I will become sheer love. And she succeeds. These tears of concern she sheds in sorrow over herself—these tears do not put out the fire; no, they are burning too brightly for that. No, these very tears make the fire flame up. But meanwhile the beloved had changed; he was no longer loving. Oh, one concern for a person! One concern can be enough for a person; no human being can endure more. If a person, when he in self-concern must confess to himself how little he has loved God until now, is troubled by the thought that meanwhile God might have

changed—then, yes, then I will despair, and I will despair at once, because then there is nothing more to wait for, neither in time nor in eternity. But therefore I take comfort in the words, and I block every escape route for me and I push aside all excuses and all extenuations and bare my breast where I will be wounded by the words that, judging, penetrate, judging "You loved only
little." Oh, only penetrate more deeply, even more deeply, you XII
healing pain, "You did not love at all"—even when such is the 277
judgment, I am in one sense aware of no pain, I am aware of an indescribable blessedness, because precisely my sentence, the death sentence upon me and my wretched love, contains something else in addition: God is unchanged love.

This is how I take comfort. And I find hidden in the words a comfort that you too, my listener, surely find precisely when you hear the words in such a way that they wound you. They do not read: One who is forgiven little *loved* little; no, they read: *loves* little. When justice judges, it balances the account, closes it. It uses the past tense; it says: He *loved* little, and thereby says that now the account is settled, we two are separated, have nothing more to do with each other.

The words, the words of love, however, read: One who is forgiven little loves little. He loves little, he *loves*; that is, this is the way it is now, now at this moment—love does not say more. Infinite love, that you remain true to yourself this way even in your slightest utterance! He loves little now, in this present instant. But what is the present instant, what is the moment—swiftly, swiftly it is past, and now, in the next moment, now all is changed; now he loves, if not much, yet he is striving to love much. Now all is changed, but not *love*; it is unchanged, unchanged the same that lovingly has waited for him, lovingly has not had the heart to be finished with him, has not had the heart to seek a separation from him but has remained with him. Now it is not justice that conclusively says: He loved little; now it is love that, joyful in heaven,[19] says: He loved little—that is, now it is changed; once it was that way, but now, now he loves much.

But then is it not really true that the forgiveness of sins is *merited*, admittedly not by works, but by love? When it is said that one who is forgiven little loves little, does this not imply that it

is love that decides the issue, whether and how far one's sins should be forgiven—and therefore, the forgiveness of sins is *merited* after all? Oh, no. A little earlier in the same Gospel (v. 42 to the end), Christ speaks of two debtors, one of whom owed much and the other little, and who both found forgiveness. He asks: Which of these two ought to love more? The answer: The one who was forgiven much. Note how we still are not entering here into the baleful region of meritoriousness, but note how everything remains within love! When you love much, you are for-
XII 278 given much—and when you are forgiven much, you love much. See here the blessed recurrence of salvation in love! First you love much, and much is then forgiven you—and see, then love increases even more. This, that you have been forgiven so much, loves forth love once again, and you love much because you were forgiven much! Here love is like faith. Imagine one of those unfortunates whom Christ healed by a miracle. In order to be healed, the person must believe—now he believes and is healed. Now he is healed—and now that he is saved, his faith is twice as strong. It is not this way: he believed and then the miracle happened and then it was all over. No, the fulfillment doubles his faith; after the fulfillment, his faith is twice as strong as it was before he was saved. So also with this matter of loving much. The love that loves much and then is forgiven much is strong, divinely strong in weakness, but even stronger is love's second time, when the same love loves again, loves because much has been forgiven.

My listener, presumably you remember the beginning of this discourse. In this solemn moment one can disturb in two ways: by speaking about something irrelevant, even though the matter is otherwise important and the discourse meaningful, or by disturbingly speaking about something that at such a moment is closest to one. "One who is forgiven little loves little"—this could seem disturbing at this very moment before you go to Holy Communion, where you indeed receive the forgiveness of all your sins. Oh, but just as something that builds up is always terrifying at first, and just as all true love is always unrest at first, and just as love of God is always sorrow at first, similarly, what seems disturbing is not always disturbing, what truly is quieting

is always disquieting at first. But is there any comparison between these two dangers—that of being quieted in false security and that of being disquieted by being reminded of the disquieting thought—of what disquieting thought?—of *the* disquieting thought that if until now one has loved only little, this, too, can be forgiven. The disquieting is strange; it is true that the one who is properly formed by this does not look as strong as the one who remained ignorant of it. But at the last moment he, through his very weakness, is perhaps the stronger; at the last
moment, through his very weakness, he perhaps succeeds where XII
the stronger one fails. 279

May God, then, bless this disquieting discourse so that it might have disquieted you only for the good, that you, quieted, might be aware at the Communion table that you are receiving the gracious forgiveness of all your sins.

II XII 281

Love Will Hide a Multitude of Sins
I Peter 4:8

Lord Jesus Christ, the birds had nests, the foxes had dens, and you XII 283
had no place where you could lay your head.[20] You were homeless in the world—yet you yourself were a hiding place, the only place where the sinner could flee. And so even this very day you are a hiding place. When the sinner flees to you, hides himself with you, is hidden in you, he is eternally kept safe, since *love* hides a multitude of sins.

I Peter 4:8. **Love will hide a multitude of sins.**

This applies in a double sense when the discourse is about human love, as we have explained more fully elsewhere.[21] The one in whom there is love, the one who loves, hides a multitude of sins, does not see his neighbor's faults; or if he sees them, he is still as one who does not see them, hides them from himself and from others. Love, in an even more beautiful sense than being in love, makes him blind, blind to his neighbor's sins. On the other side, the one in whom there is love, the one who loves, if he also has faults, imperfections, yes, even if his sins were manifold—love, that there is love in him, covers a multitude of sins.

When the discourse is about Christ's love, the words can be XII 284
taken in only one sense, that he was love did not serve to cover what imperfection there was in him—the Holy One, in whom there was no sin and in whose mouth there was no guile[22]—of course, since in him there was only love, love in his heart, and only love in his every word and all his deeds, in his whole life, in his death, until the last. In a human being love is not so perfect, and therefore, or despite that, he derives benefit, as it were, from it: while he lovingly hides a multitude of sins, love in turn does to him what he does to others and covers his sins. Thus he himself needs the love that he is showing; thus he himself draws advantage from the love in him, which nevertheless, insofar as it turns outward, hiding the multitude of sins, does not embrace the whole world as does Christ's sacrificial love, but only very few. Alas, even though it is rare enough that a human being is one who loves, no wonder, one could be tempted to say, no wonder

that a human being strives to be that, he who himself needs love and to that extent by being loving is still in a certain sense looking to his own interest! But Christ did not need love. Imagine that he had not been love; suppose that in an unloving way he had wanted to be only what he was, the Holy One. Imagine that instead of saving the world and hiding a multitude of sins he had come to the world in holy wrath to judge the world. In order to consider more fervently that it is true of him in just a single sense that his love hid a multitude of sins, imagine this, that *it* was *love*, that, as Scripture says, there is only one who is good, God, and thus it was he, he alone, the Loving One, who hid a multitude of sins, not of just a few individuals, but of the whole world.

In the brief moments prescribed, let us then speak about these words:

Love (Christ's love) *hides a multitude of sins.*

Is it not true that you have felt the need of this and on this very day you feel the need of a love that can cover sins, your sins—and this is why you are going to the Lord's table today? While it is only all too true, as Luther says, that every human being has a preacher within him[23]—he eats with him, drinks with him, awakens with him, sleeps with him, in short, is always around him, always with him, wherever he is and whatever he does, a preacher who is called flesh and blood, lusts and passions, habits
XII and inclinations—so it is also certain that deep within every
285 human being there is a secret-sharer who is present just as scrupulously everywhere—the conscience. A person can perhaps succeed in hiding his sins from the world, he can perhaps be foolishly happy that he succeeds, or yet, a little more honest, admit that it is a deplorable weakness and cowardliness that he does not have the courage to become open—but a person cannot hide his sins from himself. This is impossible, because the sin that was absolutely unconditionally hidden from himself would, of course, not be sin, any more than if it were hidden from God, which is not the case either, since a person, as soon as he is aware of himself and in everything in which he is aware of himself, is also aware of God and God is aware of him. The reason that he is so powerful, punctilious, and always very present and in-

corruptible is that he is in covenant with God—he, this secret-sharing preacher who accompanies a person everywhere, when he is awake and when he is sleeping (alas, if he does not make him sleepless with his preaching!), everywhere, in the world's noise (alas, if with his voice he does not transform the world's noise into stillness!), in solitude (alas, if he does not prevent him from feeling alone even in that most solitary place!), at the daily job (alas, if he does not make him estranged from it and like one distracted!), in festive surroundings (alas, if he does not make them like a gloomy prison for him!), in holy places (alas, if he does not keep him from going there!)—this secret-sharing preacher who accompanies a person, sharing with him secrets about what he is doing now, now at this very moment, or is leaving undone, and about the long, long ago—no, not the long ago forgotten, this secret-sharer, who has a frightful memory, takes care of that—but what was done long, long ago. A person can no more flee from this secret-sharer than he can, according to that pagan's words, ride away from care, which sits behind him on his horse,[24] and no more than, to use another metaphor, it "helps the deer to plunge ahead in order to run from the arrow that is lodged in its breast—the more violently it dashes ahead, the more firmly the arrow becomes fixed."

But today you are very far indeed from wanting to make the futile attempt to flee or to avoid this secret-sharing preacher; you have in fact given him the floor. It is true that in the confessional it is the pastor who preaches; but the true preacher is still the XII 286
secret-sharer in your inner being. The pastor can preach only in vague generalities; the preacher in your inner being is just the opposite; he speaks simply and solely about you, to you, and within you.

Sufficiently dismayed myself, I shall not make any attempt to dismay; but whoever you are, almost pure and innocent, humanly speaking—if this secret-sharing preacher preaches to you in your inner being, then you, too, sense what others perhaps sense more dismayingly, you sense a need to hide yourself. Even if you were told thousands of times and thousands of times again that it is impossible to find this hiding place, you still sense the need. Oh, if I knew how to flee to a desert island, where no human being ever came or comes; oh, would that there were a place of refuge to which I could flee—far away from myself! Would that there were a hiding place where I am so hidden that not even the consciousness of my sin can find me! Would that there were a border, however narrow, if it still makes a separation between me and my sin! Would that on the other side of a chasmic abyss there were a spot, however little, where I can stand, while the consciousness of my sin must remain on this side. Would that there were a forgiveness, a forgiveness that does not increase my sense of guilt but truly takes the guilt from me, also the consciousness of it. Would that there were oblivion!

But now this is indeed the way it is, because love (Christ's love) hides a multitude of sins. Behold, everything has become new! The Gospel has made possible what was sought and is futilely sought in paganism, what was and is a fruitless effort under the dominion of the Law. At the altar the Savior opens his arms[25] and specifically to this fugitive who wants to flee from the consciousness of his sin, flee from what is even worse than being pursued, flee from what gnaws. He opens his arms and says, "Come here to me"; and that he opens his arms already says, "Come here"; and that he, opening his arms, says "Come here" also says, "Love hides a multitude of sins."

Oh, believe him! Could you think that the one who opens his arms redeemingly to you, could you think that he is guilty of playing with words, think he is capable of using a meaningless platitude, think he is capable of deceiving you, and at the very moment—that he could say "Come here," and at the very moment when you came and he held you so embraced that it would be as if you were taken prisoner—because here, precisely here,
XII 287 there would be no forgetting, here with: the Holy One! No, this you could not believe; and if you did believe it, you of course would not come here—but blessed is the one who very literally believes that love (Christ's love) hides a multitude of sins. A loving person, yes, even if this is the most loving person, who can lovingly judge leniently, lovingly shut his eyes to your sins—oh, but he cannot shut your eyes to them. By loving talk and sympathy he can try to mitigate your guilt also in your eyes and to that extent hide it, so to speak, from you, or at least to a certain degree

hide it from you fairly well—oh, but actually to hide it from you, literally to hide it from you so that it is hidden like something that is hidden at the bottom of the sea, something no one ever gets to see any more, hidden in such a way as when what was red like blood becomes whiter than snow,[26] hidden so that sin is transformed into purity and you yourself dare to believe yourself justified and pure—this only he can do, the Lord Jesus Christ, whose love hides a multitude of sins. A human being has no authority, cannot command that you shall believe and just by commanding you with authority help you to believe. But if it requires authority even to teach, what authority is required, even greater, if possible, than the authority that commands the heaving sea to be still,[27] to command the despairing person, the one who in the agony of repentance is unable and does not dare to forget, the prostrate penitent who is unable and does not dare to stop staring at his guilt, what authority is required to command him to shut his eyes, and what authority is then required to command him to open the eyes of faith so that he sees purity where he saw guilt and sin! This divine authority he alone has, Jesus Christ, whose love hides a multitude of sins.

He hides it very literally. Just as when one person places himself in front of another person and covers him so completely with his body that no one, no one, can see the person hidden behind him, so Jesus Christ covers your sin with his *holy body*. If justice were then to fly into a rage, what more does it want—there is indeed satisfaction. If the repentance within you then feels ever so brokenheartedly that it ought to help the justice outside you to discover your guilt—there is indeed satisfaction, a satisfaction, one who makes satisfaction, who completely covers all your guilt and makes it impossible for it to be seen, impossible for justice and thereby in turn impossible for the repentance within you or impossible for you, because repentance also loses its sight when the justice to which it appeals says, I can see nothing.

He hides it very literally. Just as the mother hen, concerned, in XII
the moment of danger gathers her chicks under her wings,[28] 288
covers them, will rather lose her life than deprive them of this hiding place that makes it impossible for the enemy's eye to discover them, in the same way he hides your sin. In the same way,

because he, too, is concerned, infinitely concerned in love; he will rather lay down his life than deprive you of your safe hiding place under his love. He will rather lay down his life—yet, no, he lost his life precisely in order to ensure you a hiding place under his love. Therefore it is also not in the same way as with the hen, that is, only insofar as (or yet infinitely more than) the hen in concern covers her chicks, but otherwise not in the same way, because he hides with *his death.* O eternally secure, O blessedly safeguarded hiding place! For the little chicks there is still one danger; although they are hidden, they are still constantly in danger. When the mother has done her utmost, out of love has given her life for them, they are deprived of their hiding place. But he, on the other hand—yes, if he covered your sin with his life, then there indeed would be the possibility of the danger that they would deprive him of life and you of your hiding place. It is different when he covers your sin with his death. He would rather—if it was necessary, if everything was not decided with the one time—he would rather lay down his life once again in order to procure by his death a hiding place for you than have you deprived of the hiding place. Very literally he covers your sin just because he hides with his death. Death can, of course, set a living person aside, but one who is dead cannot possibly be set aside, and thus you cannot possibly be deprived of your hiding place. If justice then were to fly into a rage, what more does it want than the death penalty; but that penalty has been paid, and his death is your hiding place. What infinite love! There is discussion of works of love, and many can be named. But if there is discussion of love's work or the work of love, then there is, yes, then there is only one work, and, wondrously enough, you know at once whom it is about, about him, about Jesus Christ, about his atoning death, which hides a multitude of sins.

This is proclaimed at the Communion table; from the pulpit it is essentially his life that is proclaimed, but at the Communion table it is his death. He died once for the sins of the whole world and for our sins;[29] his death is not repeated, but *this* is repeated: He died also for you, you who receive in his body and blood the pledge that he died also for you, at the Communion table where

he gives you *himself* as a hiding place. O safe hiding place for XII
the sinner! O blessed hiding place, especially after first having 289
learned what it means when the conscience accuses, and the law judges, and justice punitively pursues, and then, exhausted to the point of despair, to find rest in the only hiding place that is to be found! A person, even the most loving, can at most give you mitigation, extenuation, and leave to you the extent to which you can use it, but he cannot give you himself. Only Jesus Christ can do that; he gives you himself as a hiding place. It is not a few grounds of comfort that he gives you; it is not a doctrine he communicates to you—no, he gives you himself. Just as the night spreads, hiding everything, so also did he sacrifice himself and became the hiding place behind which lies a sinful world that he saved. Through this hiding place, justice does not break, even in softened form, as when the sun's rays break through colored glass—no, powerless, it breaks against this hiding place and does not break through. He gave himself for the whole world as a hiding place, also for you, just as for me.

Therefore, my Lord and Savior, you whose love hides a multitude of sins, when I really am aware of my sin and the multitude of my sins, when before justice in heaven there is only wrath over me and over my life, when here on earth there is only one person I hate and detest, one person I would flee to the ends of the earth to avoid—myself—then I will not begin the futile attempt that only leads either more deeply into despair or to madness, but I will promptly flee to you, and you will not deny me the hiding place you have lovingly offered to all; you will shield me from the eyes of justice, rescue me from this person and from the recollection with which he tortures me; you will help me to dare—by becoming a changed, a different, a better person—to remain in my hiding place, forgotten by justice and by that person I detest.

Devout listener, it is to the love that hides a multitude of sins that you come today, seeking it at the Communion table. From the servant of the Church you have received the assurance of the gracious forgiveness of your sins. At the Communion table you receive the pledge of that. And not only that; you do not only receive this pledge in the same way as you receive from another

person a pledge that he bears this feeling for or this attitude toward you. No, you receive the pledge as a pledge that you receive Christ himself. As you receive the pledge, you receive Christ himself. In and with the visible sign, he gives you himself as a cover over your sins. Since he is the Truth, you do not find
XII out from him what truth is and now are left to yourself, but you
290 remain in the Truth only by remaining in him;[30] since he is the Way, you do not find out from him the way you are to go and now, left to yourself, must go your way, but only by remaining in him do you remain on the way; since he is the Life, you do not have life handed over by him and now must shift for yourself, but you have life only by remaining in him—in this way he is also the hiding place. Only by remaining in him, only by living yourself into him are you under cover, only then is there a cover over the multitude of your sins. This is why the Lord's Supper is called communion with him. It is not only in memory of him, it is not only as a pledge that you have communion with him, but it is the communion, this communion that you are to strive to preserve in your daily life by more and more living yourself out of yourself and living yourself into him, in his love, which hides a multitude of sins.

SUPPLEMENT

KEY TO REFERENCES

Marginal references alongside the text are to volume and page [XI 100] in *Søren Kierkegaards samlede Vaerker*, I-XIV, edited by A. B. Drachmann, J. L. Heiberg, and H. O. Lange (1 ed., Copenhagen: Gyldendal, 1901–06). The same marginal references are used in Sören Kierkegaard, *Gesammelte Werke*, *Abt.* 1–36 (Düsseldorf, Cologne: Diederichs Verlag, 1952–69).

References to Kierkegaard's works in English are to this edition, *Kierkegaard's Writings* [*KW*], I-XXVI (Princeton: Princeton University Press, 1978-). Specific references are given by English title and the standard Danish pagination referred to above [*Either/Or*, I, p. 109, *KW* III (*SV* I 100)].

References to the *Papirer* [*Pap.* I A 100; note the differentiating letter A, B, or C, used only in references to the *Papirer*] are to *Søren Kierkegaards Papirer*, I-XI^3, edited by P. A. Heiberg, V. Kuhr, and E. Torsting (1 ed., Copenhagen: Gyldendal, 1909–48), and 2 ed., photo-offset with two supplemental volumes, XII-XIII, edited by Niels Thulstrup (Copenhagen: Gyldendal, 1968–70), and with index, XIV-XVI (1975–78), edited by Niels Jørgen Cappelørn. References to the *Papirer* in English [*JP* II 1500], occasionally amended, are to volume and serial number in *Søren Kierkegaard's Journals and Papers*, I-VII, edited and translated by Howard V. Hong and Edna H. Hong, assisted by Gregor Malantschuk, and with index, VII, by Nathaniel Hong and Charles Barker (Bloomington: Indiana University Press, 1967–78).

References to correspondence are to the serial numbers in *Breve og Aktstykker vedrørende Søren Kierkegaard*, I-II, edited by Niels Thulstrup (Copenhagen: Munksgaard, 1953–54), and to the corresponding serial numbers in *Kierkegaard: Letters and Documents*, translated by Henrik Rosenmeier, *Kierkegaard's Writings*, XXV [*Letters*, Letter 100, *KW* XXV].

References to books in Kierkegaard's own library [*ASKB* 100] are based on the serial numbering system of *Auktionsprotokol over*

Søren Kierkegaard's Bogsamling [Auction-catalog of Søren Kierkegaard's Book-collection], edited by H. P. Rohde (Copenhagen: Royal Library, 1967).

In the Supplement, references to page and lines in the text are given as: 100:1–10.

In the notes, internal references to the present volume are given as: p. 100.

Three spaced periods indicate an omission by the editors; five spaced periods indicate a hiatus or fragmentariness in the text.

Lilien paa Marken og Fuglen under Himlen.

Tre gudelige Taler

af

S. Kierkegaard.

Kjøbenhavn.

Paa Universitets-Boghandler C. A. Reitzels Forlag.

Trykt hos Kgl. Hofbogtrykker Bianco Luno.

1849.

The Lily in the Field and

the Bird of the Air.

Three Devotional Discourses

by

S. Kierkegaard.

Copenhagen.

Available at University Bookseller C. A. Reitzel's Publishing House.

Printed by Royal Book Printer Bianco Luno.

1849.

SELECTED ENTRIES FROM KIERKEGAARD'S JOURNALS AND PAPERS PERTAINING TO *THE LILY IN THE FIELD AND THE BIRD OF THE AIR*

No one can serve two masters. This does not mean only the vacillating, irresolute person who does not quite know which to choose. No, the person who defiantly broke with God and heaven in order to serve his desires and drives also serves two masters, something no one can do—he has to serve God whether he wants to or not. The situation is not this simple: choose one of the two. The situation is rather this: there is only one to choose if one is actually going to serve only one master, and that is God.—*JP* I 952 (*Pap*. VIII[1] A 359) *n.d.*, 1847

See 7:3–9:12:

New Discourses on the Lilies and the Birds

But perhaps you say: Oh, I wish I were a bird, which lighter than all earthly gravity rises in the air, so lightly that it can even make itself light enough to build its nest upon the sea. Oh, I wish I were like a flower in the meadow. —This means that the poet extols as the highest happiness something to which human wish strives to return—how unreasonable to make this the teacher for the person who is to move forward.

Immediacy is poetically the very thing we wish to return to (we wish for our childhood again etc.), but from a Christian point of view, immediacy is lost and it ought not to be wished for again but should be attained again.

In these discourses, therefore, there will be a development of the conflict between poetry and Christianity,[1] how in a certain sense Christianity is prose in comparison with poetry (which is desiring, charming, anesthetizing and transforms the actuality of life into an oriental dream, just as a young girl might want to lie on a sofa all day and be entranced)—and yet it is the very poetry of the eternal.

Of course the lilies and the birds, that is, the sketching of nature, will this time have an even more poetic tone and richness of color, simply to indicate that the poetic must be put aside, for when poetry in truth shall fall (not because of a preacher's dull and dismal jawing), it ought to wear its party clothes.—*JP* II 1942 (*Pap.* VIII^{1} A 643) *n.d.*, 1848

See 39:23–26:

VIII^{1} A 644 291 Here consideration could also be given to Zeuthen's comment (which in a casual allusion in my answer[2] I hinted at wanting to consider) in a letter[3] a week ago: "that there also is a worry
VIII^{1} A 644 292 about yesterday with regard to what one has eaten—and not paid for." The difficulty is, namely, to have the day today without any presuppositions.—*Pap.* VIII^{1} A 644 May 17, 1848

From draft; see title page:

"The Lily in the Field and the Bird of the Air."
[*Deleted:* "The Bird of the Air, and the Lilies in the Field."]
Discourses.
No. 1.

In margin: draft
—*Pap.* X^{5} B 4 *n.d.*, 1849

From final copy; see title page:

S. Kierkegaard.

In margin: Final copy

No. 1.
Format and type as in *Two Upbuilding Discourses* (1843); 20 copies on thin vellum.
—*Pap.* X^{5} B 6:1 *n.d.*, 1849

From the first page proofs; see title page:

May I please have back the upbldg. discourses that you received for typesetting.—*Pap.* X^5 B 7:1 *n.d.*, 1849

From the second page proofs, with notes for the typesetter and numerous corrections (some in Israel Levin's handwriting) in the first signature, which at the bottom of page sixteen (13) has the following note in Kierkegaard's handwriting:

The nature of these page proofs is such that a *third set of proofs* is necessary.

S.K.

—*Pap.* X^5 B 8 *n.d.*, 1849

Deleted from draft; see 24:14–15:

If a lawgiver wants his laws obeyed, well, he perhaps has power he can use to compel people to obedience. Yet in this way it becomes dubious. But let him begin with his unconditionally submitting himself to the laws; then his obedience will undoubtedly compel others to obedience.—*Pap.* X^5 B 5:3 *n.d.*, 1849

Deleted from margin in draft; see 25:29–30:

. . . . . the harmony that is the movement of the celestial bodies, the almost singable sound with which everything goes in this vast complex, the echo of every point in the infinite: it is all obedience.—*Pap.* X^5 B 5:4 *n.d.*, 1849

Deleted from draft; see 31:34:

Just as a traveler who is carrying with him some valuable object knows that if all the money forwarded from home fails to reach him he still has the comfort of this treasure—[*deleted:* in the same way would] . . . . .—*Pap.* X^5 B 5:6 *n.d.*, 1849

Deleted from draft; see 33:17:

The little bird, the prey of predatory birds, seeks a hiding place in the crevices of cliffs, in the trunks of hollow trees, in a place of refuge between the branches—the poor thing, nowhere is it entirely safe.—*Pap.* X^5 B 5:10 *n.d.*, 1849

Deleted from draft; see 33:20:

It may also happen at times that the little bird is so well concealed that it can sit and see the predatory bird while the predatory bird is unable to see it; but let the little bird be on its guard. Not so with the person who by unconditional obedience is hidden in God; . . . . .—*Pap.* X^5 B 5:11 *n.d.*, 1849

Deleted from draft; see 34:28–31:

Imagine a bird busy instructing its young one, which still had no sense either of how the mother loved it or of the predatory bird's power and slyness; imagine the mother instructing it about caution with regard to the predatory bird. It will of course seem a strange exaggeration to the young bird. It does not grasp that on the one side it is precisely the mother's love that sees the danger facing the beloved as enormously great, and on the other side the mother's acquaintance with evil. Thus it will seem an exaggeration to the young one that the mother requires this unconditional obedience. It is the same for a human being with the Gospel— . . . —*Pap.* X^5 B 5:12 *n.d.*, 1849

Deleted from margin in final copy; see 39:27:

. . . . . and in all probability shrewdly diverts attention by making distinctions between things between which there is no distinction, such as whether today truly *is*, or whether you truly *are* today.—*Pap.* X^5 B 6:10 *n.d.*, 1849

See 18:12–18:

"The poet" daydreams about the exploit that he will never carry out himself, and he becomes eloquent. Perhaps he becomes eloquent simply because he is only an unhappy lover of the exploit, whereas the hero is its happy lover; consequently he becomes eloquent because the deficiency makes him eloquent. "Deficiency"—oh, in their misunderstanding people speak ill of you, as if you were only cruel and not equally compassionate, as if you only took away and never gave—deficiency essentially makes "the poet."

A passage that was not used in the first discourse in *The Lily in the Field and the Bird of the Air.*—*JP* I 167 (*Pap.* X[1] A 198) *n.d.*, 1849

The Three Devotional Discourses

In the three devotional discourses, the petition "Thy kingdom come" in the Lord's Prayer is not used, since the accent in the theme (silence) must fall most strongly on "Hallowed be thy name," and also since it comes more specifically in discourse no. 2 in the petition "Thy will be done on earth as it is in heaven," which is more appropriate to this theme (obedience).[4] Furthermore, the petition "Forgive us our trespasses as we . . . . . " is not used, because in that regard the lily and the bird cannot be the teachers; finally, the petition "Give us today our daily bread" is not used, because this petition is treated in detail in earlier discourses.[5]—*Pap.* X[1] A 252 *n.d.*, 1849

Curiously enough, in "Three Devotional Discourses"[6] I attributed to Paul the words that are by Peter: "Cast all your sorrow upon God."[7]—*JP* VI 6422 (*Pap.* X[1] A 469) *n.d.*, 1849

See 28:6–17:

It appealed to me immediately when I wrote it this way, and it still appeals to me as an epigraph for "Writings of Completion,"[8] an epigraph that could stand on the title page itself, the lines from "Three Devotional Discourses" (1849): "If for the lily, when the moment is there for it to blossom, things look as unfavorable as possible—the obedient lily simply understands only one thing: that now the moment is there."—*Pap.* X^1 A 506 *n.d.*, 1849

See 3:1–16:

X^1 A 549 350 Incidentally, it is really noteworthy that it says in the preface
to the three devotional discourses about the lily and the bird, "In
contrast to the pseudonyms, which were held out and are held
X^1 A 549 351 out with the left hand."[9] Undoubtedly it is best understood with
reference to the second edition of *Either/Or*;[10] but it has also
become significant with regard to the new pseudonym.[11]—*Pap.*
X^1 A 549 *n.d.*, 1849

[*In margin: The Three Devotional Discourses* (The Lily and the Bird) and *The Sickness unto Death* with regard to time of writing.]

It must be remembered that the three devotional discourses about the lily and the bird are the last thing I wrote. They were finished May 5, 1849. *The Sickness unto Death* is from the middle of 1848.—*JP* VI 6457 (*Pap.* X^1 A 583) *n.d.*, 1849

Tvende ethisk-religieuse

Smaa-Afhandlinger.

Af

H. H.

Kjøbenhavn.

Gyldendalske Boghandling.

Trykt hos Louis Klein.

1849.

Two Ethical-Religious

Essays.

By

H. H.

Copenhagen.

Gyldendal's Bookstore.

Printed by Louis Klein.

1849.

SELECTED ENTRIES FROM KIERKEGAARD'S JOURNALS AND PAPERS PERTAINING TO *TWO ETHICAL-RELIGIOUS ESSAYS*

Rarely does one make an attempt really to understand how it was VIII[1] A 145 71 that the life of Christ (whose life in a certain sense could not possibly have collided with anyone since it had no earthly aims) ended by his being crucified. Perhaps one fears getting to know anything of the evidence of the existence of evil in the world that is implied thereby. So one pretends as if Christ himself and God's governance ordained it this way. (Here one also learns the meaning of all the chatter that one ought not venture out in decisions but ought to wait until they come to one, since the former is—to tempt God. I wonder then, was not Christ's life a unique attempt to tempt God?) But no doubt it is both. The fact that Christ was willing to sacrifice his life does not at all signify that he sought VIII[1] A 145 72 death or forced the Jews to kill him. Christ's willingness to offer his life simply means a conception of the world as being so evil that the Holy One unconditionally had to die—unless he wanted to become a sinner or a mediocrity in order to be a success in the world. But it is unbelievable how meager a conception of an essential view of existence [*Tilværelse*] people have. They live out their lives in tomfoolery. They go out into life saying: Perhaps I will become a somebody, perhaps I will be a nobody, perhaps I will even be persecuted. What foolishness! Please, simply choose, and you do not need to guess; the specific conditions of existence can be calculated very well. If you will unconditionally risk everything for the good—then you will be persecuted, unconditionally persecuted, *tertium non datur* [there is no third possibility]. If you compromise, well, then you will certainly come to live in the ambiguity of tomfoolery, for then it is possible that you will become a somebody, but the opposite is also possible. Therefore all you sagacious pastors ought instead to say forthrightly:

We have omitted and abolished the most important view of existence; what we preach is worldly wisdom and a philistine-bourgeois gospel especially inspiring to lottery-players.

The death of Christ is the result of two factors—the Jews' guilt plus on the whole a demonstration of the world's evil. Since Christ was the God-man, that he was crucified cannot signify that the Jews at this time happened to be demoralized and that Christ came, if I may put it this way, at an unfortunate time. No, Christ's fate is an eternal fate; it indicates the specific gravity of the human race, and the same thing would happen to Christ at any time. Christ can never express something accidental.

See, now it would be an appropriate task to show how the Jews could become so enraged. But, as said, we shrink from doing this. Maybe we are afraid of getting to know too much—for example, that being high up on the world's totem pole would become evidence against one.

Distance Theology
—*JP* I 305 (*Pap*. VIII[1] A 145) *n.d.*, 1847

N.B.

"The Book on Adler" lends itself best to division into many small separate parts. It will not be understood as a whole—and it will be wearisome that it is continually about Adler, which, in my opinion is still precisely the point. Then there will be, for example, a section about the concept "Premise-authors," about the universal, the single individual, the special individual.[12] A second section: A revelation in the situation of contemporaneity.[13] A third: The relation between a genius and an apostle[14] etc. This can be done very well and then the book will be read in an entirely different way, and I will be spared mentioning Adler, for it is cruel to slay a man that way.—*JP* V 6049 (*Pap*. VIII[1] A 264) *n.d.*, 1847

VIII[1] A 271 129

The new book will be titled: **N.B.**

How did it happen that Jesus Christ could be crucified? Or: Has a human being the right to sacrifice his life for the truth?

The point is that the dogmatic discussion about Christ's atoning death has made us completely forget the event itself.

His death is an atoning death, a sacrifice he wills to make. Right. However, he was not himself responsible for being condemned to death. Here is the dialectic: he wants to save the world by his death; otherwise he cannot save it—but for all that he is not himself responsible for being persecuted and put to death.

As a rule we speak only of Christ's purity and innocence, but
here again a problem is overlooked. That is, the good and the VIII^1
true can be proclaimed in such a way that people are compelled A 271
to persecute the proclaimer. —In his first skirmishing with the 130
world, a person actually regards the world as the stronger, but when he has really felt his strength, he actually sympathizes with people for doing him wrong. Then it may occur to him (not on his own behalf, but on theirs) that he might be jacking up the price too high for them. After all, one may be so conversant with the world and with people that simply by doing what is good and true one is saying very precisely: I will be persecuted. Is this not being too hard on people? Indeed, in that way one may almost be putting a murder on their consciences. Is it not being too hard on people to structure one's own life on the most prodigious scale, to hold to it unswervingly, to compel people in a tragic kind of self-defense to put one to death? —Here I can say, as in *Fear and Trembling*,[15] that the majority do not understand at all what I am talking about. The minute a person sees that from now on he must either pare down the truth a little in order to take people along or also in a way compel them to persecute him, to take this responsibility upon themselves—is it his duty to do the former or the latter?

Thus Christ at all times must have wanted to avoid persecution (not for his own sake, for he certainly was willing to suffer, he who had come to suffer), but for the sake of people, lest he be the one who contributed to making them "guilty." —But how is it then possible that he could be put to death?

Then how he must have lived in relation to the powers (the clique) and to the lowly will be developed. How imprudently he must have lived.

Has any human being the right to hold unreservedly to the truth to such a degree that he can foresee that his contemporaries will become guilty by doing away with him? Christ is the Truth, and therefore it could not be otherwise; and furthermore his death makes it good again, since it is atoning death.

See, I am back again as before with *Fear and Trembling*. From
VIII[1] A 271 131 whom can I try to find some clarification of thoughts like these? There are not ten who can think them once I have posed them, to say nothing of before. They all think in the opposite direction, in the direction of not being afraid of risking one's life. But their thinking does not begin with that as the given in order to ask whether one has the right to do it.

See this book, p. 194 [*Pap*. VIII[1] A 307; p. 211].—*JP* V 6050 (*Pap*. VIII[1] A 271) *n.d.*, 1847

Addition to Pap. VIII[1] A 271:

> **See this book, pp. 33ff.** [*Pap*. VIII[1] A 145; pp. 207–08]
> *See journal NB*[3], p. 78 [*Pap*. VIII[1] A 469; p. 212]
> —*Pap*. VIII[1] A 272 *n.d.*, 1847

Addition to Pap. VIII[1] A 271:

> N.B. The real paradox must not be overlooked—namely, that Christ entered into the world *in order* to suffer. (See *Concluding Unscientific Postscript*, p. 460 mid. [p. 597, *KW* XII.1; *SV* VII 520]).—*JP* III 3090 (*Pap*. VIII[1] A 273) *n.d.*, 1847

See 53:

Preface

This preface contains no more than an entreaty that the reader will first practice laying aside part of his customary mode of thinking.* Otherwise it cannot help at all to begin; he will not be able to catch sight of the issue at all, because long ago he was already finished with it in the reversed position.

*(The difference is like the difference when one turns a drawing sideways)

—*Pap*. VIII[1] A 274 *n.d.*, 1847

Christ's suffering is real soul-suffering.

JP IV 4604 (*Pap*. VIII[1] A 275) *n.d.*, 1847

If I do not have the right God-fearingly to call something ungodliness that in human good-naturedness I would call weakness, then I do not have the right to sacrifice my life for the truth either, that is, to be put to death, or to let myself be put to death.—*JP* V 6051 (*Pap*. VIII[1] A 276) *n.d.*, 1847

That the Jews would have made Christ king was precisely a factor in his being crucified. When a fire is to be lighted properly, there must be a draft; but spiritually understood a draft is a double-movement. A person who immediately comes into conflict with people does not easily become a sacrifice. But the very person of whom people have been appreciatively aware—when he turns against them, when his will is not their will: this is what fans the fire and fans it to flame.

See this book, pp. 160 ff. [*Pap*. VIII[1] A 271–76; pp. 208–11].

—*JP* I 607 (*Pap*. VIII[1] A 307) *n.d.*, 1847

Authority does not mean to be a king or to be an emperor or general, to have the power of arms, to be a bishop, or to be a policeman,* but it means by a firm and conscious resolution to be willing to sacrifice everything, one's life, for one's cause; it means to articulate a cause in such a way that a person is in identity with himself about needing nothing and fearing nothing. This recklessness of infinity is authority.** True authority is present when the truth is the cause. The reason the Pharisees spoke without authority, although they were indeed authorized teachers, was precisely that their talk, like their lives, was in the finite power of seventeen concerns.

* *In margin:* that is, it is the concept of authority in immanence, not the paradoxical concept: authority.

** *In margin:* the one with authority, therefore, always appeals to the conscience, not to the understanding, intelligence, profundity—to the human being, not to the professor.—*JP* I 183 (*Pap*. VIII[1] A 416) *n.d.*, 1847

See 55:2–19:

See journal notebook[16], pp. 33ff., pp. 160ff. [*Pap*. VIII[1] A 145, 271–76; pp. 207–11].

> How was it even possible that Jesus Christ could be crucified.[*]

Once upon a time there was a man who as a child had been piously instilled by his parents with faith in Jesus Christ—but as he grew older, he could understand it less and less. "I comprehend very well," he said, "that he was willing to sacrifice his life for the truth and that he, if he sacrificed his life, sacrificed it for the truth. But what I do not comprehend is that he, who was love, did not out of love for people prevent people from committing the worst of all crimes: putting him to death."

The fact of the matter is: Christ is not love, and least of all according to the human notion of love. He was *the Truth*, absolute Truth; therefore he could not only defend letting people become guilty of his death, but he had to (it would have been impossible to defend the opposite as weakness)—that is, had to make the truth manifest in the most radical way.

[*] *In margin:* the book will be pseudonymous.

—*JP* I 316 (*Pap*. VIII[1] A 469) *n.d.*, 1847

VIII[1] A 562 261

Instructions

First of all, publish a book of essays. For this the book on Adler
VIII[1] A 562 262 can be used as I arranged it formerly. And then a new one will be added: How Was It Possible That Jesus Christ Could Be Deprived of His Life.* This essay must come out, as well as the two about the collision between the universal and the single individ-

ual and about the relation between a genius and an apostle, before I begin on the doctrine of sin.[16]—*JP* V 6114 (*Pap*. VIII^1 A 562) *n.d.*, 1848

In margin of Pap. VIII^1 A 562:

* N.B. If this essay is to be pseudonymous, I must add it as an addendum; then the title will be "Essays" by S. K., with an addendum.—*JP* V 6115 (*Pap*. VIII^1 A 563) *n.d.*, 1848

From draft of "A Cycle of Ethical-Religious Essays":

No. I.
Something on What Might Be Called
"Premise-Authors."
[*Deleted:* 1846] . . .

[*No. II.*
The Dialectical Relations: The Universal,
the Single Individual, the Special Individual.]
Addendum No. I. [*changed to:* No. II.] . . .

[*No. III.*
Does a Human Being Have the Right to Let Himself
Be Put to Death for the Truth?] . . .

[*No. IV.*
A Revelation in the Situation of the Present Age.] . . .

No. V.
A Psychological Interpretation of Magister Adler as a
Phenomenon and as a Satire upon Hegelian Philosophy
and the Present Age.
[*Deleted:* 1846.] . . .

[*No. VI.*
The Difference between a Genius and an Apostle.] . . .
—*Pap*. IX B 1–6 *n.d.*, 1848

From the preface to "A Cycle":

IX B 22 319 At some time, when the purely convulsive seizure[17] is over and the epoch of *political* ministries is past, blood will no doubt be demanded again, more blood, but blood of another kind, not that of the sacrifices slain by the thousands, no, the more costly blood, that of single individuals—of martyrs, those mighty ones who are dead, who accomplish what no living person accomplishes who has people chopped down, not even if he had them chopped down by the thousands, what even those mighty dead ones did not accomplish as living contemporaries but accomplish only as dead: to compel a raging crowd into obedience, simply because the raging crowd was allowed in disobedience to slay the martyr. The proverb says: He who laughs last laughs best, but in truth he also conquers best who conquers last, therefore not he who conquers by putting to death—O uncertain victory!—but he who conquers by being put to death—O eternal certain victory! And this sacrifice, that of obedience—for which God looks upon him well pleased, the obedient one who offers himself as the sacrifice, while he centers wrath upon the disobedience that puts to death the sacrifice—this sacrifice, this victor, is "the martyr," inasmuch as not everyone who is slain is truly a martyr! But the martyr is the ruler.

Until now, tyrants (in the form of emperors, kings, popes, Jesuits, generals, diplomats) have been able to rule and govern the world at a crucial moment, but from the time the fourth estate is established—when it has had time to establish itself in such a way that it is properly understood—it will become manifest that only martyrs are able to rule the world at the crucial moment. That is, no human being will any longer be able to rule the generation at such a moment; only the divine can do it, assisted by those unconditionally obedient to him, those who are also willing to suffer, but they are indeed the martyrs. In an older order, when the crucial moment was past, an orderly secular government took over, but from the moment the fourth estate is established, it will be seen that even when the crisis is over, the governing cannot be done *secularly*. No matter how much work and responsibility are connected with it, to rule secularly, to be

a ruler in a secular way, is an indulgence, and therefore is based upon and is possible only in proportion to this: that the far, far greatest number of people either are so completely unaware that they are not part of (political) life or are God-fearing enough not to want [*deleted:* to be part of it] to bother themselves with it. As IX
soon as the fourth estate is established, governing can be done B 22
only divinely, religiously. But religiously to rule, religiously to be 320
the ruler, is to be the suffering one; to rule religiously is suffering. Many a time these suffering ones (the rulers) will naturally, if they quite dared to have their way, wish themselves far away and say good-bye to the generation, in order either to spend their lives in the solitude of contemplation or to enjoy life, but when in fear and trembling they consider their responsibility to God, they dare not. People regard it as good fortune to be chosen to be the ruler secularly, but to be chosen to be the ruler religiously is instead like a punishment, humanly speaking—in any case a suffering, humanly speaking, the very opposite of an advantage, humanly speaking.

Displeased with and unsatisfied by the state, the Church, and everything related to them (art, science, etc. etc.), the generation, if it were allowed to have its way, would disintegrate into a world of atoms, whereby the advance would nevertheless be made that God now comes to be related to individuals neither through abstractions nor through representative individuals but becomes the one who, so to speak, takes it upon himself to bring up the generation's countless individuals, becomes himself the schoolmaster who watches over everyone, each one individually. Here thinking halts. The shape of the world would resemble—well, I do not know to what I should compare it—it would resemble an enormous Christiansfeldt,[18] and then the two most powerful opponents would be present, contending with each other over the interpretation of this phenomenon—*communism*, which would say: This way it is secularly right; there must be no distinction whatever between persons; wealth and art and science and government etc. etc. are of evil; all people should be alike as workers in a factory, as the inmates in a workhouse, dressed alike, eating the same food (made in one enormous pot) at the same stroke of the clock, in the same measure etc. etc;

pietism, which would say: This is Christianly right; there must be no distinction between persons; we should be brothers and sis-
IX B 22 321 ters, have everything in common; wealth, position, art, science, etc. are of evil; all people should be alike as once was the case in little Christiansfeldt, dressed alike, praying at specified times, marrying by drawing lots, going to bed by the clock, eating the same food out of one dish in a definite rhythm, etc. etc.

This is my view or conception of the age, the view of an insignificant person who has something of the poet in his nature, in other respects is a kind of thinker, but—yes, how often I have repeated this, to me so important and crucial, my first statement about myself—"without authority."[19]—*Pap*. IX B 22 *n.d.*, 1848

This preface[20] is, as stated, an anticipation. The book[21] was written about two years ago, with the exception of one essay,[22] which is from the end of last year. Inasmuch as this preface is dated October 1848 and since the spring of '48, when *Christian Discourses* was published, I have worked out several short works, these are in fact older than this preface, although they will be published later. But they could not be published before the present book, which they presuppose, would be published. On the other hand, the preface to this book will be understood better after the publication of those works.—*Pap*. IX B 12 *n.d.*, 1848

X[1] A 79 66

N.B. N.B.
N.B.

It was after all an act of Governance that I did not publish "The Point of View for My Work as an Author" at this time.[23] Indeed, what heavy-minded impatience! It is historical and written after a whole intermediary series of writings, which must be published first if there is any question at all of publishing it while I am alive.

Indeed, it is becoming more and more clear to me that when existence itself undertakes to preach for awakening as it is doing now, I do not dare to jack it up even more in that direction; something extraordinary like that has not been entrusted to me and scarcely can be entrusted to any human being. In a soft, refined, overcultured time, I was and ought to be for awakening. At present I ought to draw nearer to the established order.

[*In margin:* It is true that the religious, the essentially Christian, is seen to its very best advantage in such disturbed times, when, instead of becoming mild, it jacks up the price still more. That is the case with Christ, as I have shown elsewhere. But I neither dared nor have the strength to venture that far; it would be presumptuous, personally destructive, and would add to the confusion.]

I have had in mind very early the idea of ceasing to be an X^1
author; I have frequently said that the place was still vacant: an A 79
author who knew when to stop. Indeed, I actually thought of 67
stopping as early as with the publication of *Either/Or*. But I have never been closer to stopping than with the publication of *Christian Discourses*. I had sold the house and received two thousand for it. I was very tempted to use it for traveling. But I am no good at traveling and in all likelihood would just become productive, as I usually am most of all when traveling. So I stayed home, had the full harassment of the confused times, lost money on the bonds I bought, etc. During all this I continued to produce (and have written what I would not have achieved without these afflictions and a certain melancholy) but became more and more accustomed to being delayed.

Now the second edition of *Either/Or*[24] is coming out, but "A Cycle of Ethical-Religious Essays" will correlate precisely with that, and the publication will correspond to the direction I must take. What I have ready will stay there. It is gold but must be used with great care.—*Pap.* X^1 A 79 *n.d.*, 1849

All the essays (except the one on Adler) in "A Cycle" etc. could well be published. But they are to be published separately, each by itself, or at most two together, and by the pseudonyms H H,[25] F F, P P. They could then, like guerrillas, accompany the publication of the three books for awakening.[26] But precisely because their role is that of guerrillas, they must appear in doses as small as possible.—*JP* VI 6387 (*Pap.* X^1 A 263) *n.d.*, 1849

X^1 A 302 202 [*In margin:* May 4]

N.B.

In all the many reflections on my work as an author, there has been terribly much depression with which I have tormented myself of late.

The point is that I have wanted to be so terribly sagacious—instead of believing and praying. I was going to make my future secure and then sit at a remote distance and—write. Pfui! No, God surely takes care of things. And one "poet" more is really not what the times need. And in that way—first a livelihood, an appointment (for which I perhaps am not at all qualified), and then write—I would forget: to seek first God's kingdom.

That is why I have suffered so terribly. It is my punishment. I have also suffered because I have not wanted to commit myself but rather to hang loose and to shrink away from what is decisive.

This accounts for all that hypochondriacal rubbish about whether I might have placed myself too high in any of my writings, something that is so alien to my soul.

And what is the point of traveling? After all, my life is marked in such a way that any attempt to be forgotten is fruitless; and if I went abroad, I would no doubt be plagued by the thought that my journey was an escape, cowardice.

Now is exactly the moment—I can let this pass, but then there is an eternity to repent that I let it pass, and thus I become so debilitated that I am no longer a human being.

Now the two essays are being published: "Does a Human Being Have the Right to Let Himself Be Put to Death for the
X^1 A 302 203 Truth?" and "The Difference Between a Genius and an Apostle,"[27] but anonymously. [*Added:* Today, May 5, they were sent to Gjødvad.]

Life was easier for me before, but this time sagacity played badly with me. Obviously, the course of my life is becoming harder and harder—the economic situation is particularly distressing to me.

If I let this "moment" go by, then the point and position of the whole productivity is lost; then the second edition of *Either/Or* will overwhelm all of it.

But I have wanted to play the lord and master, to do the steering myself and to justify myself before God with hypochondriacal evasions, and then to take everything granted to me almost as sheer enjoyment.—*Pap*. X[1] A 302 May 4, 1849

A preface[28] to "A Cycle of Ethical-Religious Essays," a book that never came into existence because it was divided into smaller parts.

This book was written before 1848.[29] This, incidentally, is a matter of indifference, all in proportion to the extent that the book contains something of what could be called the indifference of truth to time and to all time. Either it contains some of that and then it is a matter of indifference that it was written before 1848, or it has none of that, and thus it is still a matter of indifference whether it was written before 1848, unless the year 1848 should to such a degree inhumanly have altered all conditions that what previously was wisdom has now become nonsense, and on the other hand even the stupidest nonsense has become wisdom if it is said during or after the singular year 1848, which in its "great hullabaloo" has got anybody and everybody, the whole militia, disguised as "thinkers," employed in discussion, and has granted the "thinkers" some opportunity to take a holiday.—*Pap*. X[1] A 318 *n.d.*, 1849

From draft; see 51:

Does a Human Being Have the Right to
Let Himself Be Put to Death for
the Truth?

A Posthumous Work of a Solitary Human Being.

Edited
by
H. H.

—*Pap*. VIII[2] B 134 *n.d.*, 1847

Addition to Pap. VIII^2 B 134:

N.B. This book must be very carefully written in fair copy, since I have had the good fortune of being able to write it in a period of eight hours.
Gratitude then bids me to be all the more careful in the really laborious work.
—*Pap.* VIII^2 B 135 *n.d.*, 1847

From final copy; see 49–51:

Two Ethical-Religious

Essays

by

H. H.

Edition of 525 copies; format the same as *Hverdags Historie*[30] but smaller type and printed more closely; 6 copies on vellum.

Preface

These two essays probably will [*deleted:* of course] essentially be able to interest only theologians.

H. H.

—*Pap.* X^5 B 9:1a-b *n.d.*, 1849

In margin in final copy; see p. 51:

A Poetical Venture

By

H. H.

The end of 1847

—*Pap.* X^5 B 9:2b-c *n.d.*, 1849

From draft; see 53:5–7:

The difference between the issue here and as it is for him is like the difference when one turns a drawing around.

H. H.

—*Pap.* VIII^2 B 133:1 *n.d.*, 1847

In margin in draft; see 55:35–56:1:

This picture did not make him unhappy; it was to him his love.—*Pap.* VIII^2 B 133:2 *n.d.*, 1847

From draft; see 57:14–15, changed from:

How strange, he said to himself, I never hear anyone speak of this doubt. Wherever I hear and read a presentation of this matter, it is always turned in such a way as if there were only one difficulty: that of having enough courage and faith to risk one's life. But does a human being have the right to do it? He said, if I, as innocent, am put to death, then it is indeed a terrible guilt that I place upon the others. Do I have the right to do that? Can it be so important that a person innocently suffers for the truth that he then does not prevent the others from having enormous guilt. He asked if a human being has the right to let himself be put to death for the truth. For Christ it was another matter; he was the Truth, his death the Atonement, which in turn atoned for that guilt of which the others became guilty. This he understood, although he understood that there is still the same difficult conflict with regard to Christ. But does a human being have the right to let himself be put to death for the truth?—*Pap.* VIII^2 B 133:3 *n.d.*, 1847

From draft; see 58:1:

A

Deleted: 1

—*Pap.* VIII^2 B 133:4 *n.d.*, 1847

From draft; see 58:25:

. . . . . how the doctrine of God's righteousness and the doctrine of human sin concentrically merge in the mystery of the Atonement—*JP* III 2792 (*Pap.* VIII^2 B 133:5 *n.d.*, 1847

From draft; see 58:28–30:

Dogmatics ponders the Atonement in such a way that, after all, the historical is assumed to be in order. Dogmatics wants to comprehend what is believed, that Jesus Christ was crucified for our sins.—*Pap.* VIII^2 B 133:6 *n.d.*, 1847

From draft; see 59:13:

. . . . . than*

In margin: *as it is meaninglessly expressed

[*Deleted from margin:* *just like pretending to begin (*changed from:* engage in) the impossible, to believe,]

Deleted: or rather believe the divinity and the humanity together (which is precisely to believe) than comprehend the humanity and by this very comprehending cause a split between the divinity and the humanity. The one who believes Christ's life, even if he cannot comprehend its human aspect, has nevertheless chosen the one thing needful; but the one who could comprehend only its human side has lost both Christ and faith.—*Pap.* VIII^2 B 137:3 *n.d.*, 1847

From draft; see 61:34:

Changed from: and yet almost more and more, closer and closer to despising itself because it could not shake off the yoke.—*Pap.* VIII^2 B 138:1 *n.d.*, 1847

From draft; see 65:18:

He came to the world **in order to** suffer.

Here for me as a believer everything is such that I, although I can comprehend nothing, can very well believe. As surely as I believe that Christ was God's Son, the Holy One, the Truth, so there is no offense for me in his freely choosing to suffer death and yet without having himself the slightest guilt in it, although at any moment he could have prevented it—namely, by compromising the truth somewhat—that is, by an untruth, that is, by ceasing to be the Truth and by not becoming the Redeemer. Just as one may most frequently ignore the element of freedom in his suffering and death and consider the whole thing merely as an event. But in this way there is a lowering of the dignity of Christ; because he from eternity had freely determined his death, he is also freely participating in his death, and yet just because of that, just because of that is entirely without guilt, that is, also entirely without guilt in it.—*Pap.* VIII^{2} B 133:8 *n.d.*, 1847

From draft; see 76:11–16:

But just because Christ did not as an individual human being relate himself to others but essentially related himself to the whole human race, it must all the more strongly appear that human beings are evil.

The day I become so pure and holy that I dare to call the world evil, my death sentence is signed also; but as long as I am not that, it is frivolousness to make a big splash about letting oneself be put to death for the truth.

N.B. The tone in these lines is much too profane.—*Pap.* VIII^{2} B 133:11 *n.d.*, 1847

See 79:21–80:12:

From Thoughts That Wound from Behind for Upbuilding Discourse VI[31] VIII^{1} A 564 262

Just as a child who, about to get a licking, puts a towel under his jacket, unbeknownst to the teacher, so that he will not feel the blows, so, alas, even a preacher of the Law is for good reasons helpful to the congregation by surreptitiously slipping in another figure, who is now punished—to the edification, *contentement* [satisfaction], and enjoyment of the congregation. For good reasons, because in the case of the child there is no danger involved

in being the teacher who is to administer the beating; but truly to be a preacher of the Law—yes, here the concept flips over [*slaa om*], because it means not so much to beat [*slaa*] others as to be beaten oneself. The more lickings the preacher of the Law gets, the better he is. Therefore a so-called preacher of the Law does not dare actually to administer a beating, because he knows very well and understands only all too well that those before him are not children, that the others, the ones he is to beat, the moment or those honored, esteemed, and lauded because of their serving
VIII^{1} the passions of the moment, together with their thousands, are by
A 564 far, by far the stronger ones, who will *actually* strike back [*slaa*
263 *igjen*], perhaps put him to death [*slaa ihjel*], since to be the great preacher of the Law is to be put to death. Therefore the preacher of the Law restricts himself to—beating on the pulpit. In this way he achieves his ridiculous purpose, to become the most ridiculous of all monstrosities—a preacher of the Law who is honored and esteemed, greeted with applause!—*JP* I 647 (*Pap*. VIII^{1} A 564) *n.d.*, 1848

From draft; see 85:4:

VIII^{2}
B 139:3 [*Deleted:* 3. It is something different if I in times when a tyrant
238 lived or when the concept "the times" haughtily plays lord and master, conceitedly fancies that *the single individual* is nothing—it is something different if I in such times could be inclined to set forth my thoughts, which specifically show that the one who in
VIII^{2} truth became a martyr was the stronger one, stronger than this
B 139:3 tyrant, stronger than all those thousands, who were strong
239 enough, yes, or weak enough, to put him to death, that it was he, the strong one, who had the tyrant and those thousands of weak ones in his power, that it was he who compelled them to put him to death, he who compelled them precisely when they put him to death. In my opinion, this could be a beneficial satire. Its effect, incidentally, could be strange, since surely nothing would shock the tyrant or "the times" more than for the end to be perhaps that the tyrant or "the times" put to death the very person who had championed the thesis that a human being does not dare to let himself be put to death for the truth.]

3. In other respects . . .

—*Pap.* VIII^2 B 139:3 *n.d.*, 1847

In margin in draft; see 86:15:

Those who put him to death thought they were rendering God a service.[32]—*Pap.* VIII^2 B 133:17 *n.d.*, 1847

From draft; see 87:16:

Deleted: (see *Anxiety*[33] by Vigilius Haufniensis)

—*Pap.* VIII^2 B 139:4 *n.d.*, 1847

Deleted from draft; see 87:26:

They ponder that someone has the courage to sacrifice his life for VIII^2 B 133:18 235
the truth. They think of the relation between a person and other people as purely external; each one has his part: the one to be put to death, the others to put him to death. I begin by thinking that someone has courage and ask if he has the right. I next consider that to be sacrificed is an act of freedom, and therefore the one sacrificed is a participant in his death in an altogether different sense.

My answer is: Only in the same degree as a human being in relation to others truly dares to think that he has more truth than others, only in the same degree does he dare to allow others to
become guilty against him—for the sake of the truth. No *human* VIII^2 B 133:18 236
being in relation to others, or no *Christian* in relation to Christians, dares to think he has the truth absolutely; ergo, he does not dare to use the absolute expression for absolutely being in the truth: to let others become guilty of his death.—*Pap.* VIII^2 B 133:18 *n.d.*, 1847

From draft; see 89:1:

This is, as stated, "this man's many thoughts in a brief summary." Since the whole thing is fiction, the reader will surely find it appropriate that I say nothing about this, since just because it is fiction I can, indeed, just as well say one thing as another, can say exactly what I wish, can just as well say that he wore a cap as that he wore a hat, just as well that he was tall, of medium build, had brown eyes and black hair, as to say anything else of the kind that in the situation of actuality interests a passport clerk. In another respect also, I can, inasmuch as the whole thing is fiction, say exactly what I wish with regard to his life, how he fared, what he became in the world, etc. etc. But just because I *qua* poet have a poet's absolute power to say what I wish, I will in all these respects say nothing, in order not to make sport of the reader. Yet it is true, I had nearly forgotten my own name; after all, he is dead—on the title page it says "a posthumous work"; whether he is buried is not known, but I assume it to be quite likely. [*Deleted:* And he left no family; it says on the title page: a solitary human being.]—*Pap.* VIII^2 B 139:5 *n.d.*, 1847

In margin in page proofs; see 89:13:

X^5 . . . If he had lived in [18]48, he surely would have understood
B 10:18 that, humanly speaking, it is not exactly an "awakening" that is
214 needed now; then he surely would have sat down and deliberated whether a human being has the right to let himself be put to death—in order, if possible, to halt the wild rebellion.

Deleted: If he had not already thought about the matter presumably in a thorough way, he would then have been able to sit down and deliberate whether a human being has the right to let himself be put to death in order, if possible, to halt the wild rebellion.—*Pap.* X^5 B 10:18 *n.d.*, 1849

From the third version of "The Book on Adler"; *see 99:31–38:*

Addendum II . . .

Note. But perhaps some reader recalls that Magister Kierkegaard has [*changed later to:* I have] always used the expression about himself [myself] *qua* author that he is [I am] *without authority* and used it so emphatically that it *is repeated as a formula in every preface*. Authority is a specific quality either of an apostolic calling or of ordination. To preach is precisely to use authority, and that this is what it is to preach has simply been altogether forgotten in our day when, to be sure, every theological graduate knows, even in a didactic review, how to instruct Magister Kierkegaard [me], since he [I], O fortunate age, is [am] the only theological graduate who is not informed with regard to what obviously has occupied him [me] from his [my] *Two Upbuilding Discourses* (1843) up to the present moment.—*Pap*. VIII^2 B 9:17 *n.d.*, 1847

From draft of "A Cycle":

Not to be used. IX B 24 321
[*In margin:* For essay No. II.[34]—]

Postscript for one who has read the essay

October 1848

This essay, as stated in the preface [*changed from:* like the whole collection], was written before, some of it long before, the events
that have now changed the shape of Europe.[35] If with regard to IX B 24 322
the past it was possible to say justifiably that there was a lack of action everywhere, it seems now, however, as if action enough has been taken. But it only seems so. Anyone who has a mature idea of what it is to act will easily see on closer inspection that all over Europe there has been what amounts to no action at all, that everything that has happened disintegrates into events, incidents, or insofar as something does occur, into something enormous, but without any acting personality who knows definitely beforehand what he wants, so that afterward he is able to say definitely whether what he wanted has occurred or not.

In France, for example; a republic like that really has no place in history, and unconditionally not under the rubric "action"; it finds its place better in an advertising paper under "Lost and Found." The same in the rest of Europe. Everything everywhere is an event, in many places an aping that even regarded as aping is not action, because again it is not an individual who apes something foreign and now in his own country is acting—no, the aping quite correctly consists in a kind of commotion that arises, God knows how—and then something happens. But there is no one steering, no one acting, no one who could truthfully say: I wanted this and that, and now what I wanted has occurred or it has not occurred.

Therefore the change or the incursion of the new must, once it has commenced, begin with an untruth; people must take a few days to fool one another into thinking that what occurred is what they wanted. Just as it is somewhat awkward for the particular individual to become something of sorts "one fine morning," God knows how, and thus he must see to assisting himself with various untruths, that what he has now become he has wanted from his earliest childhood etc. etc.; just as for the one who in an overexcited moment at a ball becomes engaged to a girl he does not know at all, scarcely knows who she is, it becomes a need and a temptation, out of shame, to begin with a little untruth about his having loved this girl from his earliest childhood and having proposed to her once before etc. etc.—
IX B 24 323 so also the generation finds itself in the predicament of having to give finishing touches with [*deleted:* a little] untruth in order to get history running again.

After all, they still have a little remnant of a conception of what it means to be a free rational being. In order to rescue this conception, they have to fabricate that what has occurred is what they wanted to occur—unless in the Hegelian manner they assume that it has occurred by necessity. But that the upheaval occurs and has occurred in such a way is again the old evil, this shoving of responsibility away from oneself, forced, to be sure, into something big on such a scale that finally existence must assume the paternity for what occurs in the world of free rational beings, somewhat as in nature, so that these upheavals are to be regarded meaninglessly and inhumanly as natural phenomena, and thus revolutions and republics arise in quite the same sense as there is cholera.

As far as the present essay is concerned, it is my hope that in his reading the reader will continually have had the impression that it is ethical-religious and has nothing to do with politics, that it ethically-religiously investigates how a new point of departure is procured in relation to an established order, that it comes to pass in such a way that *the point of departure is* **from above,** *from God,* *and the formula is this paradox, that an individual is used.* Humanly speaking, an individual, in comparison with the established order (the universal), is obviously infinitesimal, nothing; therefore it is a paradox that an individual is the stronger one. The explanation of this paradox can be only that it is God who uses him, God who hides behind him; but in turn God is seen for this very reason, just because the relation is a paradox. When there are hundreds of people, God is not seen; then what happens is explained as the direct result of the activity of hundreds of people, but the paradoxical constrains (insofar as it is possible to constrain freedom) one to become aware of God, of his being involved.

Politically, the whole thing, even when it comes to a decision, goes more easily, less paradoxically, more directly. Politically, one has nothing to do with God, no inconvenience from his having to be involved; *the point of departure is* **from below,** *from* IX
that which is lower than the established order, since even the most B 24
mediocre "established order" is still preferable and superior to 324
the flabbiest of everything flabby—the crowd. Nowadays, *si placet* [if you please], efforts are made in the states to bring about this irrationality, the existence of a prodigious monstrosity with many heads or, more correctly and accurately, a thousand-, according to the circumstances, a hundred-thousand-legged monster, the crowd, an irrational enormity, or an enormous irrationality, that nevertheless has physical force, the force of the shout and uproar, also an amazing virtuosity in making everything commensurable with the hands raised to vote or with the decision of fists lifted up for a brawl. This abstraction is an inhuman something whose power is certainly enormous, but whose enormous power cannot be defined humanly but can be more accurately defined as the power of a machine, that it has the power of so and so many horses—the power of the crowd is always horsepower.

This abstraction, whether it is called the public, or the majority, or the crowd, or, meaninglessly, the people, this abstraction is used politically for movement. Just as in *Gnavspil*[36] and other party games, something is put up for which the game is played, so this abstraction is the stake for which the political game is played. Truth and the like, God in heaven, etc., death, judgment, and much more, politics regards in about the same way as one finds it boring to play cards for nothing. No, cards must be played for money, and the political game must be played for the crowd, to see who can get the most *à tout prix* [at any price] on his side, or the most who with their feet go over to his side.

When one of the players sees that he has obtained the most, he hurries one evening to push forward at the head of this enormity.[*] Or more accurately, there are not even any players—this
IX is still perhaps too much a qualification of personality—the
B 24 whole thing is a game in which there nevertheless are no players,
325 like a talk although there is no one speaking, like ventriloquism. But this is certain, one evening, or possibly many evenings in succession, an enormous crowd is on its feet, surely for the organism of the state a very precarious situation that is comparable only to flatulence. This crowd of people finally becomes embittered by the friction and now demands—or, more accurately, it does not demand, it does not itself know what it wants—it merely assumes its menacing stance in the hope that something will surely happen, in the hope that the weaker party (the established government, the ruler) will perhaps become so alarmed that he will go ahead and do what neither the crowd nor the stronger ones at the head of the crowd—and the brave ones (if there are any)—have the courage to declare in specific words. Therefore, to be the stronger party is not to act but, by way of an abstract possibility, by sounds of nature, to alarm the weaker party into doing something—just as Louis Philippe[37] departed in alarm and by running away gave France a republic, or brought France into a condition out of which it became a republic (indeed, who would have thought it!). In alarm the king goes ahead and does something, and what the king does the crowd of people idolizes, maintaining that it is really the crowd that has done it.

Whereas the single individual, who in truth relates himself to a religious movement, must guard and fight with all his might

[*] *In margin:* which sings freedom songs, patriotic hymns, etc.

and utmost power lest the terrible thing should happen that this enormous abstraction would want to help him by going with its feet over to his side (since winning with the help of this is, from a religious point of view, helping untruth to win), whereas the religious individual must therefore suffer indescribably under the weight of his responsibility and his doubly reflected struggling solitariness (since he struggles alone but also to be allowed to be alone in a life-and-death struggle)—thus it goes much more easily for the political hero, and most easily of all when there is not even so much as a political hero. But if there is such a one, he takes care only to make sure of these thousands before he ventures anything, and when he has made sure of them, then
he ventures—that is, then he still does not venture anything, IX B 24 326
since in a physical way he is by far the strongest and he strives in a physical way.

But that is why almost every political movement is, instead of progress to the rational, a retrogression to the irrational. Even a mediocre government that still is organic is better than the meaninglessness that such an abstraction governs the state. The existence of this abstraction in the state (like a noxious fluid in the human organism) ultimately puts an end to a rational state. Wherever this abstraction is enthroned, there really is no governing. Obedience is given only to the one whom people themselves have established, somewhat as the idol-worshiper idolizes and worships the god he himself has fashioned—that is, people obey themselves, people idolize themselves. With the cessation of the rational state, statecraft becomes a game. Everything revolves around getting shoes on the crowd, and then getting it on one's side, voting, making noise, carrying torches, and armed, regardless, altogether regardless, of whether it understands anything or not.

Since this is the present situation and since everything these days is politics, it will not surprise me if the majority will find that the present essay treats of nothing and is preoccupied with difficulties that do not even exist. Well—so it is; it does in fact treat of God and of the God-relationship in the single individual.

—*Pap.* IX B 24 *n.d*, 1848

[*In margin:* N.B.

Something about the essay: Does a Human Being Have the Right to Let Himself Be Put to Death for the Truth?

The collision presented in the essay ("Does a Human Being Have the Right to Let Himself Be Put to Death for the Truth?") is the intellectual-ethical conflict. It is something else if, for example, one wants to force a person to commit a crime, to do something unlawful, etc. The collision is a thinker's collision with the world and people, and in order to show clearly the intellectual, the admission is made that a human being does have the right to let himself be put to death for the truth when the relation is: pagan/Christian. But in the relation Christian/Christian, where the basic truth must be common to them, where as a consequence the difference of intellectuality must emerge all the more strongly: there he is denied the right to that.—*Pap.* X^1 A 305 *n.d.*, 1849

[*In margin: N.B.*

Something about the essay: Does a Human Being Have the Right to Let Himself Be Put to Death for the Truth?]

If the essay (Does a Human Being Have the Right to Let Himself Be Put to Death for the Truth?) should end in an altogether humorous vein, then there still would be H. H.'s final additions to add:

And regarding the question of who causes or caused that person so many troubles, my answer is easy: Oh no, a human being certainly does not have the right to do it!—*Pap.* X^1 A 306 *n.d.*, 1849

[*In margin:* Ditto]

The reason that H. H.'s little humorous twist at the end of the essay (Does a Human Being Have the Right to Let Himself Be Put to Death for the Truth?) must remain is simply for the sake of earnestness. A poetical piece fancies itself to be earnestness and tries to maintain that impression in the reader; this is precisely what is less earnest in the poetical piece. The humorous twist at the end specifically manifests a consciousness that a poetical piece is never earnestness—only actuality is that. It is more or less a jest to poetize such a thing; the earnestness is to be that.—*Pap.* X^1 A 307 *n.d.*, 1849

In margin of Pap. X^1 A 307:

This is partly an exaggeration, a rigorism; moreover, the pseudonym will also be too reminiscent of the old pseudonyms, without, however, being like them. The whole passage can therefore be deleted. If there should be anything similar there, it should just be a few words, and not of humor but simply of pathos.—*Pap.* X^1 A 308 *n.d.*, 1849

[*In margin: Something about the first essay in* "Two Ethical- X^1 A 328 216
Religious Essays."]

Didacticizing about Christ's life, dividing Christ's life into paragraphs, the systematic and everything belonging to it, is nonsense. A new way had to be and has to be opened up. I have X^1 A 328 217
thought of using the poetical for that. I think that human analogies, when, please note, the qualitative difference between the God-man and human beings is observed, can contribute to illuminating it, can contribute to obtaining a fresher impression of the Gospel again. Christianity or the Gospel has become trivial to people because they have known it so long and learned it by rote. If people as they are now were without any constraint to judge Christ's life and the apostles', they really would have to judge that they were visionaries.

Thus it is above all a matter of doing *something* to make Christ's life *present*. This, I believe, is the merit of the little essay. By means of a human analogy and the poetical, possibility is conveyed instead of facticity, but possibility is what is awakening.

Furthermore, this little essay discloses and illuminates the *sympathetic* collision, without which Christ is futile and humanized.

Of the concepts, "responsibility," "sacrifice," and several others are emphasized.

Finally, this little essay contains an indirect demonstration that Christ is God. Eminent reflection and a corresponding eminent consciousness in a *human being* make him protest being put to death. Only the God-man has been able to bear the consciousness from the very beginning without letting this become a hindrance to him, so that the end would not be that he would be put to death. In a certain sense being put to death is the sort of thing that must be done immediately. Therefore most *human beings* who have been put to death have also lacked this infinite consciousness. Only in the God-man is this infinite consciousness united with absolute certainty and absolute resolution.

Ordinarily it is assumed that those who have been put to death most resembled Christ, insofar as human beings are able to. In so doing, however, it must be borne in mind that it is like this at first
X^1 sight. But in reflection, the very expression of the strongest possi-
A 328 ble human resemblance to the God-man is this, to confess that no
218 human being has the right to let himself be put to death.

There are crucial new ideas in this little essay; the whole issue is turned in a completely original way. If anyone were to think that this little essay was a reference to my life as an author, the answer must be as follows. (1) Poetically I certainly do have the right to present something like this; and if in other respects it is the case that my own life has some similarity to it, then it certainly is modesty to present such a thing poetically instead of claiming actually to be that. It is immodesty for a person to present himself as being more than he is; modesty is just to present in a poetical piece what he perhaps actually is. If I have given ten dollars to the poor, then it is immodest poetically to present someone who gave a thousand dollars (if there is any possibility of confusion). But if one actually has given a thousand dollars, then it is modest to poetize it instead of saying: I actually did do this.

But all this is unimportant, because I have a perfect right to poetize, and it is obtuse of the reader to become involved in all that nonsense about who the author is and whether he means himself.

Furthermore, H. H. has declared in the preface: This book will essentially be able to interest only theologians;[38] therefore the emphasis is on the theological yield. And finally, the second essay contains a most emphatic statement[39] in order to point out that I continually have made no pretense to be such an extraordinary. I am "without authority"; I am a genius—not an apostle, to say nothing of being deranged enough to think myself immensely higher than an apostle.

But such matters must be presented. I have made every possible effort to avoid this blather of finitude, but people might still blather themselves into it.

I would like to put a humorous twist to it at the end—it would X[1] A 328 219
be most satisfying to me—but as an accommodation I omit it. People are foolish enough, and therefore I must with great care use a unity of jest and earnestness humorously, in order not to confuse them completely.—*Pap.* X[1] A 328 *n.d.*, 1849

A word about essay no. 1 in "Two Ethical-Religious Essays" and about a companion piece to the same.

Essentially there is not even the slightest information about my life. The point about my life is simply that I am a penitent who thinks he is doing penance by suffering and thinks that ordinarily only a penitent is sufficiently cruel and tough to serve the truth, since otherwise such an elevated purity would be required that it would rarely be found among people. But to be a penitent encourages.

A companion piece to that essay could be a presentation such as this: just a penitent (thus in one sense as far as possible from purity and perfection) who voluntarily serves the truth to the point of becoming a sacrifice.

But something like this cannot be done poetically. Earnestness requires that if something like this is to be discussed it must be done directly and in my own name, directly declaring: This is my life. This is the way I have always thought of it and have done it in all the direct communications about my work as an author that lie finished.—*Pap.* X[1] A 331 *n.d.*, 1849

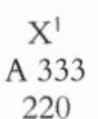

The Relation Between Two Essays by *H. H.*

To let oneself be put to death for the truth is the expression for possessing absolute truth; corresponding to this is a qualitative
X^1 A 333 221 difference [*in margin:* or as it is called in the second essay,[40] a specific difference of quality] from other people—there we have the apostle.

Therefore *no human being has a right* to this—there we have the genius.

Authority is precisely what is required, but the genius has no authority.—*JP* III 2653 (*Pap.* X^1 A 333) *n.d.*, 1849

The conclusion of the first of the two essays
was kept, but modified in such a way that the humorous element is removed, also the double-reflection, whereby the author of the poetized piece withdraws. It is now lenient and simple. For a time I had thought of adding:

If he had lived in [18]48, he surely would have understood that, humanly speaking, it is not exactly an "awakening" that is needed now; then, if he had not already answered the question, presumably in a thorough way, he could have sat down and deliberated whether a human being has the right to let himself be put to death—in order to halt the wild rebellion.[*]

This was omitted, since it diverts attention from the dogmatic contents: does a *human being* have, which is a purely dogmatic or religious issue that can be answered just as well in 47 and in 48.

The whole question is really in order to elucidate the God-man—*Pap.* X^1 A 334 *n.d.*, 1849

In margin of Pap. X^1 A 334:

[*] This was there, too: Yet it is true, I have already said this one thing about him, that he is dead—indeed, it says on the title page, his "posthumous papers." So he is dead, unless one prefers to say that he never existed, since it also says on the title page "a poetical venture."—*Pap.* X^1 A 335 *n.d.*, 1849

How witty a typographical error can be![41] In the second of the two essays, instead of "the gift [*Gave*] of being able to work miracles," it read "the inconvenience [*Gene*]."[42] —*JP* VI 6399 (*Pap.* X^1 A 336) *n.d.*, 1849

The whole postscript to essay no. 1[43] (in "Two Ethical-Religious Essays") is best omitted. Actually it involves me in a lot of nonsense. If I call it "a poetical venture," I have no right to say in the next breath that the novelistic and the poetical are unimportant; and if I declare after that that I am essentially a thinker, then there is a difficulty with the poetical form.

It is sufficient to put on the title page: poetical venture—a posthumous work of a solitary human being.

[*In margin:* But no, let it remain.]

—*Pap.* X^1 A 337 *n.d.*, 1849

The first essay (of the two essays)
is poetical, but in the same sense as a Platonic dialogue. In order to avoid pure abstraction, the didactic approach, in order to bring out personality, a personality like that is created. But no more. The novelistic in him, incidentally, is of no value, only his thought content. A work of this nature corresponds to the unity of *thinker* and *poet*. Someone like that is different from abstract thinkers in that he has a poetic element at his service, but he differs from a poet in that he essentially stresses the thought content.—*JP* VI 6400 (*Pap.* X^1 A 338) *n.d.*, 1849

The Total Production with the Addition of the Two Essays by H. H. X^1 A 351 228

The authorship conceived as a whole (as found in "A Note Concerning My Work as an Author,"[44] "Three Notes Concerning My Work as an Author,"[45] and "The Point of View for My Work as an Author") points definitively to "Discourses at the Communion on Fridays."[46] X^1 A 351 229

The same applies to the whole structure. "Three Devotional Discourses"[47] comes later and is supposed to accompany the second edition of *Either/Or* and mark the distinction between what is offered with the left hand and what is offered with the right.

"Two Ethical-Religious Essays" does not belong to the authorship in the same way; it is not an element in it but a point of view. If there is to be a halt, it will be like a point one projects in advance in order to have a stopping place. It also contains an apparent and an actual eminence: a martyr, yes, an apostle—and a genius. If any information about me is to be sought in the essays, then it is this: that I am a genius—not an apostle, not a martyr. The apparent eminence is included in order to determine all the more accurately the actual one. For most people the category "genius" is so indiscriminate that it can mean anything; for that very reason it was important to define this concept, as the two essays do by means of defining that which is infinitely qualitatively higher.

Thus the two essays appropriately have the character of a signal. But it is dialectical. It could signify: here is the stopping place; and then could signify: here is the beginning—but always in such a way that above all I take precautions not to occasion any conceptual confusion but remain true to myself in being no more or no less than a genius, or in being a poet and thinker with a quantitative "more" not customary in a poet and thinker with regard to being what one writes and thinks about. A quantitative "more," not a qualitative "more," for the qualitative "more" is: the truth-witness, the martyr—which I am not. And even quali-
X^1 tatively higher is the apostle, which I have not fancied myself to
A 351 be any more than that I am a bird. I shall guard myself against
230 blasphemy and against profanely confusing the religious sphere, which I devoutly am doing my utmost to uphold and secure against prostitution by confused and presumptuous thinking.

—*JP* VI 6407 (*Pap.* X^1 A 351) *n.d.*, 1849

The Little Book by H. H.

X^1 A 362 234 was altogether right. One cannot unceremoniously take such a difficult position, which also involves such great responsibility. So one plays an invitational low card in order to make partners of one's contemporaries. If someone stumbles over the little

book, he raises an enormous hue and cry—and he is right, because it is a very remarkable little book. But then it is he who
raised the hue and cry; now I come next. Therefore the little X^1 A 362 235
book had to be published: either with my name on it and indicated as forcefully as possible, or as it happened.—*Pap*. X^1 A 362 *n.d.*, 1849

That was a sound observation in *Wolf. Fragmenter (vom Zwecke Jesu und seiner Jünger*; para. 30[48]) about Christ's using the phrase "the kingdom of heaven" in the way the Jews understood an earthly kingdom. So there is a kind of ambiguity here, since with that Christ denounced a completely different concept. In the first of the two essays by H. H.,[49] I have shown how this is to be understood, that it belongs together with the concept of "sacrifice," this duplexity, which in fact incites passion against him, since it showed that he understood the matter spiritually.—*Pap*. X^1 A 411 *n.d.*, 1849

There is something appalling, an extremely concentrated sadness, in one single phrase in the first essay by H. H., right at the beginning of the introduction.[50] Already as a child he was an old man . . . he went on living, he never became younger. This almost insane inversion, a child who never became younger, a child who was already an old man and never became younger. Oh, what a frightful expression for frightful suffering.

And yet there is the difference that when he, if we assume this, has become an old man, he is not at all very old—because as an old man to be old like an old man is not the same as to be, as a child, old like an old man.—*JP* VI 6420 (*Pap*. X^1 A 441) *n.d.*, 1849

[*In margin:* About the review of H. H.'s book in the
Kirketidende]. X^1 A 551 351

The little book by H. H. is reviewed in the *Kirketidende*[51] (Saturday, July 21). The opinion is that it is by "a very young author who has read Mag. Kierkegaard." Splendid. What a critic! This little book is very significant. It contains the key to the greatest potentiality of all my writing, but not the one I wanted to realize. And the second essay contains the most important of all the ethical-religious concepts, the one I have deliberately omitted until its appearance there.

But I will not say anything about the book. Because to me, as I expressed earlier somewhere [*Pap.* X^1 A 351 (p. 238)], it is a false point of view, signifying that I will take another direction.

Perhaps it is even a feint on the part of the reviewer to lure me out onto thin ice.

If anything is to be written about this review, it must be done with the idea that I would stand up in defense of that "young man" and that the reviewer has done him an injustice. If it could be of any joy or compensation to him—who is a very young man according to the expert reviewer—then I can assure him that I have read the little book with unusual interest and found that it
X^1 grasped a point (the sympathetic collision) that as far as I know no
A 551 one here at home has grasped, with the exception of my pseudo-
352 nyms, and found that it properly grasped and also shed light on the perhaps most important ethical-religious concept: authority. Assuming, as the expert reviewer says, that he is a very young man, I would say to him: Young friend, keep on writing. Without reservations, you are the one I would entrust with the continuation of my work.

But nothing will be done; I will not elaborate on the point. It is just for a little fun.—*JP* VI 6447 (*Pap.* X^1 A 551) *n.d.*, 1849

X^2 Christianity and Speculative Thought
A 119 [*in margin:* Christianity and Speculative Thought]
91

Christianity is an *existence-communication* [*Existens-Meddelelse*], has entered into the world by the use of *authority. It is not to be an object of speculative thought*; Christianity is to be kept existentially on the move, and becoming a Christian is to be made more and more difficult.

Take a simple example. An officer says to a disorderly mob: Move on, please—no arguing.

No arguing—why? Because he uses authority.

Is there, then, nothing objective in Christianity or is Christianity not the object of objective knowledge? Indeed, why not? The objective is what he is saying, he, the authority. But no arguing, least of all the kind that sneaks, as it were, behind the back of the authority and finally speculates him away, too, and turns everything into speculative thought.

How, after all, can a *divine* doctrine enter into the world? By God's empowering a few individuals and overpowering them, as it were, to such a degree that at every moment throughout a long life they are willing to act, to endure, to suffer everything for this doctrine. This, their unconditional obedience, is the form of their authority. They use the authority and appeal to God, but they also support it with their unconditional obedience. If you will not do this voluntarily, well, then we are prepared to suffer everything, and then we will find out who is the stronger. It is like being at an auction. People want to frighten the one sent from God, show him all the horrors, but he says: I bid nevertheless, because my unconditional obedience, in which I myself am (X^2 A 119 92) also compelled, makes it possible to outbid you in endurance, so that you cannot outbid me. He endures, then, and finally he dies. Now he is compelling. Now he compels the generation and thereby brings the divine doctrine to bear upon the generation. His unconditional obedience, which was the support, becomes itself an explanation of his having had divine authority, something he himself has said. As long as he is living and striving, he really uses the most unconditional obedience, because he cannot get a willing ear for his divine authority; but then he dies, and now the authority has all the greater effectiveness.

The two small pieces by H. H. are very instructive.—*JP* I 187 (*Pap.* X^2 A 119) *n.d.*, 1849

[*In margin:* On the occasion of H. H.] 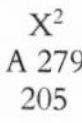

On the Occasion of H. H.

No matter how one conceives of simplicity after (on the other side of) reflection, it is never exactly like the simplicity of imme-

X^2 A 279 206 diacy; it will be recognizable precisely by the continuous accompaniment of reflection, but it is ethically subordinated.

This is the difference between the martyr of immediacy and the martyr of reflection; therefore the immediate martyr cannot have genuine sympathetic collisions.

It is easy enough to make out as if one had thought reflection through; then the simple conclusion would come forth just like a simple conclusion of immediacy, never striven for by any reflection. This looks splendid, but it is the same sort of rubbish as all the Hegelian talk about doubting and then arriving at certainty[52] etc.—only those who have never attempted anything indulge in such talk, only those who are most remote from attempting it in earnest.—*JP* IV 4457 (*Pap.* X^2 A 279) *n.d.*, 1849

[*In margin*: About Peter.]

X^2 A 280 206

About Peter[53]

Peter came down in December. He told me that he had delivered an address at the last convention,[54] where he had talked about Martensen[55] and me, and was surprised that I had not heard of it. He went on to say that in the same lecture he actually had directed his remarks against R. Nielsen[56] and a certain H. H. At that point I told him that I myself am H. H. He was somewhat stunned by that, for he very likely had not read much of the little book, fully convinced that it was not by me. We discussed it a little. Then Peter said: Well, there isn't much point in talking further about it, since I now have to write up the address first. So he wrote up the address. He dealt very briefly with H. H. and also observed that he certainly had a remarkable similarity to S. K.[57] God knows what he actually said at the convention.

It is an awkward situation, especially when one wants to be a man of conscience etc.

X^2 A 280 207 Lately, in a way that at least jars on me, he has taken up the Scriptural phrase: "All is yours."[58] He also uses it in the address. Once in an earlier conversation I reproached him, saying that there was a certain integrity that requires one to give the source[59] of certain thoughts and expositions, to which he answered: It is not at all necessary, for "All is yours" applies to the true believer.—*JP* VI 6557 (*Pap.* X^2 A 280) *n.d.*, 1849

[*In margin*: About H. H.] X^2 A 285 209

About H. H.

Peter finds it inconsistent that when one says, "Only the person who is silent becomes a martyr,"[60] one is in fact saying that.[61] Quite true; *aber* [but] that happened because I wanted to take a new direction at just that point. See, my dear Peter, here is a consistency of which you are not aware.

But in the book itself a martyrdom is still made possible—namely, to be put to death because one has defended the thesis that a human being does not have the right to let himself be put to death for the truth, since one's contemporaries would regard this as enormous arrogance.

And finally it was and is my view that part of a step such as
being put to death for the truth is that one's contemporaries are X^2 A 285 210
helped to share the guilt in an appropriate way, that an invitation to participate is extended, for otherwise the responsibility is too great.

Incidentally, all this and much more is noted in the journal [*for example Pap.* X^1 A 302, 305, 306, 328, 334; pp. 218–19, 232, 233–35, 236] of the period when I published H. H.

But, after all, such things cannot be brought out without betraying the secret machinery; on the other hand I perceive that Peter is not a particularly resourceful *combinateur* [combiner or weaver of dialectical strands].—*JP* VI 6562 (*Pap.* X^2 A 285) *n.d.*, 1849

A few words occasioned by the review X^5 B 11 214
of *Two Ethical-Religious Essays* by H. H.
in the Scharling and Engelstoft journal[62]

There exists a theological journal by S. and E. It has existed for some years, undergone changes, acquired a new title—a change that meant no more than if it had come to read E. and Sch.

instead of Scharling and E. There is not much to say about this journal; only this much is certain, it has never been involved in paradoxes.

X^5 B 11 215 How lacking in plan this journal is can be shown by the fate of Mag. K.'s writings. Mag. K. has been an author for several years now, but until now this journal has found no place for a review of anything of his—indeed, why should there be a place for this in a journal that is occupied with itself to such an extent that it reviews its own reviews. For a period M. K.'s books were merely mentioned, and a note informed the reader that the editorial staff had not received any free copies. This presumably means that if the editorial staff does not receive any free copies it does not review a book. Therefore, a literary journal does not, as one would suppose, have an obligation to its subscribers—no, it levies a tax on the author; one must provide free copies in order to be so fortunate as to be reviewed. Mag. K. did not do so and was so fortunate—not to be reviewed. So some time passed. The journal came out—Mag. K's book was mentioned and it was stated that the editorial staff had received no free copy. [*In margin:* This was, it seems to me, strange enough, but we still had not received enough of the strangeness; something even more strange happened.] Later the method was changed somewhat. The book by Mag. K. was mentioned, a few words were said about it, and to that was added that it was desirable that someone would undertake to review it, that it was inexplicable that no one as yet had reviewed them etc. [*in margin:* these books, "which are especially suitable for review." So says our only journal, which has not reviewed them itself but has variously repeated that they were suitable for review, conduct that obviously is just not suitable for a literary journal]. Once again, a strange way of talking. It is the only journal we have; but instead of reviewing the books, it repeats: It is strange. But enough of this.

Last year a little book by H. H. came out. It has had a curious fate in the literature. The author has been treated as a negligible person, a follower of Mag. K. In the *Kirketidende*[63] it says that the
X^5 B 11 216 author is a very young man. Later in the *Kirketidende*,[64] Dr. K., first cavalier spokesman of the clerical conference (now vocal member of Parliament), tossed off a few words in the greatest

haste. [*In margin:* Then a theological graduate, Hiorth,[65] leaped to his assistance and said that H. H. was a *Schüpler* (follower) of Mag. K.] Now finally our hard-working, good-natured, and zestful Prof. Scharling comes along with a few words in his journal. One essay is titled: Is a human being allowed to let himself be put to death for the truth? The reviewer thinks the author to be a follower of Mag. K. but on the whole is without discernment—he only wishes that he would apply his talents to a more worthy subject. And the reviewer is a professor in theology. The issue, and the way H. H. has posed it, is absolutely essentially related to the fundamental question of Christianity. There is scarcely any question that lies closer to a Christian than this: Does a human being have the right to let himself be put to death for the truth? But someone who relates himself to Christianity in terms of acquiring an official position and a livelihood—well, to him this can seem the most remote of all questions.*

But since people have been busy enough making this little book a trifle, perhaps they will allow me (and perhaps I also owe it to the author) to say that my judgment is totally different, that I regard it as significant, that I could almost be tempted to be envious of this author.

* Christianity entered into the world by existentially answering the question: Does a human being have the right to let himself be put to death for the truth—but of course at that time there were no professors of theology; indeed, they are not mentioned once in the N.T. "The professor" is a later invention, from a quieter time, when the question borders on nonsense, whereas the earnestness of life and the truth of Christianity is the professor-position.—*Pap.* X^5 B 11 *n.d.*, 1849

Basilius the Great, Bishop of Caesarea in Cappadocia † 379, said it very well.

In opposition to the allegorists, he says, "As far as I am concerned, when I hear the word 'grass,' I understand grass; I take plants and fish and animals and cattle, everything just as it is said, *for I am not ashamed of the Gospel.* Others have sought with certain *παραγωγαί* [word-twistings] and *τροπολογίαι* [interpretations] to procure for Scripture a certain venerableness by means of their own ingenuity." (See Clausen's *Hermeneutik*,[66] p. 165).

So it is as H. H.[67] has maintained, that everything about the lofty and the profound and the amazingly beautiful etc. is affectation that does not like to obey the simple, or actually does not like to *obey*, and therefore leads the whole thing over into other categories, just as the Romans, when they felt that they could not shake off Augustus' yoke, made up the fiction that he was a god, a substituting of other categories.—*Pap.* X^2 A 533 *n.d.*, 1850

X^3 A 637 413 *Concerning the First Essay in H. H.'s Two Essays*

It is stated there that a person has power to act only as long as he is silent. If one is actually to become a martyr, he must not say it.[68]

X^3 A 637 414 In his convention address, Peter observed that there was an inconsistency here: here it was said.[69] —Yes, quite right, for it was precisely because there had to be a halt along that line. Furthermore, by taking such a step a person ought to prompt people to act accordingly. And it is one thing to say: I will let myself be put to death, and another thing anonymously and thus poetically to introduce these thoughts and in this way still open the possibility of a martyrdom—people would become so furious because he defended the principle that a human being does not have the right to let himself be put to death for the truth that they would put him to death for that reason.

All this is recorded in the journals of that period [for example, *Pap.* X^1 A 305, 328; X^2 A 285; pp. 232, 233–35, 243], and it actually is redundant to make this entry, but I do it only to save rummaging around in the old journals in order to make sure. —*JP* VI 6704 (*Pap.* X^3 A 637) *n.d.*, 1850

That Christ Permitted the Situation to Develop to the Point of His Being Put to Death Is Not a Direct Prototype [Forbillede] *for a*
X^5 A 87 99 *Human Being.*

I am thinking of the turn that H. H. (*Two Ethical-Religious Essays*) gave to the matter. Christ is Love—how then could he have the heart to permit people to become guilty of his death; would it not be love to ease up a little? In answer to this, H. H.[70] points particularly to the other side, that Christ is also the Truth and therefore could not yield but had to let it reach its climax.

But there is also another vantage point in the matter that, as far X^{5} A 87 100 as I remember, H. H. does not call attention to, namely, the fact that Christ let the situation develop to the point of his being put to death is love itself, because his death is indeed the Atonement, the Atonement also for the sin of those who took his life. If he had not been put to death, he would not have attained his destiny, for he did in fact come to the world to suffer and die.

But it is not possible for any human being to come into this situation. No human being has the right to think that his sufferings will be atoning or beneficial for others in the sense that in solitary knowledge only he would know of it together with God. No, this would be the law for being more than human. No, as a human being he must let God govern and counsel and himself use his understanding and every permissible means to avoid suffering.—*JP* II 1921 (*Pap.* X^{5} A 87) *n.d.*, 1853

"Ypperstepræsten" – "Tolderen" – "Synderinden",

tre Taler

ved Altergangen om Fredagen.

Af

S. Kierkegaard.

Kjøbenhavn.

Forlagt af Universitetsboghandler C. A. Reitzel.

Trykt hos Kgl. Hofbogtrykker Bianco Luno.

1849.

"The High Priest"—"The Tax Collector"

"The Woman Who Was a Sinner,"

Three Discourses

at the Communion on Fridays.

By

S. Kierkegaard.

Copenhagen.

Published by University Bookseller C. A. Reitzel.

Printed by Royal Book Printer Bianco Luno.

1849.

SELECTED ENTRIES FROM KIERKEGAARD'S JOURNALS AND PAPERS PERTAINING TO *THREE DISCOURSES AT THE COMMUNION ON FRIDAYS*

See 127:23–24,130:1–133:13:

The Pharisee and the Tax Collector

The one lifted his eyes up
The other cast his eyes down
how one who truly prays lifts his eyes up
and how he casts them down.

—*JP* IV 3927 (*Pap.* VIII[1] A 635) *n.d.*, 1848

Sept. 1 IX A 266 151

Friday Sermon

On Wednesday evening when I had my discourse[71] ready for today, I almost threw it away and chose this theme, which has gripped me so powerfully.

It will be based on this passage in Hebrews: We have a high priest who has been tested in all things, yet without sin.[72]

How Christ put himself in our place.

(1) The one who is suffering always complains that the one who wants to comfort him does not put himself in his place. One person can never quite do this in relation to another—there is a boundary. But Christ did it.[*] He was God and became man; thus he put himself in our place. And in every way he put himself in every sufferer's place. If it is poverty and need—he too was poor. If it is ignominy etc.—he too was scorned. If it is fear of death—he too suffered death. If it is sorrow for one deceased—he too wept for Lazarus. If it is sadness for the confusion and corruption in the world—he too wept over Jerusalem.[**]

(2) Tested in all things [*deleted:*—yet without sin]. He was
IX tempted just as you are. Here it is exactly the same, that the one
A 266 who feels the temptation says that the other person does not
152 understand him, does not put himself in his place. But Christ put himself in your place. To be developed.

(3) Yet without sin. In this respect he did not put himself in your place. Yet in another sense he did: Christ's *atoning death*, he died for you, suffered the punishment of sin in your place.[†]—*JP* IV 3928 (*Pap.* IX A 266) September 1, 1848

In margin of Pap. IX A 266:

[*] He *is able* to have sympathy with our weaknesses—for he was tested in all things the same way (this is the condition for sympathy), and he must have sympathy with our weaknesses, for it was precisely in order to be able to have sympathy with our weaknesses that through his own voluntary decision he was tested in all things.—*JP* IV 3929 (*Pap.* IX A 267) *n.d.*

Addition to Pap. IX A 266:

[**] Yes, in one sense he more than put himself in our place, because the hardest of all is to have been rich and then to become poor, to have been happy and then to become unhappy; no human being was ever tested in such a reversal as that: to be God and then to become a poor servant, to come from heaven down to earth.—*JP* IV 3930 (*Pap.* IX A 268) *n.d.*

In margin of Pap. IX A 266:

[†] (3) He put himself completely in your place, was tested in all things in the same way—yet without sin.

. . . . . And when punitive justice here in the world or in the judgment hereafter seeks the place where I, a sinner, stand with all my guilt, with my many sins, it does not find me; I no longer stand at that place, I have left it and someone else stands at my place in my place; I stand saved beside this other one, him, my Redeemer, who put himself in my place—for this accept my gratitude, Lord Jesus Christ.

Here presumably the discourse is essentially finished—and then just a few words to those who are going to Communion.

—*JP* IV 3931 (*Pap.* IX A 269) *n.d.*

The Difference between the Pharisee and the Tax Collector IX A 272 153

(1) The tax collector stood far off by himself.
The Pharisee presumably has chosen the top place, where he stood by himself.

(2) The Pharisee talks with himself.
The tax collector talks with God.

To be sure, the Pharisee fancies that he is talking with God, but it is easy to see that it is a delusion. This is a big difference.

(3) The tax collector casts his eyes down.
The Pharisee presumably in pride lifts his eyes up.

(4) The Pharisee *thanks* God—and yet actually blasphemes him.
The tax collector accuses himself, prays—honors God.

(5) The tax collector went home justified. IX A 272 154

Assuming even that the Pharisee went up justified—the way he went up into God's house became a guilt that he in any case took home. Probably it escaped him completely that among other things his guilt was going up into the house of the Lord *in this way*; if he had stayed home he would have had one guilt fewer.

—*JP* IV 3932 (*Pap.* IX A 272) *n.d.*, 1848

Text for a Friday Sermon

Just the verse from the gospel about the tax collector and the Pharisee:

but the tax collector stood far off by himself and did not even dare lift up his eyes, but said: God, be merciful to me, a sinner.[73]

You, however, are now closer—you are now about to go up to the Communion table, even though you are still far off. But in a sense the Communion table is the place where one is closest to God.

In margin: In the inwardness of the consciousness of his sin (and this inwardness determines the distance) the Christian stands still further away—and yet at the foot of the altar he is the closest to God that it is possible to be. This being far off and near, whereas the Pharisee in his presumptuous forwardness was near—and far off.

"He went home to his house justified."[74] This is to be used in the conclusion.—*JP* IV 3933 (*Pap*. X^1 A 428) *n.d.*, 1849

From draft; see 109:

The High Priest—The Tax Collector—
The Woman Who Was a Sinner
Three Discourses at the Communion on Fridays

[*In pencil:* In that case the three texts could perhaps be printed right in the front on the back of the title page. Hebrews 4:15: For we have not a high priest etc. Luke 18:13: And the tax collector stood far off etc. Luke 7:47: Her many sins are forgiven her, because she loved much].

Deleted: Perhaps the title can simply be:
Three Discourses at the Communion
on Fridays.
—*Pap*. X^5 B 25:1 *n.d.*, 1849

From draft; see 111:2–7:

[*Deleted:* May he kindly receive the little book that I more than gladly dedicated to him. Oh, how different everything within the encompassing enclosure of the holy is from the worldliness outside! If he actually does appropriate it, I then become the debtor.] Sept. 8 [*changed from:* 10],[75] 1849. . . .—*Pap*. X^5 B 25:2 *n.d.*, 1849

From draft; see 113:3:

[*In pencil:* No. 1]
Discourse at the Communion
on Fridays.
[*In margin:* See journal NB^7 p. 17 (*Pap*. IX A 266; pp. 251–52).]

Hebrews 4:15.
[*In margin:* written about the middle of 1849.]
—*Pap.* X^5 B 25:3 *n.d.*, 1849

To the passage (in the discourse "The High Priest," Hebrews 4): that gold is virtue, that might is right, that the crowd is truth,[76] could have been added: that the outcome is the judgment. It is the same kind of category as the others.—*Pap.* X^2 A 209 *n.d.*, 1849

From draft; see 125:1–3:

[*In pencil:* No. 2]
Friday Sermon.
Luke 18:13.
—*Pap.* X^5 B 25:4 *n.d.*, 1849

From draft; see 135:1–3:

[*In pencil:* No. 3]
Friday Sermon.
—*Pap.* X^5 B 25:5 *n.d.*, 1849

From draft; see 140:32:

[*Deleted:* when the tears did not (convulsively) burst forth through some resistance but she dissolved in tears, then if someone asked her, "Why are you crying?" she would have to say, "Oh, I do not know that myself"]—in this way she has forgotten herself completely.

Deleted from margin: and if you would compare her to a dying person, who when he wakes up in the blessed hereafter might say: Where am I?—*Pap.* X^5 B 25:7 *n.d.*, 1849

From final copy; see 141:27–33, changed from:

He says—presumably also in order to deal gently with the love, since, although it would not disturb her to hear it said directly, "You sinned much"—he says, "Her many sins are forgiven her, because she loved much." He speaks of her as if she were absent, and yet she is present; he changes her into a picture, and yet she is actually present; it is as if he were telling a parable, and yet it is an actual story that is taking place at that very moment before the eyes of all those present. It is as if he said:—*Pap.* X^5 B 26:8 *n.d.*, 1849

Deleted from margin in draft; see 141:27–33:

X^5 B 25:8 236 In the same way the mother speaks of the child when she really
wants to express how she, in order to defend him properly
against those who would do him harm, hides him, as it were,
X^5 B 25:8 237 within herself, as if he did not actually exist, because to such a
degree he is, as she says, her own "mother's little boy"—to that
degree mother love swallows, as it were, the child.—*Pap.* X^5 B
25:8 *n.d.*, 1849

The sinner, who after all was a woman and a woman who was a sinner, dared go to see Christ at the Pharisee's house, where the Pharisees were all together at a feast—Nicodemus,[77] who regarded himself as a righteous man, dared go to him only at night.—*JP* IV 4024 (*Pap.* X^2 A 29) *n.d.*, 1849

The prototypes are anonymous or eternal pictures: "the tax collector," "the woman who was a sinner"—a name distracts so easily, sets tongues wagging, so that one comes to forget oneself. The anonymous prototype constrains a person to think of himself insofar as this can be done.—*JP* II 1856 (*Pap.* X^2 A 36) *n.d.*, 1849

About the three Friday discourses (The High Priest, The Tax Collector, and The Woman Who Was a Sinner)

they are related to the last pseudonym, Anti-Climacus.[78]
—*JP* VI 6515 (*Pap.* X^2 A 126) *n.d.*, 1849

About the three discourses (The High Priest, The Tax Collector, The Woman Who Was a Sinner)

They are now delivered to the printer.

(1) I must have a place of rest, but I cannot use a pseudonym as a place of rest; they are parallel to Anti-Climacus,[79] and the position of "Discourses at the Communion on Fridays" is once and for all designated as the place of rest of the authorship.

(2) Since at this time there is an emphasis on my pseudonym (Climacus), it is important for the stress to be in the direction of upbuilding.

Again, what love on the part of Governance, that what I need and must use always lies finished and ready.

(3) The preface is reminiscent of the two upbuilding discourses of 1843, because to me it is very important to emphasize that I began at the outset as a religious author; it is of importance for the repetition.—*JP* VI 6519 (*Pap.* X^2 A 148) *n.d.*, 1849

If it had been possible, the reconciliation with "her"[80] would have occurred simultaneously with the three discourses (The High Priest, The Tax Collector, The Woman Who Was a Sinner), which contain in the preface—for the sake of a repetition of the entire authorship—a repetition of the preface to the two upbuilding discourses of 1843, a book I knew she read at the time.—*JP* VI 6545 (*Pap.* X^2 A 217) *n.d.*, 1849

The Woman Who Was a Sinner

The woman who was a sinner is present almost as if only in effigy,[81] and yet she is the one around whom the action centers—the one who is present.—*JP* IV 4044 (*Pap.* X^3 A 566) *n.d.*,1850

En opbyggelig Tale.

Af

S. Kierkegaard.

Kjøbenhavn.
Forlagt af Universitetsboghandler C. A. Reitzel.
Trykt hos Kgl. Hofbogtrykker Bianco Luno.
1850.

An Upbuilding Discourse.

By

S. Kierkegaard.

Copenhagen.

Published by University Bookseller C. A. Reitzel.

Printed by Royal Book Printer Bianco Luno.

1850.

SELECTED ENTRIES FROM KIERKEGAARD'S JOURNALS AND PAPERS PERTAINING TO *AN UPBUILDING DISCOURSE*

From draft; see 259:1–7:

An Upbuilding Discourse
[*Changed from:* "The Woman Who Was a Sinner."
(*Deleted*: A) Christian Discourse.]
[*Deleted:* Discourse at the Communion on Fridays.]
By
S. Kierkegaard.

—*Pap.* X^5 B 115:1 *n.d.*, 1850

From final copy; see 259:1–7:

An Upbuilding Discourse.
[*Changed from:* "The Woman Who Was a Sinner."
Christian Discourse.]
By
S. Kierkegaard.
Deleted: Available at Reitzel's Publishing House

—*Pap.* X^5 B 116:1 *n.d.*, 1850

From draft; see 147:

A possible preface to the upbuilding discourse "The Woman Who Was a Sinner." X^5 B 117 312

> If neither "The Accounting"[82] nor *Two Discourses at the Communion on Fridays*[83] is published but only the upbuilding discourse, which is to be dedicated to my father, the following preface could perhaps be used.

X^5 B 117 313

Preface

What was first said in my first book of upbuilding discourses, in the Preface to *Two Upbuilding Discourses* in 1843, that this book "seeks that single individual [*hiin Enkelte*]"; what was repeated verbatim in the Preface to each new collection of upbuilding discourses; what was pointed out, after I had exposed myself to the laughter and the insults of the crowd and thus, as well as I could, contributed to evoking awareness by dedicating the next large work, *Upbuilding Discourses in Various Spirits*, 1847, to "the single individual [*den Enkelte*]"; what the world revolution in 1848 certainly did not witness against or render untrue—emphasis upon the single individual—let me repeatedly remind [readers] of this. [*In margin:* If for the sake of recollection it is possible for a thinker to manage to concentrate all his thinking in one single idea, this has been granted to me, the upbuilding author, whose entire thinking is essentially contained in this one thought: the single individual.]

"The single individual"—of course, the single individual religiously understood, that is, understood in such a way that everyone, unconditionally everyone, yes, unconditionally everyone, just as much as everyone has or should have a conscience, can be this [*denne*] single individual and should be that, can stake his honor in willing to be that, but then also can find blessedness in being what is the expression for true fear of God, true love for one's neighbor, true humanity [*Menneskelighed*,] and true human equality [*Menneske-Lighed*]. Oh, if only some might achieve it, if it is not, although the task for all, too high for all of us, yet not too high in such a way that it should be forgotten, forgotten as if it were not the task or as if this task did not exist [*deleted:* in November 1850], so that we may at least learn to forsake not only the mediocre but also the indifferent half measures that reject an established order, yet without advancing to become in an extraordinary sense the single individual, but rather schismatically organizing parties and sects, which are neither the one nor the other.

November 1850
—*JP* II 2033 (*Pap.* X^5 B 117)

From final copy; see Pap. X^5 B 117:

Preface

What [same as pp. 262:2–11] untrue; [*deleted addition in margin:* then what next—for now comes something entirely new and something quite differently earnest—what existence took upon itself to inculcate radically, what the world revolution in 1848 frightfully taught me to verify and further understand,]: emphasis [same as 262:12–26] human equality.

November 1850 . . .

—*Pap*. X^5 B 118 November 1850

From draft; see 147:3:

The beginning of December [*changed from:* November] 1850.
—*Pap*. X^5 B 115:2 *n.d.*, 1850

Deleted from margin of draft; see 149:3:

Introduction

That a woman is presented as a prototype will not be disturbing, because one can learn much from a woman. Ordinarily a woman does not have as many thoughts as a man, but neither does she have as many half-thoughts; she is totally absorbed in one thing; "one" is her element (one wish, one thought, etc.). She has mainly feelings and passion; she has heart, and from the heart, in a different sense, proceeds life. The man, with his thoughts and intentions and resolutions, easily becomes frustrated, disappoints himself by getting very close and then breaking off. The woman does not trifle in that way, plunges into the decision. By way of thinking, there is perhaps more earnestness in the man; by way of passion and decision, there is more earnestness in the woman.—*Pap*. X^5 B 115:3 *n.d.*, 1850

Deleted from final copy; see 151:8:

I have seen the one who, rich, in the twinkling of an eye became poor and for whom everything then for a long time or forever became of no importance; but this is not sorrow over one's sin.—*Pap.* X^5 B 116:4 *n.d.*, 1850

Deleted from final copy; see 151:16:

I have seen a dying person for whose failing eyes and heart everything becomes of no importance; but this is not sorrow over his sin. I have seen . . . . .

—*Pap.* X^5 B 116:6 *n.d.*, 1850

To Taler

ved Altergangen om Fredagen.

Af

S. Kierkegaard.

Kjøbenhavn.

Forlagt af Universitetsboghandler C. A. Reitzel.

Trykt hos Kgl. Hofbogtrykker Bianco Luno.

1851.

Two Discourses

at the Communion on Fridays.

By

S. Kierkegaard.

Copenhagen.

Published by University Bookseller C. A. Reitzel.

Printed by Royal Book Printer Bianco Luno.

1851.

SELECTED ENTRIES FROM
KIERKEGAARD'S JOURNALS AND PAPERS
PERTAINING TO
*TWO DISCOURSES AT THE COMMUNION
ON FRIDAYS*

Friday Discourses.

This can become a regular form of writing.

3 Discourses at the Communion on Fridays.

No. 1. Luke 7:47. "But one who is forgiven little loves little."

No. 2. I Peter 4:7[8]. Love will hide a multitude of sins.

At "the Communion table" it is especially true that *love,* namely, Christ's love, will hide a multitude of sins. In the strictest sense Christ's reconciliation was love's work or "the work of love" *κατ' ἐξοχήν* [in the eminent sense].

[*Deleted:* No. 3. I Corinthians 11:31,32.

Can be used some other time.]

—*JP* VI 6494 (*Pap.* X^2 A 39) *n.d.*, 1849

In margin of Pap. X^2 A 39:

No. 3. Luke 24:31 could be used. The very fact that he be- X^2 A 40 30
comes invisible to me is the sign that I recognize him: he is indeed the object of faith, a sign of contradiction, consequently in a certain sense must become invisible when I recognize him. He
is the prototype, must therefore become invisible so that the imi- X^2 A 40 31
tator can be like him.

At the Communion table he is invisibly present, and yet in verse 30 it truly says that it was when he blessed the bread, broke it, and gave it to them that they recognized him.—*JP* VI 6495 (*Pap.* X^2 A 40) *n.d.*, 1849

Text for a Friday discourse—see journal NB[12], pp. 226 and 227 [*Pap.* X^2 A 39, 40; p. 269]. The one under the quoted text no. 3 was not used.—*Pap.* X^2 A 127 *n.d.*, 1849

From page proofs; see 267:7:

Changed from: Available at bookseller P. G. Philipsen's.
—*Pap.* X^5 B 138:1 *n.d.*, 1851

From draft; see 162:

The two discourses at the Communion are to be published
On the back of the title page there is the date:
End of 1849.
The dedication from "The Accounting"[84] is to be used here.
The preface will be Note no. 3.[85]
—*Pap.* X^5 B 132 *n.d.*, 1849–51

See 163:

For
"The Accounting."
The dedication will read
To One Unnamed
whose name will one day be named
is dedicated
etc.
then the line "and will—*be named*" goes out
—*Pap.* X^5 B 261 *n.d.*, 1849–50

See 163:

The Dedication to Regine Schlegel,
if there can be such a thing during my *lifetime*, could very well be used in the front of a small collection of Friday discourses but properly belongs to the writings on my work as an author. Inas-

much as I appear so decisively in the character of the religious, which I have wanted from the very beginning, at this moment *she* is the only important one, since my relationship to her is a *God*-relationship.

The dedication could read:
To R. S.—with this little book is dedicated an authorship,
which to some extent belongs to her,
by one who belongs to her completely.

Or with a collection of Friday discourses: To R. S. is dedicated this little book

—*JP* VI 6675 (*Pap.* X^5 B 263) *n.d.*, 1849

See 163:

To a contemporary,
whose name must still be
concealed, but history will
name—be it for a short time or long—
as long as it names mine,
is dedicated
with this little book
the whole authorship, as it
was from the beginning.

—*JP* VI 6676 (*Pap.* X^5 B 264) *n.d.*, 1849

Deleted from draft of "Three Notes" in Point of View:

Three "Notes" Concerning
My Work as an Author

Appendix

by

S. Kierkegaard

—*Pap.* IX B 63:1 *n.d.*, 1848

From draft of "Three Notes" in Point of View; *see 165–66:*

Contents

No. 1. For the Dedication to "That Single Individual."[86]
No. 2. A Word about the Relation of My Work as an Author to "That Single Individual."[87]
No. 3. Preface to "Friday Discourses."[88]

—*Pap.* IX B 63:3 *n.d.*, 1848

From draft, with numerous changes, of "Three Notes" in Point of View; *see 165–66:*

No. 3.

Preface to "Friday Discourses"

Two (no. II and III) of these discourses (which still lack something essential in order to be, and therefore were not called, "sermons") have been given in Frue Church.

An authorship that began after *Either/Or* and advanced step by step seeks here its decisive place of rest, at the foot of the altar, from which a beginning can be made in another sense, where the author, personally most aware of his own imperfection and guilt, does not call himself a truth-witness but a singular kind of thinker and poet, nor does he say that he has had anything new to bring, but that he has tried to think through the old once again, if possible more inwardly.* . . .

In margin: * *Note.* See S. K. postscript to Johannes Climacus's *Concluding Postscript.*[89] Cop. Feb. 1846.

—*Pap.* IX B 63:14 *n.d.*, 1848

Notation with ms. of Point of View; *see 165–66:*

Note no. 3 has been used; so it will be only

"Two Notes"

Perhaps the title of the book could be:

"The Single Individual."

Two Notes Concerning My Work as an Author.

—*Pap.* X^5 B 187 *n.d.*, 1851

From draft; see 165–66:

To the typesetter
the smallest possible brevier

Preface

An authorship [same as 165:2–11.] [*Deleted:* Turned this way, I have nothing further to add, unless—incredible!—it should occur to someone (something I would have to deplore profoundly as almost derangement!) to ask me—for which I have truly given no occasion—do I think I have a closer relation to God? To such I would answer: No, oh no, far from it! There lives no human being, unconditionally no human being, in Christendom there has never lived any human being, who is not equally close to God, loved by him. I really think, however, that there perhaps are not many who, like me, have day in and day out been employed in the blessed occupation of keeping in mind that he—alas, not because of his virtue—is loved by him. But it is not my fault if others ignore or disdain the love that is lavished upon them just as richly as upon me.]

As I turn [*same as 166:11–17.*]

[*Deleted:* 1849.]

S.K.

—*Pap.* X^5 B 133 *n.d.*, 1849

From draft; see 165–66:

To the typesetter: in the smallest brevier.

Preface.

An authorship [essentially the same as *Pap.* X^5 B 133.] (I am unaware of having stood in any other author's way of anything earthly that he may have wished to achieve; I myself have achieved nothing. What as a danger corresponds with conceptual correctness to "the single individual," what was the danger, according to my conception, at the time in Denmark, to become the butt of the market town spirit's pettiness and envy, which, heaping up blather, could easily have become dangerous, and at every moment, especially in prosperous times, can become dangerous for the little country that does not even in its language participate in a larger whole—obedient to God, loving my idea, in sympathy with every worthy effort here at home, I have voluntarily exposed myself to this. If this was a crime, then I confess it, then I am guilty. But according to my conceptions it will be just as difficult for my contemporaries to be able to "forgive" me this "crime" as it is impossible for me, even with the best of will, to be able to request forgiveness for this crime, which, personally understood, my treasure and possession, I indeed also wish to take with me to the grave.)

1849

—*Pap.* X^5 B 135 *n.d.*, 1849–51

From draft; see 165–66:

This is no. 3 of Three Notes, which consequently is omitted there; so the title becomes "Two Notes," as is also pointed out on the folder of the draft. [*Deleted:* Note no. 3 is to be checked with this, which is from memory.]

To the typesetter:
in the smallest brevier.

Preface. . .

—*Pap.* X^5 B 136 *n.d.*, 1849–51

From draft; see 169:10:

Three Discourses at the Communion on Fridays

[*Deleted:* Part one. Friday sermon.]

In margin: See Journal NB^{12}, p. 226 (*Pap.* X^2 A 39–40; p. 269).

[*Deleted:* Luke 7:47: But one who is forgiven little loves little.]

No. 1.

—*Pap.* X^5 B 130:1 *n.d.*, 1849

See 169:27–35:

To pray oneself out is something like crying oneself out, as we say.

And when you have prayed yourself out completely, then there is only one thing left: Amen.—*JP* III 3436 (*Pap*. X[1] A 388) *n.d.*, 1849

See 169:27–35:

Theme for an upbuilding discourse.
The Art of Arriving at an Amen.

It is not very easy. There always seems to be something to add. A resolution, the resolution of faith.—*JP* III 3437 (*Pap*. X[1] A 389) *n.d.*, 1849

In margin of Pap. X[1] A 389.

How close the comic always is to the highest pathos; at this point one could very well think of Peer Degn, who at one time could recite the whole litany in Greek but now could only remember that the last word was: Amen.[90]—*JP* III 3438 (*Pap*. X[1] A 390) *n.d.*, 1849

Deleted from draft; see 172:24–173:9:

Justice demands the fulfillment of the Law—how severe; love X[5] B 130:3 333
demands but one thing—how lenient, and yet the most severe judgment precisely because the demand is the most lenient. The one who demands his right immediately is severe, but the one who forgives and forgives and now forgives for the seven-times-seventieth time: this is no judgment, and yet it is the most severe judgment. Justice makes the guilt manifest by demanding; love, which demands nothing, makes the guilt greater and greater by continually forgiving. Name the most terrible, the most loathsome sins, say of someone that he is guilty of them; take another person of whom it must be said that there was no love in him—[*deleted:* which judgment is the more severe!] and it is not justice

X^{5} B 130:3 334 that says it. No, it is love, the forgiving love; love, which itself is almost brought to despair over it, does not say it judging but suffering—which judgment is the more severe? Think of that woman who was a sinner, the one discussed in the passage from which our text is taken. Of her it is said: She sinned much; hear that together with this judgment: He loved little [91]—which is the more severe judgment. The severity lies precisely in this, that love, the forgiving love, is changed into judgment, since, unlike justice, which wants to make the guilt manifest, love on the contrary wants to hide it by forgiving and pardoning—and see, now the guilt becomes more frightfully manifest.—*Pap.* X^{5} B 130:3 *n.d.*, 1849

X^{4} A 351 203

About Myself

Now they are being printed.[92] Oh, I feel inexplicably, unspeakably happy and calm and confident and overwhelmed.

X^{4} A 351 204 Infinite Love! I have suffered much during the past days, very much, but then it comes again. Once again an understanding of my task is clear to me but with greater vividness, and even though I have blundered seventeen times—nevertheless an infinite love in its grace has made it all completely right.

Infinite Love! It is blessed to give thanks, but a person perhaps never feels his wretchedness and sin more than when he is overwhelmed in this way, just as Peter said: Depart from me, for I am a sinful man [93]—on the very occasion of the great catch of fish.—*JP* VI 6772 (*Pap.* X^{4} A 351) *n.d.*, 1851

X^{4} A 380 227

The Review of My Two Latest Books.[94] August 13

In *Flyveposten* [95]there is one in which it is stated, "It appears from this that the author now considers his work as an author virtually at an end."

This is really odd. Imagine an author's declaring explicitly that he now intends to lay down his pen, and let us assume that this author is still a young man; what then will the "journal," the critical intermediate authority, ordinarily do? It will say: Well, it must not be taken altogether literally; it may be for a time, or perhaps he will begin again in another manner etc. etc.—in short, the journal will write it up to mean that the author will continue.

But the situation is this. I have in no way said that I am ceasing to be an author, as the journal adequately demonstrates by having to confine itself to saying: It appears—and then what does the journal do? It takes it upon itself to circulate the news that I am going to stop, it takes it upon itself to be instrumental in getting me to stop.

This is very amusing! I must have a friend, a patron, who is interested in this and perhaps for some time has been interested in my quitting as an author damn soon. [*In margin:* Perhaps he would even be glad to see me leave the country—but it would be ungrateful of me, who must say as did Peer Degn: Should I forsake a congregation that loves and esteems me and which I in turn love and esteem?[96]]

Strangely enough, quite accidentally today I saw the same article in *Fyens Avis*[97] and with no indication that it was from *Flyveposten*, but otherwise the identical article, except that the word "brilliant" was left out.

Thus it seems that my friend and patron must have sent it to X^4 A 380 228
Fyens Avis himself. Perhaps he has sent it to several provincial newspapers—all for the purpose that I might stop writing.

This could be one interpretation. Maybe the whole thing is nothing but journalistic clumsiness that immediately sees to getting something put in circulation that can be chattered about, such as: Am I actually going to stop etc.—for then the content of the books is of no importance.—*JP* VI 6779 (*Pap.* X^4 A 380) August 13, 1851

EDITORIAL APPENDIX

ACKNOWLEDGMENTS

Preparation of manuscripts for *Kierkegaard's Writings* is supported by genuinely enabling grants from the National Endowment for the Humanities and gifts from the Dronning Margrethes og Prins Henriks Fond, the Danish Ministry of Cultural Affairs, the Augustinus Fond, the Carlsberg Fond, the General Mills Foundation, the Jorck Fond, the Lutheran Brotherhood Foundation, and Gilmore and Charlotte Schjeldahl.

The translators-editors are indebted to Grethe Kjær and Julia Watkin for their knowledgeable observations on crucial concepts and terminology.

Per Lønning, Wim R. Scholtens, and Sophia Scopetéa, members of the International Advisory Board for *Kierkegaard's Writings*, gave valuable criticism of the manuscript on the whole and in detail. Jack Schwandt and Julia Watkin helpfully read the manuscript. Regine Prenzel-Guthrie, associate editor of *KW*, scrutinized the manuscript. Nathaniel Hong, associate editor of *KW*, scrutinized the manuscript and prepared the index.

Acknowledgment is made to Gyldendals Forlag for permission to absorb notes to *Søren Kierkegaards samlede Værker* and *Søren Kierkegaards Papirer.*

Inclusion in the Supplement of entries from *Søren Kierkegaard's Journals and Papers* is by arrangement with Indiana University Press.

The book collection and the microfilm collection of the Kierkegaard Library, St. Olaf College, and Gregor Malantschuk's annotated set of *Søren Kierkegaards samlede Værker* were used in preparation of the text, Supplement, and Editorial Appendix.

Matters concerning the electronic manuscript were handled by Francesca Lane Rasmus and Nathaniel Hong. The volume was guided through the press by Marta Nussbaum Steele.

COLLATION OF *THE LILY IN THE FIELD AND THE BIRD OF THE AIR* IN THE DANISH EDITIONS OF KIERKEGAARD'S COLLECTED WORKS

Vol. XI Ed. 1 Pg.	*Vol. XI Ed. 2 Pg.*	*Vol. 14 Ed. 3 Pg.*
5	9	127
8	11	129
9	13	131
11	15	132
12	16	132
13	17	133
14	18	134
15	19	135
16	20	136
17	22	137
18	23	138
19	24	139
20	25	140
21	27	141
22	28	143
23	29	144
24	31	145
25	32	145
26	33	146
27	34	147
28	35	148
29	36	149
30	37	150
31	39	151
32	40	152
33	41	153
34	43	154
35	44	155
36	45	156
37	46	157
38	47	158
39	48	158
40	49	159
41	50	160
42	51	161
43	52	162
44	53	163
45	55	164
46	56	165

COLLATION OF *TWO ETHICAL-RELIGIOUS ESSAYS* IN THE DANISH EDITIONS OF KIERKEGAARD'S COLLECTED WORKS

Vol. XI Ed. 1 Pg.	*Vol. XI Ed. 2 Pg.*	*Vol. 15 Ed. 3 Pg.*	*Vol. XI Ed. 1 Pg.*	*Vol. XI Ed. 2 Pg.*	*Vol. 15 Ed. 3 Pg.*
51	63	11	82	97	39
57	69	15	83	98	40
59	71	17	84	99	41
60	72	17	85	100	42
61	73	18	86	101	42
62	74	20	87	102	43
63	74	20	88	103	45
64	76	21	89	104	45
65	77	22	90	105	46
66	78	23	91	107	48
67	79	24	95	111	51
68	80	25	96	112	51
69	81	26	97	113	52
70	83	28	98	114	53
71	84	28	99	115	54
72	85	29	100	116	55
73	86	31	101	118	56
74	87	32	102	119	57
75	89	33	103	120	58
76	90	34	104	121	59
77	91	35	105	122	60
78	92	36	106	124	61
79	93	37	107	125	62
80	95	38	108	126	63
81	96	39	109	127	64

COLLATION OF *THREE DISCOURSES AT THE COMMUNION ON FRIDAYS* IN THE DANISH EDITIONS OF KIERKEGAARD'S COLLECTED WORKS

Vol. XI Ed. 1 Pg.	*Vol. XI Ed. 2 Pg.*	*Vol. 14 Ed. 3 Pg.*	*Vol. XI Ed. 1 Pg.*	*Vol. XI Ed. 2 Pg.*	*Vol. 14 Ed. 3 Pg.*
247	277	169	266	296	185
251	281	173	267	297	186
252	282	173	268	298	187
253	283	174	269	299	188
254	284	175	273	303	193
255	285	176	274	303	193
256	286	177	275	305	194
257	287	178	276	306	195
258	289	179	277	307	196
259	290	180	278	308	197
263	293	183	279	309	198
264	293	183	280	311	199
265	295	184			

COLLATION OF *AN UPBUILDING DISCOURSE* IN THE DANISH EDITIONS OF KIERKEGAARD'S COLLECTED WORKS

Vol. XII Ed. 1 Pg.	*Vol. XII Ed. 2 Pg.*	*Vol. 17 Ed. 3 Pg.*	*Vol. XII Ed. 1 Pg.*	*Vol. XII Ed. 2 Pg.*	*Vol. 17 Ed. 3 Pg.*
249	295	13	255	301	18
250	295	13	256	303	19
251	297	14	257	304	20
252	298	15	258	305	21
253	299	16	259	306	22
254	300	17			

COLLATION OF *TWO DISCOURSES AT THE COMMUNION ON FRIDAYS* IN THE DANISH EDITIONS OF KIERKEGAARD'S COLLECTED WORKS

Vol. XII Ed. 1 Pg.	*Vol. XII Ed. 2 Pg.*	*Vol. 17 Ed. 3 Pg.*	*Vol. XII Ed. 1 Pg.*	*Vol. XII Ed. 2 Pg.*	*Vol. 17 Ed. 3 Pg.*
267	313	27	279	326	38
271	317	31	283	328	41
272	317	31	284	328	41
273	319	32	285	330	42
274	320	33	286	331	43
275	321	34	287	332	44
276	322	35	288	333	45
277	323	36	289	334	46
278	325	37	290	336	47

NOTES

THE LILY IN THE FIELD AND THE BIRD OF THE AIR

TITLE PAGE. See Supplement, pp. 198–99 (*Pap.* X^5 B 4, 6:1, 7:1, 8).

1. See Historical Introduction, p. xiii.
2. The quotations are freely cited from *Two Discourses* (1843). See *Eighteen Discourses*, p. 5, *KW* V (*SV* III 11).
3. See *Four Discourses* (1844), in *Eighteen Discourses*, p. 179, *KW* V (*SV* IV 73).
4. See Supplement, p. 202 (*Pap.* X^1 A 549).
5. Matthew 6:24–34. See *Christian Discourses*, *KW* XVII (*SV* X 14–15), and *Judge for Yourself!* p. 149, *KW* XXI (*SV* XII 423–24).
6. With reference to the following four paragraphs, see Supplement, pp. 197–98, 200–01 (*Pap.* VIII^1 A 643; X^1 A 198).
7. The Kingfisher (*Alcedo ispida*). See *JP* I 1023 (*Pap.* II A 612).
8. See Matthew 18:2–4.
9. Cf. Genesis 35:18. Benjamin, son of the right hand, or son of the South, may also be rendered as "son of joy."
10. Matthew 6:33.
11. Cf. *Judge for Yourself!*, pp. 110–13, *KW* XXI (*SV* XII 391–93) and *The Moment*, no. 7, in The Moment *and Late Writings*, *KW* XXIII (*SV* XIV 248–50).
12. See Matthew 19:21.
13. Proverbs 9:10.
14. See Philippians 2:12–13.
15. See Acts 1:7.
16. A line in the first stanza of the hymn *Med Sorgen og Klagen hold Maade* (the author's name is not given) in *Tillæg til den evangelisk-christelige Psalmebog* (Copenhagen: 1847), 610, p. 50. In 1848 Kierkegaard sketched some discourses on this theme. See *JP* VI 6277, 6278, 6280 (*Pap.* IX A 421, 498, 500).
17. With reference to the following sentence, see Supplement, pp. 200–01 (*Pap.* X^1 A 198).
18. Proverbs 6:6.
19. With reference to the following five paragraphs, see Supplement, p. 197 (*Pap.* VIII^1 A 359).
20. Cf. *Either/Or*, II, pp. 157–78 (*SV* II 143–61).
21. Cf. Acts 17:28.
22. For continuation of the paragraph, see Supplement, p. 199 (*Pap.* X^5 B 5:3).
23. See Matthew 4:10; Mark 12:30.

24. Cf. Matthew 6:10.

25. See Matthew 10:29.

26. With reference to the remainder of the sentence, see Supplement, p. 199 (*Pap.* X^5 B 5:4).

27. This obvious inversion of the relation of the speeds of light and sound is inexplicable, but so the text reads.

28. With reference to the following sentence, see Supplement, p. 201 (*Pap.* X^1 A 506).

29. See Romans 15:5.

30. For continuation of the text, see Supplement, p. 199 (*Pap.* X^5 B 5:6).

31. Cf. *Fear and Trembling*, p. 9 and note 2, *KW* VI.

32. For continuation of the text, see Supplement, p. 200 (*Pap.* X^5 B 5:10).

33. With reference to the following phrase, see Supplement, p. 200 (*Pap.* X^5 B 5:11).

34. See James 1:13.

35. See I Thessalonians 5:3.

36. With reference to the following two clauses, see Supplement, p. 200 (*Pap.* X^5 B 5:12).

37. Cf. I Thessalonians 5:16.

38. See Supplement, p. 198 (*Pap.* VIII^1 A 644).

39. For continuation of the sentence, see Supplement, p. 200 (*Pap.* X^5 B 6:10).

40. Cf. Romans 8:20.

41. See Psalm 102:26.

42. I Peter 5:7. See Supplement, p. 201 (*Pap.* X^1 A 469).

43. Cf. Luke 23:43.

TWO ETHICAL-RELIGIOUS ESSAYS

TITLE PAGE. See Supplement, p. 200 (*Pap.* X^5 B 9:1a-b).

1. With reference to the essay title page, see Supplement, pp. 217, 219, 220, 236 (*Pap.* X^1 A 263; VIII^2 B 134, 135; X^5 B 9:2b-c; X^1 A 335).

2. With reference to the following paragraph, see Supplement, pp. 210–11, 221 (*Pap.* VIII^1 A 274; VIII^2 B 133:1).

3. With reference to the following paragraph, see Supplement, p. 212 (*Pap.* VIII^1 A 469).

4. See Supplement, p. 239 (*Pap.* X^1 A 441).

5. In the Danish text of *Two Ethical-Religious Essays*, the initial letter of pronouns referring to Christ is not consistently in lower or upper case. In keeping with *Pap.* X^5 B 33b:13, in which Kierkegaard apologizes to the printer for changing capital *H* to lower case in the page proofs of *Practice in Christianity*, the lower case is used throughout the present work.

6. See Supplement, p. 221 (*Pap.* VIII^2 B 133:2).

7. With reference to the remainder of the sentence, see Supplement, p. 221 (*Pap.* VIII^2 B 133:3).

8. See Supplement, p. 221 (*Pap*. VIII[2] B 133:4).

9. See Luke 23:34.

10. With reference to the remainder of the sentence, see Supplement, p. 222 (*Pap*. VIII[2] B 133:5).

11. With reference to the following sentence, see Supplement, p. 222 (*Pap*. VIII[2] B 133:6).

12. See Supplement, p. 222 (*Pap*. VIII[2] B 137:3).

13. See John 6:15.

14. With reference to the following four paragraphs, see Supplement, p. 239 (*Pap*. X[1] A 411).

15. See, for example, Luke 19:37–40.

16. See Matthew 6:24.

17. Mark 15:34.

18. With reference to the remainder of the sentence, see Supplement, p. 222 (*Pap*. VIII[2] B 138:1).

19. See John 18:36.

20. See Shakespeare, *Hamlet*, III, 1, 56; *William Shakspeare's Tragiske Værker*, I-IX, tr. Peter Foersom and Peter Frederick Wulff (Copenhagen: 1807–25; *ASKB* 1889–96), I, p. 97; *W. Shakspeare's dramatische Werke*, I-VIII, tr. Ernst Ortlepp (Stuttgart: 1838–39; *ASKB* 1874–81), I, p. 289; *Shakspeare's dramatische Werke*, I-XII, tr. August Wilhelm v. Schlegel and Ludwig Tieck (Berlin: 1839–41; *ASKB* 1883–88), VI, p. 63; *The Complete Works of Shakespeare*, ed. George Lyman Kittredge (Boston: Ginn, 1936), p. 1167.

21. See Matthew 6:33

22. See John 19:19–22.

23. See Mark 15:13.

24. See, for example, John 10:30.

25. Luke 13:2.

26. See Matthew 26:53.

27. For continuation of the text, see Supplement, pp. 222–23 (*Pap*. VIII[2] B 133:8).

28. See Philippians 2:12.

29. On this Socratic theme, see *Sickness unto Death*, pp. 87–96, *KW* XIX (*SV* XI 199–207).

30. With reference to the remainder of the paragraph, see Supplement, p. 223 (*Pap*. VIII[2] B 133:11).

31. "Spoonerism" is the closest equivalent of the Danish *bakke snagvendt* for *snakke bagvendt* (speak backward). The English term comes from William A. Spooner (1844–1930), Warden of New College, Oxford. Examples: "a half-warmed fish" ("a half-formed wish"); "You [a failing student] have tasted two worms, and you will leave Oxford by the first town drain" ("You have wasted two terms, and you will leave Oxford by the first down train").

32. With reference to the remainder of the paragraph, see Supplement, pp. 223–24 (*Pap*. VIII[1] A 564).

33. I Corinthians 9:26.

34. See *Fragments*, pp. 20–21, *KW* VII (*SV* IV 190).

35. According to an ordinance of Dec. 18, 1767, a malefactor who, out of life-weariness, committed a murder punishable by execution was not to be executed but be put to hard labor in irons for life and on the anniversary of the murder be publicly whipped. The ordinance was revoked in 1833.

36. See, for example, *Two Ages: The Age of Revolution and the Present Age, A Literary Review*, pp. 7–12, *KW* XIV (*SV* VIII 8–12).

37. See Supplement, pp. 224–25 (*Pap.* VIII² B 139:3).

38. With reference to the following sentence, see Supplement, p. 225 (*Pap.* VIII² B 133:17).

39. See Supplement, p. 225 (*Pap.* VIII² B 139:4).

40. For continuation of the paragraph, see Supplement, p. 225 (*Pap.* VIII² B 133:18).

41. See Luke 23:34.

42. With reference to the following paragraph, see Supplement, pp. 225–26 (*Pap.* VIII² B 139:5; X¹ A 337).

43. See Supplement, pp. 232–33, 226 (*Pap.* X¹ A 305–08; X⁵ B 10:18).

44. The *Adler* manuscript, version IV (*Pap.* VIII² B 7:8, 9:17), has the following essay, with minor differences, as an addendum.

45. See *JP* V 5181 (*Pap.* I A 328).

46. In Greek the word means "one who is sent."

47. The *Adler* manuscript, version I (*Pap.* VII² B 235, pp. 141–50), was used as the manuscript for the following nine pages of the essay.

48. See Supplement, p. 237 (*Pap.* X¹ A 336).

49. With reference to the following three paragraphs, see Supplement, pp. 211–12 (*Pap.* VIII¹ A 416).

50. See *The Concept of Anxiety*, p. 59, *KW* VIII (*SV* IV 329).

51. Cf. Psalm 51:10–12.

52. With reference to the following note, see Supplement, pp. 226–27 (*Pap.* VIII² B 9:17).

53. See the prefaces in *Eighteen Discourses*, pp. 5, 53, 107, 179, 231, 295, *KW* V (*SV* III 11, 271; IV 7, 73, 121; V 79); *Three Discourses on Imagined Occasions*, p. 5, *KW* X (*SV* V 175). See also Corsair *Affair*, Supplement, p. 173, *KW* XIII (*Pap.* VII¹ B 38); *On My Work*, in *Point of View*, *KW* XXII (*SV* XIII 494).

54. See Ephesians 2:19.

55. See, for example, *Sickness unto Death*, pp. 99, 117, 126, 127, *KW* XIX (*SV* XI 210, 227, 235, 237).

56. See Matthew 7:29.

57. See Matthew 28:18.

58. See Plato, *Phaedo*; *Platonis quae exstant opera*, I-XI, ed. Friedrich Ast (Leipzig: 1819–32; *ASKB* 1144–54), I, pp. 472–610; *Udvalgte Dialoger af Platon*, I-VIII, tr. Carl Johan Heise (Copenhagen: 1830–59); *ASKB* 1164–67, 1169 [I-VII]), I, pp. 1–189; *The Collected Dialogues of Plato*, ed. Edith Hamilton and Huntington Cairns (Princeton: Princeton University Press, 1963), pp. 41–98.

59. An allusion to Nicolai Frederik Severin Grundtvig (1783–1872), Danish pastor, poet, and politician. See, for example, *JP* V 5752, 5753 (*Pap.* V A 94, 95).

60. See I Corinthians 4:13. The part of the manuscript of *Adler* version I (*Pap.* VII^2 B 235, pp. 141–50), used as the final copy for part of "The Difference between a Genius and an Apostle," ends here. The remainder of the essay is version IV of Addendum II in *Adler* (*Pap.* VIII^2 B 7:9–10, 9:18).

61. II Corinthians 6:10.

62. See Philippians 4:7.

63. For a contemplated postscript, see Supplement, pp. 227–31 (*Pap.* IX B 24).

THREE DISCOURSES AT THE COMMUNION ON FRIDAYS

TITLE PAGE. See Supplement, p. 254 (*Pap.* X^5 B 25:1).

1. See Historical Introduction, *Eighteen Discourses*, *KW* V, pp. xvii-xxi.
2. With reference to the remainder of the preface, see Supplement, p. 254 (*Pap.* X^5 B 25:2).
3. *Eighteen Discourses*, p. 5, *KW* V (*SV* III 11).
4. With reference to the following heading and discourse, see Supplement, pp. 251–53, 254–55 (*Pap.* IX A 266–69; X^5 B 25:3).
5. See John 6:68.
6. See Mark 9:50.
7. See Matthew 11:28.
8. See Luke 9:58.
9. See Mark 10:35–37.
10. With reference to the following three clauses, see Supplement, p. 255 (*Pap.* X^2 A 209).
11. See Matthew 4:1–11.
12. With reference to the following heading and discourse, see Supplement, pp. 251, 253, 253–54 (*Pap.* VIII^1 A 635; IX A 272; X^1 A 428).
13. See Luke 18:9–14.
14. See Luke 18:9.
15. See Luke 18:11.
16. See Luke 14:8–10.
17. See Luke 10:38–42.
18. With reference to the following heading, see Supplement, p. 255 (*Pap.* X^5 B 25:5).
19. See Matthew 11:28.
20. See John 4:16.
21. See I John 4:18.
22. See Luke 7:37–50.
23. See Luke 7:37–38.
24. See Ecclesiastes 7:2.
25. The confessional.

26. For continuation of the sentence, see Supplement, p. 255 (*Pap.* X^5 B 25:7).

27. See Supplement, p. 257 (*Pap.* X^3 A 566).

28. With reference to the following four sentences, see Supplement, pp. 255–56 (*Pap.* X^5 B 26:8).

29. See Supplement, p. 256 (*Pap.* X^5 B 25:8).

AN UPBUILDING DISCOURSE

TITLE PAGE. See Supplement, p. 261 (*Pap.* X^5 B 115:1, 116:1).

1. See Supplement, pp. 261–63 (*Pap.* X^5 B 117, 118).
2. See *Two Discourses* (1843), *Eighteen Discourses*, p. 5, *KW* V (*SV* III 11).
3. See Supplement, p. 263 (*Pap.* X^5 B 115:2).
4. See Supplement, p. 263 (*Pap.* X^5 B 115:3).
5. See I Corinthians 14:34.
6. See Luke 1:38.
7. See Luke 2:19.
8. See Luke 8:15.
9. See Luke 2:35.
10. See Luke 11:41–42.
11. For continuation of the text, see Supplement, pp. 263–64 (*Pap.* X^5 B 116:4).
12. For continuation of the text, see Supplement, p. 264 (*Pap.* X^5 B 116:6).
13. See John 11:4.
14. See Matthew 6:17–18.
15. John 12:4–6.
16. See Luke 7:41–43.
17. See Proverbs 16:32.
18. See John 1:29.
19. See John 15:13.

TWO DISCOURSES AT THE COMMUNION ON FRIDAYS

TITLE PAGE. See Supplement, p. 270 (*Pap.* X^5 B 138:1, 132).

1. See Supplement, pp. 272–74 (*Pap.* IX B 63:3, 63:14; X^5 B 187; X^5 B 133, 135, 136).
2. *Postscript*, pp. 629–30, *KW* XII.1 (*SV* VII 548–49).
3. Toward the altar.
4. See Supplement, p. 274 (*Pap.* X^5 B 130:1).
5. See John 12:47.
6. See John 6:68.
7. See John 3:17, 3:19.
8. See Matthew 11:28, the theme of Part One of *Practice*, pp. 3–68, *KW* XX (*SV* XII v-65).
9. With reference to the following sentence, see Supplement, p. 275 (*Pap.* X^1 A 388–90).

10. See John 20:23.
11. See Genesis 7–8.
12. See Genesis 11:1–9.
13. See Genesis 19:1–29.
14. With reference to the remainder of the paragraph, see Supplement, pp. 275–76 (*Pap*. X^5 B 130:3).
15. Cf. Psalm 139:7–12.
16. See Genesis 4:13–15.
17. Cf. Galatians 6:7.
18. II Corinthians 5:20.
19. Cf. Luke 15:7.
20. See Matthew 8:20; Luke 9:58.
21. See *Works of Love*, pp. 280–99, *KW* XVI (*SV* IX 267–85).
22. Cf. John 8:46; Isaiah 53:9.
23. The source has not been located.
24. Horace, *Odes*, III, 1, 40; *Q. Horatii Flacci opera* (Leipzig: 1828; *ASKB* 1248), p. 65; *Horace The Odes and Epodes*, tr. C. E. Bennett (Loeb, Cambridge: Harvard University Press, 1978), p. 171: But Fear and Threat climb to the selfsame spot the owner does; nor does black Care quit the brass-bound galley and even takes her seat behind the horseman.
25. Most likely a reference to Thorvaldsen's altar statue in Vor Frue Church, Copenhagen.
26. See Isaiah 1:18.
27. See Matthew 8:26–27.
28. See Matthew 23:37.
29. Cf. Hebrews 7:27, 9:12.
30. Cf. John 14:6.

SUPPLEMENT

1. See p. 18.
2. *Kierkagaard: Letters and Documents*, Letter 175, *KW* XXV.
3. *Af Søren Kierkegaards Efterladte Papirer*, I-VIII, ed. Hans Peter Barfod and Hermann Gottsched (Copenhagen: 1869–81) IV, pp. 397–98.
4. See pp. 24–35.
5. See, for example, *Christian Discourses*, *KW* XVII (*SV* X 19–41).
6. See p. 41.
7. I Peter 5:7.
8. See *JP* VI 6271 (*Pap*. IX A 390).
9. Freely quoted. See p. 3.
10. See note 24 below.
11. Anti-Climacus, the pseudonymous author of *Sickness unto Death* (July 30, 1849) and *Practice* (September 27, 1850).
12. See *Adler*, Addendum I, *KW* XXIV (*Pap*. VII^2 B 235, pp. 33–53).
13. Ibid. (pp. 74–93).
14. Ibid. (pp. 136–50). See also *Two Essays*.

15. See *Fear and Trembling*, p. 8, *KW* VI (*SV* IV 59–60).

16. See *JP* V 6110 (*Pap*. VIII[1] A 558).

17. See note 29 below.

18. Christiansfeldt is a small Danish town in southern Jylland, founded by a denomination of Moravian Brethren (*Herrnhuter Brüdergemeinde*). Kierkegaard's father and the family of Emil Boesen, Kierkegaard's closest friend, were associated with the group in Copenhagen during Kierkegaard's early years.

19. See Historical Introduction, p. ix.

20. See Supplement, pp. 214–16 (*Pap*. IX B 22); see also *Pap*. IX B 10.

21. "Does a Human Being Have the Right to Let Himself Be Put to Death for the Truth?" pp. 51–89.

22. No. III in "A Cycle of Ethical-Religious Essays." See Supplement, p. 213 (*Pap*. IX B 1–6)

23. *The Point of View* was published posthumously in 1859 by Peter Christian Kierkegaard.

24. The second edition of *Either/Or* and *The Lily in the Field and the Bird of the Air* were published May 14, 1849. See Historical Introduction, pp. x–xiv.

25. See p. 47.

26. The three parts of *Practice in Christianity*, eventually published September 17, 1850.

27. *Two Essays* was published May 19, 1849.

28. See Supplement, pp. 214–16 (*Pap*. IX B 22).

29. The year 1848 was a time of internal upheaval in many European countries. Most notable was the February Revolution in Paris, during which the Second Republic was proclaimed. In Denmark there was an additional element, war with Prussia. In the context of the old Slesvig-Holsten issue, Prince Frederick of Augustenburg put himself at the head of a provisional government proclaimed in Kiel in March 1848. A Danish army subdued the rebels north of the Eider River. A new national assembly of Germany decided to incorporate Slesvig, and a Prussian army under Wrangel drove the Danes back. On August 26, 1848, an armistice was signed in Malmø, and the government of the two duchies was entrusted to a commission composed of two Prussians, two Danes, and a fifth member by common consent of the four. War was renewed between March and July 1849, and a second armistice was signed between Prussia and Denmark. Germans in the duchies increased their army under General Willesen. The Danes trapped Willesen's army at Isted on July 23, 1849. In 1850 Prussia concluded a treaty with Denmark and gave up claim to the duchies. In London, May 8, 1852, the leading European powers signed a treaty concerning the succession after Frederik VII, and there was no further outbreak until his death in 1863. From 1848 on, the financial situation of the country was precarious and inflation rampant.

On March 21, 1848, as the result of earlier events, movements, and an enormous demonstration at Christiansborg, King Frederik VII (King Christian VIII had died January 28, 1848) agreed to the dissolution of the ministries. Thereupon the March government, the Moltke-Hvidt government, was formed and Frederik VII declared that he now regarded himself as a constitutional monarch. A constitutional Assembly convened in November 1848, and King Frederik signed the new constitution June 5, 1849.

30. *Two Ages*, *KW* XIV (*SV* VIII 3–105).

31. The Roman numeral indicates the position of the discourse in the manuscript of Part III of *Christian Discourses*, "Thoughts that Wound from Behind—for Upbuilding," *KW* XVII (*SV* X 222–32).

32. See John 16:2.

33. *The Concept of Anxiety*, pp. 93–96, *KW* VIII (*SV* IV 363–66). See also *Sickness unto Death*, pp. 44–47, *KW* XIX (*SV* XI 156–59).

34. Essay II ("The Dialectical Relations: The Universal, the Single Individual, the Special Individual") in "A Cycle" was Addendum I in version III of *Adler*. See Supplement, p. 213 (*Pap*. IX B 2); *Pap*. VIII^2 B 9:13.

35. See note 29 above.

36. For other references to the Danish game of *Gnavspil*, see *Fear and Trembling*, p. 100, *KW* VI (*SV* III 147); *Fragments*, p. 22, *KW* VII (*SV* IV 191).

37. Louis Philippe (1773–1850), king of France (1830–48), came to power in the July revolution of 1830 and abdicated during the revolution in February 1848. He fled ignominiously to England, where he died in 1850.

38. P. 49.

39. P. 99 fn.

40. Cf. p. 100.

41. Cf. *Either/Or*, I, p. 20, *KW* III (*SV* I 4).

42. Pp. 97–98.

43. P. 89.

44. "A Note" refers to "The Accounting," *On My Work*, in *Point of View*, *KW* XXII (*SV* XIII 489–501).

45. The "Three Notes Concerning My Work as an Author" intended as appendices to *Point of View* were: (1) "For the Dedication to 'That Single Individual,'" (2) "A Word about the Relation of My Work as an Author to 'That Single Individual,'" and (3) "Preface to 'Friday Discourses.'" Eventually no. 3 was omitted. A shortened version of no. 3 was used as the preface to *Two Discourses at the Communion on Fridays* (1851). See Supplement, pp. 271–72 (*Pap*. IX B 63:1,3,14).

46. See *Christian Discourses*, *KW* XVII (*SV* X 245–317).

47. See pp. 1–45.

48. Hermann Samuel Reimarus, *Von dem Zwecke Jesu und seiner Jünger: Noch ein Fragment des Wolfenbüttelschen Ungenannten*, ed. Gottfried Ephraim Lessing (Braunschweig: 1778), pp. 112–17.

49. Pp. 59–63.

50. P. 55.

51. *Dansk Kirketidende*, IV, 43, July 22, 1849, col. 718–19.

52. See, for example, *Fear and Trembling*, pp. 5–7, *KW* VI (*SV* III 57–59).

53. Søren Kierkegaard's brother Peter Christian (1805–1888), Grundtvigian adherent and pastor of Pedersborg parish 1842–56.

54. Pastoral convention in Roskilde, October 30, 1849. See *JP* VI 6550, 6558, 6559 (*Pap.* X^2 A 256; X^6 B 130, 131); *Letters*, Letter 240, *KW* XXV.

55. Hans Lassen Martensen (1808–1884), professor of theology, University of Copenhagen, and Court Chaplain and later Mynster's successor as Bishop of Sjælland.

56. Rasmus Nielsen (1809–1884), professor of philosophy, University of Copenhagen, and author of *Mag. S. Kierkegaards "Johannes Climacus" og Dr. H. Martensens "Christelige Dogmatik"* (1849), in which he was critical of Martensen.

57. See Peter C. Kierkegaard, "*Roskilde Præstconvent den 30te Oktober 1849*," *Dansk Kirketidende*, 219, December 16, 1849, col. 191.

58. See I Corinthians 3:22.

59. In his journals Kierkegaard was very careful about giving detailed bibliographical information about his reading referred to in the journal entries.

60. See pp. 55–57.

61. See notes 53, 54, 57 above.

62. *Nyt Theologisk Tidsskrift*, ed. Carl Emil Scharling and Christian Thorning Engelstoft, I, 1850, p. 384.

63. *Dansk Kirketidende*, IV, 43, July 22, 1849, col. 718.

64. See note 44 above.

65. Jens Mathias Hjorth, review of Rasmus Nielsen, *Evangelietroen og den moderne Bevidsthed*, *Nyt Theologisk Tidsskrift*, 285, December 4, 1849, p. 137.

66. Henrik Nicolai Clausen, *Det nye Testaments Hermeneutik* (Copenhagen: 1840; *ASKB* 468).

67. See pp. 103–05.

68. See note 60 above.

69. See notes 53, 54, 57 above.

70. See pp. 64–65.

71. "The High Priest," see pp. 113–24.

72. Hebrews 4:15.

73. Luke 18:13.

74. Luke 18:14.

75. On September 8, 1840, Kierkegaard proposed marriage to Regine Olsen, who gave her acceptance on September 10, 1840.

76. P. 118.

77. See John 3:2.

78. The pseudonymous author of *Sickness unto Death* and *Practice*.

79. See note 78 above.

80. Regine Olsen. See *JP* VI 6537–44 (*Pap.* X^2 A 210–16); *Letters*, Letter 239, *KW* XXV.

81. See p. 141.

82. "The Accounting" was published August 7, 1851, as part of *On My Work*.

83. *Two Discourses at the Communion on Fridays* was published August 7, 1851.

84. For drafts of a dedication to "The Accounting," see Supplement, pp. 270–71 (*Pap*. X^5 B 261, 263–64). See also *Pap*. X^5 B 262.

85. See Supplement, pp. 271–72 (*Pap*. IX B 63:1,3, 14; X^5 B 187).

86. *Point of View*, *KW* XXII (*SV* XII 591–98).

87. Ibid. (599–610).

88. Part Four of *Christian Discourses*, *KW* XVII (*SV* XII 247–344).

89. *Postscript*, pp. 629–30, *KW* XII.1 (*SV* VII 548–49).

90. See Ludvig Holberg, *Erasmus Montanus*, I, 4; *Den Danske Skueplads*, I-VII (Copenhagen: 1788; *ASKB* 1566–67), V, no pagination; *Comedies by Holberg*, tr. Oscar James Campbell, Jr., and Frederic Schenck (New York: American-Scandinavian Foundation, 1935), p. 126.

91. See Luke 3:47.

92. *On My Work* and *Two Discourses on Fridays* (August 7, 1851).

93. See Luke 5:8.

94. See note 92 above.

95. *Flyveposten*, 181, August 7, 1851.

96. See Holberg, *Erasmus Montanus*, I, 4; *Danske Skueplads*, V, no pagination; *Comedies*, p. 127.

97. *Fyens Avis*, 187, August 9, 1851.

BIBLIOGRAPHICAL NOTE

For general bibliographies of Kierkegaard studies, see:

Jens Himmelstrup, *Søren Kierkegaard International Bibliografi*. Copenhagen: Nyt Nordisk Forlag Arnold Busck, 1962.

International Kierkegaard Newsletter, ed. Julia Watkin. Launceton, Tasmania, Australia, 1979–.

Aage Jørgensen, *Søren Kierkegaard-litteratur 1961–1970*. Aarhus: Akademisk Boghandel, 1971. *Søren Kierkegaard-litteratur 1971–1980*. Aarhus: privately published, 1983.

Kierkegaard: A Collection of Critical Essays, ed. Josiah Thompson. New York: Doubleday (Anchor Books), 1972.

Kierkegaardiana, XII, 1982; XIII, 1984; XIV 1988; XVI, 1993; XVII, 1994; XVIII, 1996.

Bruce H. Kirmmse, *Kierkegaard in Golden Age Denmark*. Bloomington: Indiana University Press, 1990.

François H. Lapointe, *Sören Kierkegaard and His Critics: An International Bibliography of Criticism*. Westport, Connecticut: Greenwood Press, 1980.

Søren Kierkegaard's Journals and Papers, I, ed. and tr. Howard V. Hong and Edna H. Hong, assisted by Gregor Malantschuk. Bloomington, Indiana: Indiana University Press, 1967.

For topical bibliographies of Kierkegaard studies, see *Søren Kierkegaard's Journals and Papers*, I-IV, 1967–75.

INDEX

ADVISORY BOARD

KIERKEGAARD'S WRITINGS